THE ORGANISATION OF THE FIRM

In recent years there has been a growth in work on the organisation of the firm. The same period has also seen a corresponding rise in literature dealing with the organisation of the multinational firm, but the two literatures have developed quite separately, even though insights from each have much to offer the other. This unique collection of essays from respected academics aims to bridge this gap, addressing questions of the theory of the firm and international business.

The material is presented in three sections:

- The first section deals with theoretical issues underpinning multinational enterprise. These are the issues of information, re-engineering and change management and international trade.
- The second section concentrates on the inter-firm relationships of multinationals, assessing the interplay of cooperation and adversarial behaviour.
- The third section deals with applications of the principles presented in the first two sections. The applications concern the defence equipment industry, the world automobile industry and corporate governance under European Union Regulations.

The Organisation of the Firm is aimed at researchers and students in the field of international business, and is likely to appeal to advanced undergraduates and postgraduates, as well as academics.

Ram Mudambi is Senior Lecturer in Strategy in the School of Business at the University of Buckingham. He has taught at several universities in the US including Cornell, Purdue and the University of North Carolina at Chapel Hill. He has published widely in the area of multinational strategy, particularly focusing on foreign direct investment.

Martin Ricketts is Professor of Economic Organisation at the University of Buckingham. Since 1992 he has been a Trustee of the Institute of Economic Affairs and Chairman of their International Advisory Council. His main research interests are Industrial Policy, Public Finance, Public Choice, Housing Policy, New Institutional Economics, and Austrian Economics. His publications include *The Economics of Business Enterprise: An Introduction to Economic Organisation and the Theory of the Firm* (Second Edition, 1994).

ROUTLEDGE STUDIES IN BUSINESS ORGANISATION AND NETWORKS

1. DEMOCRACY AND EFFICIENCY IN THE ECONOMIC ENTERPRISE
Edited by Ugo Pagano and Robert Rowthorn

2. TOWARDS A COMPETENCE THEORY OF THE FIRM
Edited by Nicolai J. Foss and Christian Knudsen

3. UNCERTAINTY AND ECONOMIC EVOLUTION
Essays in Honour of Armen A. Alchian
Edited by John R. Lott Jr

4. THE END OF THE PROFESSIONS?
The restructuring of professional work
Edited by Jane Broadbent, Michael Dietrich and Jennifer Roberts

5. SHOPFLOOR MATTERS
Labor–management relations in 20th-century American manufacturing
David Fairris

6. THE ORGANISATION OF THE FIRM
International business perspectives
Edited by Ram Mudambi and Martin Ricketts

THE ORGANISATION OF THE FIRM

International business perspectives

Edited by Ram Mudambi and Martin Ricketts

Routledge
Taylor & Francis Group
LONDON AND NEW YORK

First published 1998
by Routledge
2 Park Square, Milton Park, Abingdon, Oxfordshire OX14 4RN

Transferred to Digital Printing 2005

Simultaneously published in the USA and Canada
by Routledge
711 Third Avenue, New York, NY 10017

Routledge is an imprint of the Taylor and Francis Group, an informa business

First issued in paperback 2015

Typeset in Garamond by Pure Tech India Ltd, Pondicherry

British Library Cataloguing in Publication Data
A catalogue record for this book is available from the British Library

Library of Congress Cataloging in Publication Data

The organisation of the firm: international business perspectives /
edited by Ram Mudambi and Martin Ricketts.
p. cm.
Includes bibliographical references and index.
1. International business enterprises. 2. Industrial organisation.
I. Mudambi, Ram, 1954– . II. Ricketts, Martin J. HD62.4.0735 1997
658'.049–dc21
97–8357
CIP

ISBN 978-0-415-14298-4 (hbk)
ISBN 978-1-138-88091-7 (pbk)

CONTENTS

FIGURES

TABLES

LIST OF CONTRIBUTORS

Alistair Alcock is Senior Lecturer in Law at the University of Buckingham, UK. Formerly Director, Corporate Finance, UBS- Phillips & Drew.

Peter J. Buckley is Professor of Managerial Economics and Director of the Centre for International Business at the University of Leeds, UK.

John Burton is Professor of Business Administration at the University of Birmingham, UK.

Martin J. Carter is a Senior Research Fellow at the Centre for International Business at the University of Leeds, UK.

Mark Casson is Professor of Economics at the University of Reading, UK.

Keith Hartley is Professor of Economics and Director of the Centre for Defence Economics at the University of York, UK.

Susan R. Helper is Associate Professor of Economics and a Fellow of the Center for Regional Economic Issues at Case Western Reserve University, Cleveland, USA.

Richard Lamming is CIPS Professor of Purchasing and Supply Management at the University of Bath, UK.

James R. Markusen is Professor of Economics at the University of Colorado, Boulder, USA and a Fellow of the National Bureau of Economic Research (NBER), USA.

Susan McDowell Mudambi is Lecturer in Marketing at the Open University Business School, Milton Keynes, UK.

Ram Mudambi is Senior Lecturer in Strategy in the School of Business at the University of Buckingham, UK.

Martin Ricketts is Bernard Sunley Professor of Economic Organisation and Dean of the School of Business at the University of Buckingham, UK.

Mari Sako is Reader in Industrial Relations at the London School of Economics and Political Science, UK.

ACKNOWLEDGEMENTS

The core of this volume consists of papers that were given at the September 1995 ESRC Industrial Economics Study Group meeting at the University of Buckingham. The editors wish to thank the Study Group and its convenor, Professor Steve Thompson for providing the funding that made the meeting possible.

Two chapters are developments of papers that have appeared earlier. Chapter 4 by Markusen is a development of 'The Boundaries of Multinational Enterprises and the Theory of International Trade', *Journal of Economic Perspectives*, 9 (2), pp. 169–89, 1995. Chapter 6 by Mudambi and Mudambi is a development of 'From Transactions Cost Economics to Relationship Marketing: A Model of Buyer-Supplier Relations', *International Business Review*, 4 (4), pp. 419–33, 1995. We should like to thank the American Economic Association and Elsevier Science respectively for cooperation with regard to including these papers.

Chapter 9 by Sako, Lamming and Helper is a reprint of 'Supplier Relations in the UK Car Industry – Good News/Bad News', *European Journal of Purchasing and Supply Management*, 1 (4), pp. 237–48, 1995. We thank Elsevier Science for permission to reprint this paper.

1

ECONOMIC ORGANISATION AND THE MULTINATIONAL FIRM

Ram Mudambi
and
Martin Ricketts

1. Organisations in Economics

Managers and other people bound up with the everyday world might be forgiven for thinking that economic principles have little to say about the internal organisation of firms. Even textbooks of 'managerial economics', until very recently, would tend to describe firms in terms of sets of cost curves rather than in terms of organisational features. Having learned that average cost cannot be rising unless it falls short of marginal cost, aspiring business practitioners heave a sigh of relief and turn to more obviously 'relevant' concerns in the fields of marketing, organisational behaviour, or business strategy. This is regrettable because economic analysis has produced a powerful paradigm for analysing organisational structure and because the separation of the economic from the management literature leads to a proliferation of jargon which is unnecessary and confusing.

It was Ronald Coase (1937) who, in a celebrated paper, set out the elements of the modern economic approach to organisations. Coase studied firms in the United States in an attempt to understand what determined the scope of their operations. In the 1930s students were aware that some firms were 'vertically integrated' and others specialised in a particular part of the productive process. They also recognised that some firms produced a wide range of products while others kept within a very confined area. The problem was to find some explanation for these differing structures. Coase proposed a simple answer.

Transacting in markets and organisation within a firm are alternative methods of coordinating economic activity. Firms can choose whether to buy an input from another firm or to make it themselves. In making this choice they will have to compare the cost of internal organisation with the cost of using markets. Recognition of the fact that, in Coase's words, 'there is a cost of using the price mechanism' therefore formed the foundation stone of his analysis. In the absence of transaction costs, all transactions could take place across markets and there would appear to be no rationale for structures called firms at all.[1] Where transacting is costly, however, the firm will undertake those activities for which internal organisation has a net advantage. The boundary of the firm is located where the costs of 'internal' organisation and 'external' markets are finely balanced.

Coase established clearly, therefore, that efficient organisation was about economising on the costs of transacting. The whole approach has since come to be called the 'transactions cost paradigm'. He also introduced the idea that firm and market were substitutes and that, as the scope of a firm increased, transactions were 'internalised'. For this reason, the Coasian theory of the firm is sometimes referred to as the 'internalisation' theory. Originally, the focus of attention of Coase's theory was on vertical integration and the scope of the firm. More recently, however, Coasian reasoning has been used by economists investigating the growth of the multinational enterprise.

2. The Cost of Transacting

Although Coase's paper was recognised as an important contribution, and was reprinted in the early 1950s by the American Economic Association, it was not until the 1970s that his insights were systematically developed further. The literature is now extensive and a full survey cannot be attempted here. However, attention has focused on four broad (and inter-related) issues. Below they are discussed very briefly in turn under the headings – coordination costs, policing costs, bargaining costs, and government imposed costs.

Coordination costs

The simple problem of coordinating one person's activities with another suggests that 'internalisation' can reduce transactions costs. The most obvious examples are in the field of continuous flow operations where the absence of inventories of intermediate products requires the perfect coordination of upstream and downstream processes and suggests that control within an organisation will be more effective than contracting at arm's length. More generally, the costs of gathering and disseminating information may (up to a point) be reduced by internalisation. If so, internalisation may assist in the process of mutual adjustment to changing circumstances. In Chapter 2 Mark Casson develops this perspective, which accords closely with Coase's original conception.

Policing costs

Within the economics tradition, the general problem of contract enforcement has been seen as central to the analysis of institutional structure. If people or firms cannot be relied upon to honour agreements, economic organisations must be structured so as to encourage cooperative behaviour even where information is imperfect and allows opportunities for cheating. 'Moral hazards' or 'hidden actions', for example, occur when one person, in pursuing some personal objective, acts detrimentally to the interests of another with whom he or she has a contractual relation. A classic example would be the action of driving less carefully in the knowledge that another person is providing insurance cover. The tendency to shirk when not being observed raises the same type of problem.[2] 'Adverse selection' or 'hidden information' occurs when suppliers of high quality goods and services find it costly to differentiate themselves from suppliers of low quality products. Obviously everyone will claim to be high quality suppliers if there are no cheap means of putting these claims to a decisive test. The result is that prevailing prices will seem discouragingly low to high quality suppliers and attractively high to low quality suppliers – hence the term 'adverse' selection.[3] In the following sub-sections, a brief account is given of how some of these contractual problems affect business structure and how the problem of 'contract enforcement' underlies organisational form.

The policing of effort (principal and agent)

The literature on principal and agent is concerned with the design of mechanisms to induce a suitable degree of effort from one party (the agent) even where there are costs of monitoring and enforcement.[4] Franchising, for example, has been analysed within a principal–agent framework.[5] No monitoring is required to induce effort if a franchisee pays a fixed fee to a franchiser for the use of a resource such as a brand name and keeps all the remaining profit. On the other hand, this system loads the risk-bearing costs onto the franchisee and, where there are multiple franchisees, provides no protection against shading on quality and the consequent degradation of the value of the brand. Monitoring by the franchiser moves the arrangements closer to 'internal organisation' and away from arm's length contract. The incentive to monitor is provided by a royalty on sales which gives the franchiser a continuing interest in the value of the brand name.

Contractual arrangements in principal–agent theory are therefore determined by a complex balancing of conflicting forces. Effort incentives can be achieved by accepting greater risk-bearing costs – a large franchise fee and low royalty. Monitoring costs can substitute for greater costs of risk bearing – a lower fee and larger royalty element. Thus risk aversion on the part of franchisees, a franchised resource vulnerable to free riding, and low monitoring costs on the part of franchisers tend to yield 'internal' firm-like arrangements. High monitoring costs, risk neutrality on the part of franchisees and a franchised resource which is not vulnerable to free riding will tend to produce 'external' market-like arrangements.

Policing quality

Where the quality of inputs cannot be ascertained at low cost, for example by simple inspection, and where the value of the final product is very dependent upon all suppliers meeting exacting standards, closer integration between stages of production is encouraged. 'Internalisation' may give a buyer much greater control over the actual processes of production in upstream activities. It may also give rights of inspection and improve information flows. Thus if the proper treatment and display of a product is important, manufacturers integrate into distribution; or if the condition of a raw material is critical and depends upon production methods, a manufacturer may integrate backwards to secure reliable supplies.

Policing property rights

Perhaps the main consideration for theorists of the multinational enterprise has been the role of this form of organisation in the protection of new information. When new knowledge can be protected by patents or copyright, its value can accrue to the originator through licensing agreements. Classic examples include process innovations such as float glass. In many instances, however, legal protection is unreliable and the costs of transacting in information is prohibitive. The buyer uncertainty problem (the difficulty of a buyer assessing the value of information in advance of its receipt) and opportunism (the danger that once in receipt of new information the buyer will have ample incentive to repudiate a prior assessment of its value) combine to make trade in information very hazardous.

'Internalisation' can therefore be seen as a way of exploiting vulnerable information. Organisations such as multinational enterprises protect valuable information and exploit its profit-making potential by using it internally. If licensing the information to firms in other countries is ineffective or contractually hazardous then they respond by expanding their own activities internationally.

Policing restrictive agreements

Profits can be made not only by gains in efficiency but also by exploiting or creating a monopoly position. Early work by Hymer (1960) developed the view that multinational organisation was a form of horizontal integration aimed at stifling competition. The multinational firm was an alternative to a simple agreement to control output and prices in the various markets or to the establishment of a cartel. Hymer did not link this observation closely to the Coasian transaction costs tradition, but later writers (see Caves 1996) have noted that alternatives such as cartels tend to break down, especially in dynamic and uncertain conditions, and that Hymer's work can be seen as an implicit comment on the high transaction costs of policing international restrictive agreements.

There is a direct connection between the licensing problem discussed above (p. 4) and the cartel problems at issue here. As Casson (1987) notes, a firm wishing to sell access to a new technology may license overseas producers. If so, the value of the licenses will be undermined by competition between the licensed producers unless royalty terms are very carefully specified. A multinational enterprise can be seen as a more reliable method than an international cartel of suppressing such competitive forces.

In a similar tradition, internalisation can also be seen as a means of enforcing price discrimination. A monopolist selling in several different markets will wish to charge higher prices in those markets where elasticities are lower. This objective will be undermined if arbitrage is possible and low price purchasers can make profits by re-selling to higher price purchasers. By integrating forward into those businesses with elastic demands for the monopolist's output, the monopolist can prevent arbitrage from taking place. Forward integration can also prevent downstream firms from substituting other inputs for the one supplied by the monopolist.

Bargaining costs

'Hold up' and the problem of specific assets

'External' contracts are particularly likely to fail where an agreement requires one of the parties to invest in highly transaction-specific resources. A supplier required to invest in equipment which had a virtually zero value for alternative purposes would be vulnerable to 'hold up'. The buyer might try to renegotiate terms and force down the price. Technically, the return on a specific asset is a form of rent – a payment in excess of the minimum required to keep it in its existing employment. This rent is then vulnerable to opportunistic raids by the buyer who knows that the supplier cannot credibly threaten to use the resource elsewhere. Bargaining over the distribution of this pool of rent may be extremely costly and disruptive. In the case of physical capital the obvious solution is for the buyer to finance it and then lease it to the supplier. This is sometimes called quasi-vertical integration. Where the proper use and maintenance of the equipment is important and costly to monitor from outside, however, full vertical integration is the likely response. Williamson (1985) sees asset specificity (particularly human asset specificity) and the implied vulnerability to opportunism as a key explanation of the development of internal governance in place of classical contract.

The introduction of new products and processes

Radical innovation and the huge uncertainty which surrounds it can give rise to particularly intractable bargaining problems. This is not simply a matter of asset specificity, although investment in new and specialised assets may be required of upstream or downstream firms in the supply chain. Bargaining problems often relate more to the differing perceptions of risks and possibilities which may be held by the participants than to fears about 'hold-up' and dependency. Large costs of communication or education may be associated with product or process innovation. This observation leads to the idea that the multinational enterprise is a means of economising on the costs of 'technology transfer' – costs which are 'transactional' in nature. Bertin and Wyatt (1988), for example, argue that the multinational may be less concerned with the internalisation and policing of 'leaky' information than is commonly assumed. Multinational expansion may indicate the 'difficulty' rather than the 'ease' of transferring technology across national boundaries.

Internalising production externalities

Where there are technical interdependencies between firms so that the production activities of one firm yield economies or diseconomies to others, a case for integration can be made. In the absence of internal organisation, adjustments to allow for 'external effects' may either not be made at all because transaction costs prove to be prohibitive, or may involve such bargaining problems that the social advantages of coordination are substantially offset by the costs of achieving them. 'Economies of scope' – the cost savings derived from producing a range of products within a single firm rather than in a set of firms each producing a single product, derive from internalising these 'external' effects.

If production externalities transcend national boundaries it is clear that multinational expansion can be seen as a means of 'internalising' externalities. This idea is closely associated with the subject matter of policing property rights discussed above. The 'leaking away' of information about technical improvements to rivals or producers in related areas is a form of external effect. In the absence of secure and negotiable property rights, integration is encouraged.

It is worth emphasising here, however, that the 'internalisation' of an externality and the 'internalisation' of a transaction are not quite the same thing. As Casson (1987) is at pains to point out, the 'internalisation' theory of the firm is a wider theory than a theory of the 'internalisation' of externalities. Even in a world with no external effects and with perfectly secure property rights in all resources, 'internalisation' will still be chosen where information, coordination, bargaining or other transaction costs are high enough.

Costs imposed by governments

Some transaction costs are directly created by government policy. Tariffs and other trade taxes result in impediments to transacting across national boundaries. Quotas are designed to keep the level of transacting below some specified limit. Where direct exports are an alternative to production in an overseas market, the existence of tariff barriers will reduce trade flows in the final product and encourage multinational production. Tariffs act as a supplement to transport costs and result in a wider geographical spread of production facilities and a smaller trade in goods than would otherwise occur.

3. Exploiting Firm Specific Knowledge

The protection and exploitation of new information as a driving force of multinational expansion has already been emphasised (pp. 4–6). Some information is highly firm specific, however, and not very transferable across markets. The danger of imitation is not great because the information takes the form of 'know how' embodied in the people which make up the team. It may have been accumulated gradually over time as a result of experience in operating the firm's routines and procedures and it may be difficult for any person or small group of people to re-create the right conditions elsewhere. Economists in the 'Austrian' tradition refer to this type of knowledge as 'tacit knowledge' – knowledge that cannot simply be written down in codified form and communicated quickly and effectively to other people and organisations. Some types of knowledge and skill can be accumulated only by experience over time.

Writers on economic organisation have drawn attention to firm-specific capabilities (Chandler 1992) in the form of the 'core competencies' of a firm, its sources of 'competitive advantage' (Porter 1990) or its 'architecture' (Kay 1992). The jargon varies but the underlying approach to the firm and its organisation is similar. In the modern world, the assets which give rise to a competitive edge frequently consist of reputation, networks of contacts, firm-specific procedures and general 'know-how' which cannot be transferred to others at low cost. The multinational firm exploits these assets by geographical expansion (internalisation) because licensing is ineffective and because the alternative of direct exports faces transport costs, tariffs or other trade restrictions.

This combination of firm-specific advantages (also called 'ownership advantages') with significant transport costs or tariff barriers ('location advantages') and high costs of transacting in information (or 'internalisation advantages') gives rise to Dunning's 'eclectic' or 'Ownership-Location-Internalisation (OLI)' theory of the multinational firm. Critics have argued that the internalisation of a transaction may reduce costs even where ownership advantages are not present and that therefore the latter are not a strictly necessary precondition for multinational expansion.[6] Nevertheless, the increasing significance of non-tradable ownership advantages is widely seen to be an important source of multinational expansion and is consistent with much of the empirical evidence about the characteristics of multinational firms.

Markusen (1997) surveys this empirical evidence and draws attention to the relatively high ratio of research and development expenditure-to-sales in multinational firms; the large share of professional and technical workers in employment; the importance of product differentiation and advertising; the significance of new and technically complex products in the output of the multinational; and the relatively high value of intangible assets to total market value.[7] All these observations are consistent with the view that ownership advantages play an important role in motivating international expansion. In the following sections we look at the ways that these issues have been handled in some of the management literature.

4. Decision-Making in the Multinational Firm

International business, as an area of academic study, is typically composed of two related subject areas. The first is the study of the international business environment, while the second is the study of the firm in this environment. The first subject area is more concerned with macro-considerations, taking as its unit of analysis entire countries or groups of countries while the second is more narrowly focused, taking as its unit of analysis the individual firm. We are concerned with the organisation of the firm. Our concern is therefore with micro aspects and it is this second subject area of international business that we focus on. All the functional areas of business have some relevance to our topic of study. However, as might be expected, areas related to management structures are most closely related to our area of interest.

By necessity, a multinational firm is a multi-unit enterprise. Practical decisions in multinational firms deal with both the oversight of the entire firm as well as with linkages between its constituent units. All these decisions can be placed into three basic categories. The first category is made up of decisions relating to the organisation and control of the existing enterprise and its affiliated units. The second consists of decisions relating to entry modes into new areas including the design of relationships between the new units and the centre. The third consists of decisions relating to the location of the various activities of the organisation.

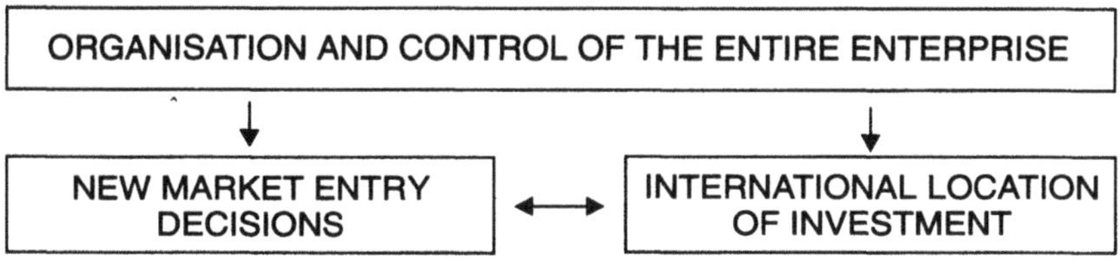

Figure 1.1 The relationship between the decision categories

Success in the first of these categories may be seen to be a prerequisite for success in the next two. In other words, organisation and control of the existing enterprise is a basis for expansion, which encompasses new entry, as well as the location of such entry. Appropriate entry modes and location choice are mutually-related choices. Thus, the relationship between the decision categories may be summarised as in Figure 1.1.

Transaction costs analysis

In the theory of the firm, the driving force underlying organisation is the minimisation of transaction costs. In the strict sense of Coase, transaction costs arise from participating in market transactions, and the underlying choice is a dichotomous one involving the comparison of these costs with the cost of making the product (vertically integrating). This revolutionary insight can be easily extended to analyse situations where the firm faces a continuum of intermediate choices. Many of these intermediate choices have become significant in western business relations decades after Coase's seminal work and more recently several others have appeared through an observation of Japanese management practices.

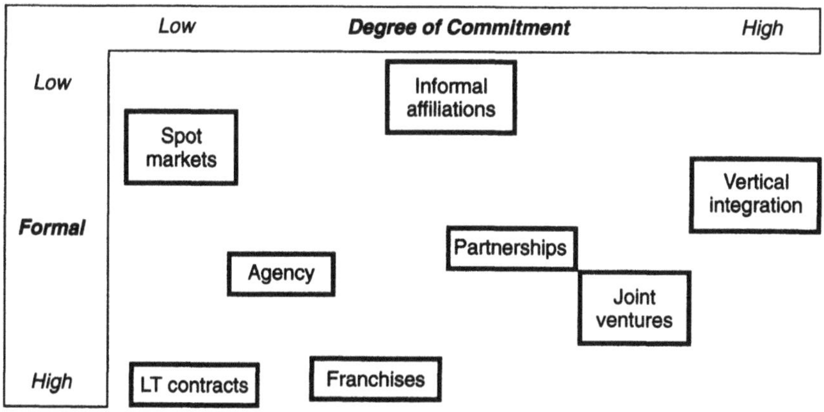

Figure 1.2 Vertical relationships

Firms today choose from a multiplicity of intermediate organisational forms, from spot markets at one extreme through various forms of inter-firm cooperation, to vertical integration, at the other extreme. It is worthwhile to outline briefly inter-firm organisational forms, using the degree of commitment between the parties and the degree of formalisation of the terms of the relationship as joint measuring rods.

Various kinds of transaction costs arise in all inter-firm relationships in Figure 1.2. For example, agents may require monitoring, franchises may encourage free riding, long term contracts may suffer from problems arising from bounded rationality and joint ventures may lead to 'hold-up'. In designing inter-firm relationships, all the considerations of transaction costs analysis need to borne in mind.

The practical application of transaction costs analysis

Applying the results of economic theory to the practical issues of international business requires systematically breaking down the processes undertaken by the firm into their constituent transactions. Then, in each of the above three classes of decisions (Figure 1.1), the important goal of research is identifying the nature and sources of transaction costs associated with each alternative. It will then be possible to design an organisational structure and logistical pattern of operation that will minimise transaction costs and consequently maximise efficiency and profits.

The disaggregation of the firm can be carried out from two different perspectives. The first perspective is to split up the firm in terms of the activities undertaken with regard to its outputs. This is called *value chain disaggregation*. The second perspective is to split up the firm in terms of the functional activities that it undertakes. This is called *functional disaggregation*. Both of these forms of disaggregation are relevant to the multinational firm.

Value chain disaggregation

The value chain identifies a sequential chain of activities which are chronologically linked. This linkage is the crucial element which identifies the chain. According to McKinsey & Co., the value chain forms a 'business system' (Grant 1995). A simplified view of such a system is presented in Figure 1.3. The activities involved are business activities as opposed to merely stages of production. In fact, the stages of production can be seen to be subsumed within the value chain. The decisions with regard to procurement, parts production and raw materials are all part of the manufacturing link of the chain.

The considerations of transaction costs underlie the firm's decisions not only with regard to the make-or-buy considerations within the manufacturing link of the chain, but also with regard to all inter-linkages in the chain. Thus, decisions on whether the firm should develop its own technology or

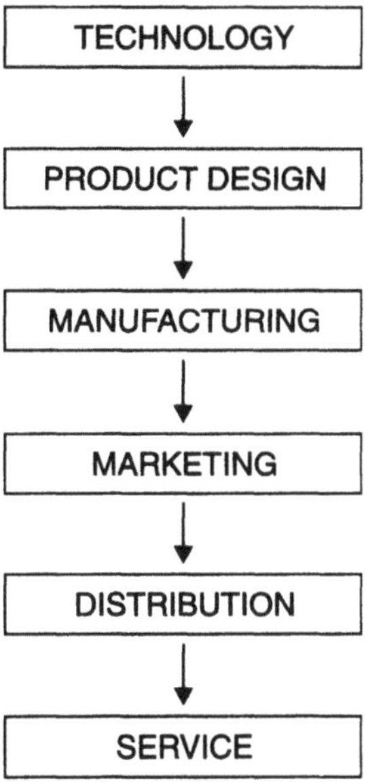

Figure 1.3 The value chain as a business system

license it from others are based on the costs of internal development as compared with the transaction costs involved in license fees and the probability of holdup. At the other end of the chain, decisions with regard to managing service are based on a comparison of internal operating costs with the transaction costs involved in a market relationship with a quantification of the associated problems of moral hazard and free ridership.

Functional disaggregation

While it may be argued that value chain analysis views the firm vertically, functional analysis views the firm horizontally. Principal functions may be portrayed as in Figure 1.4. As may be seen, several links in the value chain also appear as business functions, for example, manufacturing and marketing. Further, several functions impinge all the operations of the firm, for example, corporate management and R&D, while others are more narrowly focused. The key element of functional disaggregation is the recognition of the importance of overheads.

Porter (1985) calls narrow-focus functions (the bottom of Figure 1.4) primary activities and broad-focus functions (the upper part of Figure 1.4) support activities.

Transaction costs appear in an examination of a functionally-disaggregated firm in much the same way as they appear in a firm disaggregated using the value chain. Their appearance may be more subtle, however, since many

CORPORATE MANAGEMENT			
MANAGEMENT INFORMATION			
RESEARCH AND DEVELOPMENT			
PRODUCT DESIGN	MANUFACTURING	MARKETING	SALES AND DISTRIBUTION

Figure 1.4 Functional disaggregation of the firm

aspects will appear through an assessment of an identification of the firm's comparative advantage. These considerations may lead one firm to concentrate its manufacturing in one country and rely on export to service other markets while leading another to spread its manufacturing activities over many locations.

5. New Market Entry Modes

Since a multinational firm is, by definition, a firm with operations in several countries, a key feature of such a firm is the structure of the multifarious relationships among activities which are separated by political boundaries. However, there are two schools of thought with regard to the 'nationality' of multinational firms. On the one side is the view propounded by Porter (1990), that firms have home bases which establish their identity and critical managerial behaviours. On the other side is the view associated with senior business executives like Reuter and Barnevik (Barnevik 1994; Taylor 1991) that the multinational firm is a 'stateless' enterprise, which has no nationality. It may be argued that the latter view is a particularly European one, and has been formed in firms which are necessarily internationally-oriented and composed of diverse groups. This necessity arises from the small national markets and cultural diversity found in Europe (Henzler 1992). It is worth noting that Barnevik himself is associated with ABB, a multinational with strong ties to Sweden and Switzerland, both tiny national markets.

Thus, we will proceed under the assumption that is traditional in international business, namely that multinational firms have a home country and a nationality. While there may be some firms whose nationality is difficult to pin down, such firms represent a relatively small proportion of all multinationals. And even such firms must undertake headquarters functions and make decisions regarding the nature of relationships between the headquarters and the firm's operating units.

The structure of these relationships can vary from a pure export-orientated approach typified by the Japanese automobile firms in the 1970s (see, for example, Keller 1993) to the loose confederations typified by early European multinationals like Unilever (Bartlett and Ghoshal 1989). The relationships can be changed over time, but the decisions driving such change can be derived from the basic principles underlying the initial decisions regarding entry into overseas markets.

Exporting is often regarded as the first step into a foreign market, but its persistence as a viable strategy mode, even in the largest multinationals, suggests that it still has an important role to play. The sequentialist school has made much of the typically-observed pattern of proceeding from export to licensing to foreign direct investment (FDI) (see Buckley and Ghauri 1991). Exporting itself has often been analysed as a sequential process (Hood and Young 1979), with 'anticipatory exports' (exports from the home country in anticipation of building or acquiring a foreign plant), 'associated exports' (complementary exports after the establishment of the subsidiary) and 'balancing exports' (which occur when the foreign plant is operating at capacity).

Market-entry decisions can be understood as a specific application of transaction costs analysis. Therefore the overriding consideration in the design of the relationship between the headquarters and the overseas market is the location of the firm's capital.[8] If it is retained in the home country then relationship with the foreign market is said to be transactions based. However, if the firm's capital is located in the foreign market, the relationship with the foreign market is based on FDI. A short taxonomy of foreign market entry modes is provided in Figure 1.5.

Transactions-based relationships require the foreign facility to be controlled through contract, and the flow of payments from the foreign market to the firm's headquarters consists of payments for goods or payments for services (royalties, license fees, etc.). In contrast, FDI-based relationships allow the firm to manage the foreign facility directly and the flow of payments to headquarters largely consists of returns to invested capital (repatriated profits, debt service, etc.).

TRANSACTION BASED	Exporting	Spot transactions
		Long term contracts
		Foreign distributor/agent
	Licensing technology/trademarks	
	Franchising (Licensing with fully packaged business system)	
FOREIGN DIRECT INVESTMENT	Joint venture	Marketing/distribution only
		Fully integrated
	Fully owned subsidiary	Marketing/distribution only
		Fully integrated

Figure 1.5 Overseas market entry decisions – modes of foreign market entry

While FDI confers greater control on headquarters, it is regarded as the more risky form of entry in terms of capital committed, but has been found to be the most effective in securing market share and strategic competitive advantage. This is reported by Buckley *et al.* (1987). With transactions-based modes, some control is sacrificed for a lower level of financial risk. When put in these terms, it may be seen here that the fundamental choice is reduced to one between the firm and the market.

6. International Location of Investment

FDI has increased enormously over the last thirty years. The total value of global FDI was estimated at US$ 105 billion in 1967. By 1984 it had climbed to an estimated US$ 596 billion and by 1993 it was estimated at US$ 2,125 billion (United Nations 1994). In order to understand these increases, it is necessary to examine how firms choose to locate capital investments.

Location in the international context is typically investigated within a partial equilibrium framework under the umbrella of Dunning's (1977) Ownership-Location-Internalization (OLI) paradigm. Applying this framework typically requires weighing up three sets of factors: country resources, firm-specific resources and tradability issues. Country resource conditions are items such as the local competitive situation, infrastructure, relative labour costs and demand conditions. Firm-specific competitive advantages are unique capabilities of the firm that are not easily transferable to other locations. Tradability issues include transport costs, exchange rate dynamics, tax considerations and tariffs and regulatory constraints. Research has shown that tradability issues can often become dominant (Wheeler and Mody 1992, Mudambi 1995).

The production of any good is composed of a vertical chain of activities, whose input requirements vary considerably. Therefore, the firm must take account of the differential advantages of different countries for each stage of the value chain. These considerations create some of the strongest driving forces underlying multinational production arrangements.

In this context, the strategic location decision is made up of two components. The first concerns the optimal location for a given activity considered independently and the second concerns the importance of linkages between the activity and the other activities of the firm. The importance of the first component in the overall decision increases as that of the second declines and vice versa. In other words, if the linkages between the firm's activities are unimportant then the location of each activity can be determined largely independently of all other activities. However, if these linkages are critical, then determining the optimal location for each activity in isolation will have little value.

This decision process may be implemented in three steps, as follows:

Activity	Requirements	Location
Design	• Technical expertise • Design and fashion expertise • Marketing information	USA
Component manufacture	• Skilled and unskilled labour • Sophisticated machinery • Materials-leather, canvas, rubber, plastics	Taiwan, S. Korea
Assembly	• Unskilled labour • Simple machinery	Thailand, the Philippines

Figure 1.6 Nike: production of sports shoes
Source: Based on Harvard Business School Cases 9–385–328 and 9–386–037, 1985.

1 Definition of key activities;
2 Identification of principal requirements underlying the execution of each activity;
3 Identification of locations which meet the requirements from step 2.

This process yields a short list of locations. The firm must finally decide on the location which best meets all its corporate objectives.

An illustration of this process is provided in Figure 1.6, which describes the international location decisions of Nike, an American footwear multinational (Harvard Business School 1985a, 1985b and Business Week 1994). Actually 100 per cent of Nike's output is produced by subcontractors, most of them outside the US. These subcontractors are divided into three distinct groups, ranked in terms of the closeness of their relationship to Nike and consequent role in the multinational's overall strategy. Thus Nike provides an object lesson in the interlinkage between the international location of production and foreign market entry modes.

7. Organisation and Control

The key decision that must be made by the overall management of a multinational firm is the balance between economies of scale (globalisation/centralisation) and product differentiation (localisation/decentralisation). Multinationals have evolved and changed through time in their approach to this question. Bartlett and Ghoshal (1989) identify three phases in the development of the multinational.

The first phase is the pre-Second World War period, which is called the era of the European multinationals like Unilever, ICI, Philips and Courtaulds. These companies are described as 'multinational federations' and each national subsidiary was permitted a high degree of operational independence, undertaking its own product development, manufacture and marketing.

Parent-subsidiary relations revolved around the appointment of senior managers to subsidiaries (governors), authorisation of major capital expenditures and the flow of dividends to the parent. Such structures were a natural reaction to a period when transport and communication was relatively expensive and unreliable and national markets were highly differentiated.

The second phase encompasses the decades following the Second World War and is called the era of American multinationals. These include companies like GM, Ford, Caterpillar, Procter & Gamble and Coca-Cola. While subsidiaries of these companies enjoyed a high level of autonomy, the key feature of these US multinationals was the dominant position of the firm's domestic operations. Since the US was the largest and most affluent market in the world, the US operations of these firms acted as the source of much of the product and process technology as well as manufacturing and marketing 'know-how'. The major competitive advantage of the foreign subsidiaries was their access to the expertise developed in domestic operations.

The third phase covers the 1970s and 1980s and relates to the rising power of Japanese multinationals across a range of manufacturing industries from steel and shipbuilding to electronics and cars. The key identifying characteristic of the Japanese multinationals of this period was their use of a global manufacturing strategy based on a centralised domestic production hub. The prime competitive advantage of these firms was their highly-trained and motivated domestic workforce as well as a range of innovative management techniques.

Today we observe multinationals from all three phases actively competing in the global marketplace, which seems to indicate that no one organisational form is dominant. However, over the last decade, virtually all multinationals seem to be converging towards attempting to extract both scale and differentiation advantages. This has been aided, in part, by the falling costs of customisation which has reduced the sharpness of the globalisation/localisation strategic choice. This, in turn, has been based on making better use of information and making subsidiaries function as global partners. Such a coordination and control structure has been called a 'networked global organisation'

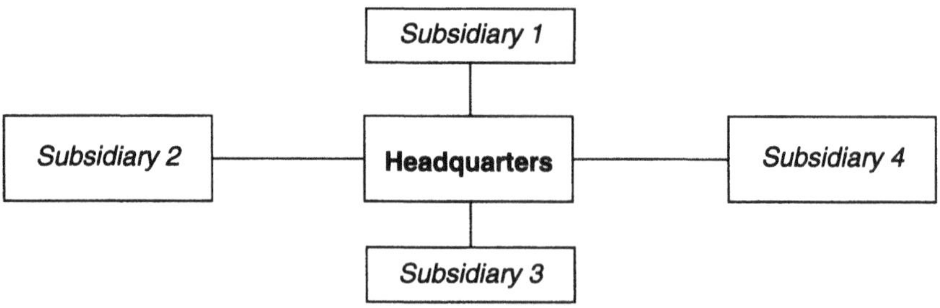

Figure 1.7a Non-networked multinational organisation

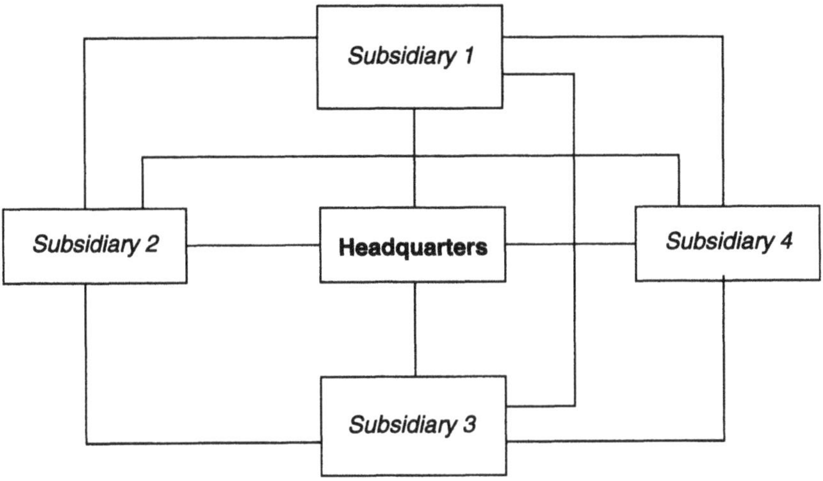

Figure 1.7b Networked global organisation

(Gross *et al.* 1987). Its functioning is dependent upon a much larger number of information channels, as depicted in Figures 1.7a and 1.7b.[9]

Thus, while European, US and Japanese non-networked multinational organisational firms relate to differing headquarters–subsidiary relations as depicted in Figure 1.7a, the networked global organisation is based on entirely new inter-subsidiary relationships.

The operationalisation of such networking typically occurs by identifying the comparative advantages of each subsidiary and giving that subsidiary a global role related to these advantages. Thus, a UK subsidiary may be designated the global source for a particular product, while a German subsidiary may be designated the global source for another. This leads to intra-firm movement of components and finished goods and mimics the workings of free trade. Examples of firms which have implemented such organisation include Ciba–Geigy (sinced merged with Sandoz to form Novartis), ICI and Philips (Czinkota *et al.* 1996: 712–38).

Concluding Remarks

It is our objective to introduce a collection of works aimed at bridging the divide between the theory of the economic organisation of the firm and the applied work in international business dealing with the multinational firm.[10] Both these disciplines share an interest in the logistics, organisation and control of the multinational firm. This interest centres both on the internal organisation of the firm itself including a determination of its boundaries, as well as the organisation of its relationships with external entities. As we have noted, the early literature in international business (for example, Buckley and Casson 1976, Dunning 1981, etc.) was an explicit application of the theoretical principles of economic organisation to the multinational firm. However, in the large literature in international business which followed these pioneering efforts, paradigms from other social sciences were brought to bear, but in much of the work the fundamental principles of economic organisation have been marginalised. Further, in the two decades since Dunning's and Buckley and Casson's original contributions, there have been many developments in the theory of economic organisation which have not yet found their way into the international business literature. Thus, in many ways, this collection of papers adopts a 'back to basics' approach to international business.

Notes

1 Demsetz (1995) criticises this view by emphasising specialisation as the defining characteristic of production within a firm. A world of single people contracting across markets, on this interpretation, would be a world of specialised single person 'firms'.

2 The classic paper proposing the firm as a solution to a moral hazard problem is Alchian and Demsetz (1972).

3 Akerlof (1970) is the seminal paper.

4 Classic references include Holmstrom (1979). An overview is provided in Pratt and Zeckhauser (eds) (1985).

5 See Rubin (1978), Martin (1988) and Dnes (1992).

6 See Casson (1987) p. 35. 'Dunning thus uses Coasian theory in a thoroughly non-Coasian way'.

7 See also Caves (1996).

8 The location of capital is used here to represent equity and therefore control. As pointed out by Buckley *et al.* (1992), the key feature of FDI is control from the parent.

9 It is straightforward to see that the number of information channels required to run a non-networked multinational organisation with 'n' subsidiaries is n, i.e. one to each subsidiary. However, to run a networked global organisation, an additional nC_2 information channels (one between each pair of subsidiaries) are required. Thus total number of channels required is

$$^{n}C_2 + n = n(n+1)/2$$

10 In international business it is common to differentiate between multinational firms, global firms, transnational firms and so on. We use the term multinational firm to refer to the class of all such firms, i.e. all firms which have significant operations in more than one country.

Part I

THEORETICAL ISSUES

INTRODUCTORY NOTE

Part I is made up of contributions which consider the multinational enterprise from the perspective of transactions cost theory. Casson emphasises the costs of collecting and disseminating information. This focus derives directly from Coase. However, Casson is not content merely to contrast the market with the firm but wishes to predict the circumstances in which alternative types of firm – centralised or decentralised, autocratic or consultative – will emerge. He develops a model of internal organisation, analyses its properties and explores its implications for the multinational firm.

Buckley and Carter draw attention to the connection between the collection and interpretation of information in a team and the role of entrepreneurship. To organise a business process, they argue, is to organise an entrepreneurial team. The authors compare different 'architectures' of a company operating in two countries – separate decisions, sequential decisions, decisions made by a joint board or decisions made by one of the parties (parent choice). They argue that information, coordination and motivation losses and the costs incurred in mitigating these losses will vary with the decision process adopted. As with the chapter by Casson, this contribution by Buckley and Carter follows the theory of teams in concentrating more on information and coordination problems rather than on the problem of motivation.

The final chapter in Part I concerns the relationship between the multinational enterprise and the theory of international trade. Markusen points out that direct exports and foreign investment are substitute forms of organisation. Traditional theories of international trade provide no rationale of the multinational enterprise but Markusen's chapter presents a model in which such enterprises arise naturally depending upon configurations of transport costs, plant specific and firm specific fixed costs. He notes, however, that if firm specific advantages could be marketed, licensing would be a viable alternative to the multinational. Markusen's chapter therefore includes a section on the transaction costs of trading in certain types of knowledge and reviews the advantages of 'internalisation' from the point of view of the multinational enterprise.

2

THE ECONOMICS OF INTERNAL ORGANISATION WITH SPECIAL REFERENCE TO THE MULTINATIONAL ENTERPRISE

Mark Casson

1. Introduction

Internalisation theory (Buckley and Casson 1976) relates the theory of the multinational enterprise (MNE) conceptually to the theory of the firm. The theory of the MNE is a theory about a firm that is spread out over space. In this theory, space has been subdivided politically into the territories of different national states. Internalisation theory explains how the organisational boundaries of the firm interact with the location of its activities to determine whether or not it becomes an MNE. This theory is more general than ordinary theories of the firm because these ordinary theories of the firm ignore the spatial dimension and implicitly confine their attention to a firm's operations within a single nation state.

In developing a general theory, however, a special theory is often a useful preliminary step. In this chapter, therefore, the first step in developing an economic theory of the internal organisation of the MNE is taken by concentrating attention on a very simple case. In this case there are just two countries: the firm produces in one of them and sells in another. Once the key insights have emerged from this analysis, they are extended and generalised to the more complex case of several production locations and several national markets typical of the modern MNE.

The theory of internalisation derives from the Coasian approach to the firm. Coase's insight addresses head-on the question of where the boundaries of the firm are drawn: the scope of the firm's activities expands up to the margin where the cost of internalising an additional market is just equal to the benefit of replacing the corresponding external market. External markets need to be replaced because of imperfections – i.e. deviations from the Walrasian ideal. Coase (1937) originally emphasised the costs of price discovery as the major imperfection. Later work has highlighted the costs of writing comprehensive legally-enforceable contracts and the limited scope of property rights in knowledge too (Williamson 1975; Casson 1979).

While the Coasian approach is quite satisfactory as an explanation of the boundaries of the firm, the same cannot be said of its explanation of internal organisation. It might be expected that the Coasian approach would analyse the best form of internal organisation in order to identify the minimum cost of an internal market with which the costs of an external market should be compared. It turns out, however, that a separate account of internal organisation needs to be grafted on to the Coasian approach in order to perform this task (see Sah and Stiglitz 1986, Bolton and Dewatripont 1994). The strength of the Coasian approach lies more in identifying the costs of the external market than in identifying the costs of the internal one. In the Coasian literature, for example, the costs of internalisation are sometimes imputed to the setting of shadow prices within a decentralised firm and at other times to the bureaucratic operations of a hierarchy in a centralised one. Williamson (1985) has attempted to integrate internal organisation into an analysis of the boundaries of the firm using a simple typology, but this only predicts in the broadest terms how the fit between boundary and internal organisation is formed.

This chapter tackles the issue from a different standpoint. Building upon recent work by Radner (1992), Casson (1994, 1995a) and Carter (1995) it uses the economic theory of teams developed by Marschak and Radner (1972) to explain the internal organisation of the firm. The major insight of this approach is that organisation can only be fully understood from an economic standpoint when it is recognised that the firm's environment is continuously volatile and that the information about the environment which is needed for decision-making is costly to collect. The owner of a firm faces a trade-off between the efficiency with which he allocates resources within the firm and the cost of the resources that he allocates to the collection of information instead. The more resources he allocates to collecting information, the higher his expected operating profit will be. But beyond a certain point, an increase in his expenditure on information will not increase his expected net profit, because investment in information, like investment in any resource, encounters diminishing marginal returns. There is an optimum point at which the marginal contribution to expected operating profit from collecting and processing an additional item of information is just equal to the expected costs involved. The rules and procedures employed to process this optimal amount of information determine the efficient organisational structure of the firm.

The present chapter develops this approach, and extends it from the internal organisation of the firm to the organisation of external markets as well. It uses the concepts of volatility and information cost to examine the negotiation strategies that will emerge in the external market as an analogue of the administrative procedures of the internal one. It compares the efficiency of internal and external arrangements under different patterns of volatility and different structures of information costs. By invoking the principle that the most efficient arrangement will, in the long run, be selected, it predicts the choices between firm and market in different economic environments. Not only does it predict whether the firm or the market will prevail; it also predicts what kind of firm will emerge, and what kind of market the firm is a substitute for.

The analysis shows that the advantage of the firm over the market is greatest where there are multiple sources of volatility that can be identified in advance, and where a synthesis of information from these sources routinely needs to be carried out. The major problem with the market alternative to the firm is that the incentive to bluff is difficult to remove. Bluffing distorts the allocation of resources both *directly*, through misleading price quotations, and *indirectly* by discouraging those who bluff from discovering the true value of what they are bluffing about. This denies access to the information required to implement a sophisticated decision rule. When substitutions between resources are easy to make the incentive to bluff is constrained by competitive threats, but when complementarities predominate this is no longer the case. Complementarities therefore play to the strengths of the firm and exacerbate the weaknesses of the market.

To simplify the discussion it is assumed that bluffing is confined to information about the state of the environment, and that bluffing about the quality of the product is not an issue. It is assumed that product quality can be ascertained without cost; the consequences of relaxing this (and other assumptions) are considered in Casson (1996b).

The rest of the chapter is structured as follows: Section 2 introduces a simple model of the internal organisation of the firm; Section 3 analyses the market alternative; the comparison between them is effected in Section 4. Possible extensions of the model are discussed in Section 5, and applications to the MNE in Section 6. Section 7 concludes by relating the model to wider issues raised by the continuing debate on the nature of the firm.

2. Modelling Organisation: Rational Choice with Costly Information

The market environment

Consider a firm which has innovated a new product or, by some other means, gained control of a market niche. The exploitation of this niche involves two activities: one upstream and one downstream. The simplest case, considered here, is where the upstream activity produces the product and the downstream activity distributes it to customers. There are many other possibilities, though: for example, the upstream and downstream activities may be adjacent stages of a vertical production sequence. In the case of the MNE, the upstream and downstream activities are located in different countries. The important thing is that uncertainty impinges on both activities and that these activities are linked by intermediate product flow. Information needs to be collected on both activities to fully coordinate the flow of product through the internal market that links them. In the simple case discussed here the intermediate product is wholesale finished product ready for distribution to consumers, while in the case of multi-stage production, it is semi-processed product instead.

Uncertainty relates to discrete states of the environment. Consumer demand is continuously disturbed by a stochastic factor, such as fashion, which impinges systematically on every individual. As a result, the state of demand confronting the distribution activity in any given period may be either good, $s_1 = 1$, or bad, $s_1 = 0$. Production takes place in a single plant, in which cost conditions are disturbed by changes in the scarcity of manual labour or raw materials. The state of supply in any given period may be either good, $s_2 = 1$, or bad, $s_2 = 0$.

The internal wholesale market is coordinated by setting the appropriate value of output, x. It is assumed that the firm faces a discrete choice whether to produce a marginal batch of output ($x = 1$) or not ($x = 0$). Intra-marginal output is ignored; indeed, to simplify the discussion it is assumed that the marginal batch is the only batch of output produced. The consequences of relaxing this assumption are considered later on. Output sells for P_1 when demand conditions are good, and for $P_0 < P_1$ when conditions are bad. It costs c_1 to produce when supply conditions are good and $c_0 > c_1$ when conditions are bad. Thus operating profit is $\pi(s_1, s_2, x)$ given by

$$\begin{aligned} &\pi(s_1, s_2, 0) = 0 && (s_1, s_2 = 0, 1) \\ &\pi(0,0,1) = P_0 - c_0 && \pi(0,1,1) = P_0 - c_1 \\ &\pi(1,0,1) = P_1 - c_0 && \pi(1,1,1) = P_1 - c_1 \end{aligned} \tag{1}$$

It is further assumed that $c_1 < P_0 < c_0 < P_1$, which means that production is profitable whenever *either* demand *or* supply conditions are good. Production is unprofitable only when both conditions are bad.

Disturbances are random, serially independent, and uncorrelated. In other words, demand and supply shocks are transitory rather than permanent, and are unrelated to each other. In each period demand conditions are good with probability p_1 and supply conditions are good with probability

$p_2 (0 \leq p_1, p_2 \leq 1)$. The probability $p(s_1, s_2)$ that the environment is in state s_1, s_2 is then

$$p(0,0) = (1 - p_1)(1 - p_2) \quad p(0,1) = (1 - p_1)p_2$$
$$p(1,0) = p_1(1 - p_2) \qquad p(1,1) = p_1 p_2 \tag{2}$$

For an informed choice of output to be made, information on the state of the environment must be gathered before the output decision is made. It is, however, more costly to gather the information before the decision than afterwards. This is because a special investigation is required before the decision is made, whereas the state of the environment tends to become apparent once the consequences of the decision manifest themselves to those involved. Information on each aspect of the environment s_j, is gathered separately because there are no economies of gathering them together. It is assumed for simplicity that the observation $\hat{s}_j$ is perfectly accurate:

$$\hat{s}_j = s_j \qquad (j = 1, 2) \tag{3}$$

The optimisation problem

Because the shocks are transitory rather than permanent, there is no advantage to memorising previous states of the market. The state of the market does not 'evolve' and the nature of the uncertainty remains the same from one period to the next. The owner of the firm therefore faces essentially the same decision problem in each period. Telescoping all future decisions into the present as part of a single inter-temporal contingent plan reveals that it is optimal to defer decisions on future output to the future periods in which the relevant information becomes available. This means that the maximisation of expected net present value at the outset is equivalent to the maximisation of expected net profit v on a period-by-period basis. The optimal plan is encapsulated by a procedure to be applied in each successive period. The firm is thus an organisation geared to the routine implementation of this procedure.

Let the set of feasible procedures be K. Any procedure k in K structures the gathering of information $\hat{s}_1$, $\hat{s}_2$ and its use in the output decision in a particular way:

$$x = x(\hat{s}_1, \hat{s}_2, k) \tag{4}$$

The kth procedure incurs an expected information cost $i(k) \geq 0$.

A risk-neutral owner maximises expected net profit

$$v = \sum_{i=1}^{2} \sum_{j=1}^{2} p(s_1, s_2)\pi(s_1, s_2, x) - i(k) \tag{5}$$

while a risk-averse owner maximises v subject to a no-loss constraint. This involves a different concept of risk-aversion from the one conventionally employed, but is particularly useful because it leaves the objective (5) unchanged and merely restricts the admissible set of strategies to a subset K' of K, such that

$$\pi(s_1, s_2, k) \geq 0 \text{ for } k \in K' \tag{6}$$

The concept implies that owners regard breaking even as absolutely crucial, but are tolerant of uncertainty about the amount of positive profit that they make. Note that for analytical simplicity the constraint (6) is specified in terms of gross profit, and not in terms of the net profit described in equation (5).

The structure of information costs

It is assumed that there are three people in the firm who can make observations: the owner (individual 0), the marketing manager who distributes output (individual 1) and the production manager who requisitions inputs (individual 2). Information on demand conditions is most readily collected by the marketing manager, who incurs an observation cost $b_1 > 0$ before the decision is made, and zero afterwards. Similarly, information on supply conditions is most readily collected by the production manager, who incurs an observation cost $b_2 > 0$ before the decision is made and zero afterwards. It costs the owner $B_j > b_j (j = 1, 2)$ to observe conditions for himself before the decision is made, and $b_0 \geq 0$ thereafter. The inequality constraint on B_j implies that the owner is systematically disadvantaged so far as the collection of information is concerned, because information arises most naturally as a byproduct of the activities that the managers carry out.

The natural response for the owner is to delegate the collection of information to the managers. To do this he must overcome three problems, however. The first is the cost of communication. Because information on the state of the environment is tacit, it costs $m \geq 0$ to communicate the state to the owner. The second problem is deceit. Observations generate private information. In the absence of moral restraints it may pay managers to misreport conditions. By pretending that conditions are bad when in fact they are good the production manager can inflate the production budget to provide a surplus $c_0 - c_1$ for himself, while the marketing manager can reduce the sales target to generate a surplus $P_1 - P_0$ for himself. The owner must therefore check out the situation after the output decision has been made, if he has not done so before, to determine for himself the budget that is required to implement the output plan. This also allows him to check on any report that was given before the decision was made, and so overcomes the third problem, of shirking by a manager who does not make a proper observation even though he has been given a budget for the purpose.

In the light of all this it is assumed that while owners may delegate the collection of the information required for the output decision, they do not delegate the setting of budgets once this decision has been made, but set these budgets themselves. Collecting this information on both production and distribution incurs a cost $2b_0$. Managers respond to this by always reporting truthfully when they are consulted prior to the output decision.

While information is costly to communicate, decisions on output are not. Orders can be issued by the decision-maker at no cost. This means that it pays to localise decision-making at the point of observation unless the rule employed to take the decision is costly to communicate in itself (see Table 2.3).

The opportunity costs of the managers' time and of the owners' time are ignored. Effectively they are treated as fixed costs which must be incurred whatever procedure the firm adopts. In the case of the managers this is not unreasonable since their information gathering is a natural byproduct of their other work, but it is much more questionable where the owner is concerned. It is also assumed that managers are in competitive supply and can be replaced at will. This ensures that all the profits of coordination accrue to the owner of the firm.

The set of procedures

A procedure involves two steps. The first specifies what information is to be collected and the second specifies how the information that has been collected is to be used. The first decision is actually the more sophisticated one, despite the fact that conventional theories of the firm tend to focus on the second instead. Once it is known what information has been collected, it is fairly straightforward to determine the appropriate level of output.

Because there are four possible states of the environment, in each of which the firm may decide to produce or not, there are $2^4 = 16$ possible rules for fixing output. Given the restrictions on cost and price imposed above, however, there are just five rules which dominate the rest (see Table 2.1). They comprise the rule Y1, which is optimal when full information is available, the rules Y2 and Y3 which require only one item of information each, and Y4 and Y5 which can be applied when no information is available at all.

Which output rule is appropriate depends upon the first stage decision. This decision concerns the variables $z_1(k), z_2(k)$, which govern whether the respective observations $\hat{s}_1$, $\hat{s}_2$ are made. The procedures comprising K may be derived by enumeration from the decision tree shown in Figure 2.1. Economic intuition suggests, and calculations confirm, that under the assumed conditions there are just seven dominant procedures according to the profit criterion, each of which is associated with a particular output rule. The

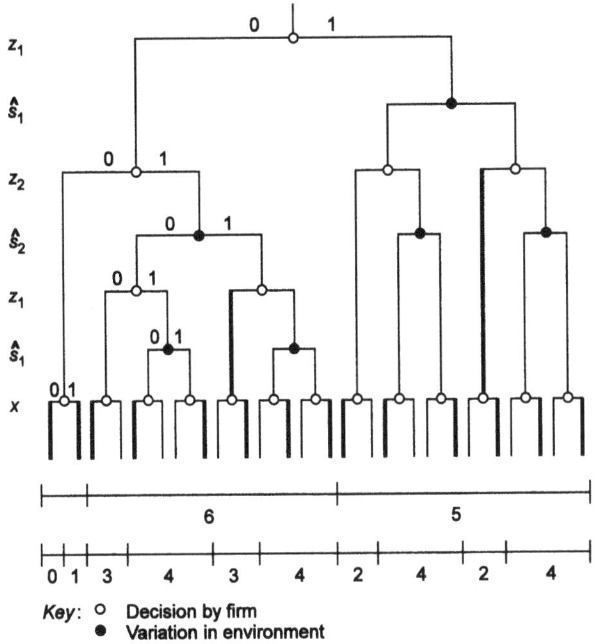

Figure 2.1 Decision tree for all investigation procedures

Notes:
The solid lines indicate the choices made when output rule Y2 applies in the full information case.
The figure indicates how the options 5 and 6 encompass the regular procedures 2–4.
The final revelation of the true states s^1, s^2 has been suppressed from the bottom of the figure in the interests of clarity.

Table 2.1 Five dominant output rules

			States $(\hat{s}_1, \hat{s}_2)$		
Reference	(0,0)	(0,1)	(1,0)	(1,1)	*Formula*
Y1	0	1	1	1	$x = \hat{s}_1 + \hat{s}_2 - \hat{s}_1\hat{s}_2$
Y2	0	0	1	1	$x = \hat{s}_1$
Y3	0	1	0	1	$x = \hat{s}_2$
Y4	0	0	0	0	$x = 0$
Y5	1	1	1	1	$x = 1$

dominance relations apply equally to the set K and the subset K' defined above. The dominant procedures are listed in Table 2.2.

The *regular procedures*, indexed $k = 0, 1, \ldots, 4$, involve investigations which are decided upon in a single step. The most sophisticated of these – procedure 4 – involves a commitment at the outset to collecting information on both sets of conditions. The *option procedures* $k = 5, 6$ involve two-step decisions. They defer the decision on a second investigation until the results of the first observation are known. Note that the use of the term 'procedure' is particularly appropriate in the two-step case because of the sequential nature of the investigation process.

Table 2.2 Dominant investigation procedures

k	z_1	z_2	*Description*	*Dominant output rule*	*Acceptability under risk aversion*
Regular					
0	0	0	No investigation; no output	Y4	Yes
1	0	0	No investigation; always produce	Y5	No
2	1	0	Investigate only demand and produce if and only if good	Y2	Yes
3	0	1	Investigate only supply and produce if and only if good	Y3	Yes
4	1	1	Investigate demand and supply simultaneously and produce provided at least one of them is good	Y1	Yes
Option					
5	1	$1 - \hat{s}_1$	Investigate demand initially and investigate supply too if conditions are bad	Y1 if $\hat{s}_1 = 0$ Y2 if $\hat{s}_1 = 1$	Yes
6	$1 - \hat{s}_2$	1	Investigate supply initially and investigate demand too if conditions are bad	Y2 if $\hat{s}_2 = 0$ Y3 if $\hat{s}_2 = 1$	Yes

It is assumed that individual managers report observations only to the owner and not to each other. There are four reasons for this. The first is that the information reported is of a tacit nature, as noted above, and benefits from being received and interpreted by someone with breadth of knowledge, such as the owner, rather than by another functional specialist, such as the other manager. The second is that the owner may be conveniently located at a communications hub, reducing the transmission costs associated with reporting the information. The third consideration is that it is more difficult for the owner to check the accuracy of a report which has been made to another manager and not directly to himself. The final, and most fundamental consideration, is that the costs of explaining the relevant decision rule to the manager who receives the communication may be too great. While each manager may be capable of understanding and applying a rule that relates to a single item of information that he collects himself, it may be too difficult for him to apply a rule that synthesises this information with information supplied by other people.

Table 2.3 Optimal assignments of personnel under alternative procedures

k	*Owner (0)*	*Responsibilities prior to output decision* *Manager 1*	*Manager 2*
0/1	Give output instructions	Receive output instructions	
2	Delegate output decision to 1	Observe demand conditions and implement output rule. Give instructions to 2	Receive output instructions from 1
3	Delegate output decision to 2	Receive output instructions from 2	Observe supply conditions and implement output rule. Give instructions to 1
4	Instruct 1 and 2 to observe and report. Give output instructions	Report demand conditions to 0. Receive output instructions	Report supply conditions to 0. Receive output instructions
5	Instruct 1 to observe and report. Depending on result, instruct 2 to observe and report. Give output instructions	Report demand conditions to 0. Receive output instructions	Await instruction whether to observe supply conditions. Receive output instructions
6	Instruct 2 to observe and report. Depending on result, instruct 1 to observe and report. Give output instructions	Await instruction whether to observe demand conditions. Receive output instructions	Report supply conditions to 0. Receive output instructions

Table 2.4 Information costs incurred by alternative procedures under optimal assignments

k	*i(k)*
0	0
1	$2b_0$
2	$2b_0 + b_1$
3	$2b_0 + b_2$
4	$2b_0 + b_1 + b_2 + 2m$
5	$2b_0 + b_1 + (1 - \hat{s}_1)b_2 + (2 - \hat{s}_1)m$
6	$2b_0 + b_2 + (1 - \hat{s}_2)b_1 + (2 - \hat{s}_2)m$

It follows that the synthesis involved in procedures 4–6 is effected by the owner himself. The implementation of procedure 2 is delegated to the marketing manager, and procedure 3 to the production manager. It is assumed for simplicity that each manager can implement the relevant output rule in a costless way. It only remains to consider whether, under these conditions, the owner might not be better off collecting all the information directly for himself. As noted earlier, it costs the owner B_j to observe s_j for himself. Conversely, it costs the owner $b_j + m$ to learn the information from the relevant manager, and b_0 to check its veracity afterwards. Provided, therefore, that $B_j > b_0 + b_j + m (j = 1, 2)$, the collection of information will be delegated along the lines described above. It is assumed that this condition is always satisfied.

Comment

The key feature of this formulation is that the set of dominant institutional arrangements has been restricted, by a judicious choice of assumptions, to just seven possibilities, each of which has a plausible real-world interpretation. The seven possibilities span the four organisational characteristics listed in Table 2.5. These characteristics have much to say about the style and structure of organisation implied by the choice of a particular procedure. It is particularly interesting to note the distinction between a decentralised organisation and a consultative one, since this is often fudged in the literature on organisational behaviour. Procedures 2 and 3 are decentralised but not consultative because they delegate decisions to managers who do not consult others before they take their decisions, whilst procedures 4–6 are both centralised and consultative because although the owner takes the decision he does so only after consulting one, and possibly both, of the managers.

Table 2.5 Organisational style and structure under different investigation procedures

		Style and structure		
k	*Decentralised*	*Consultative*	*Marketing-led*	*Production-led*
0/1	–	–	–	–
2	√	–	√	–
3	√	–	–	√
4	–	√	–	–
5	–	√	√	–
6	–	√	–	√

Example

To illustrate the solution method, consider the numerical example shown in Figure 2.2, where

$$P_0 = 4 \qquad P_1 = 8$$
$$c_0 = 2 \qquad c_1 = 6 \tag{7}$$

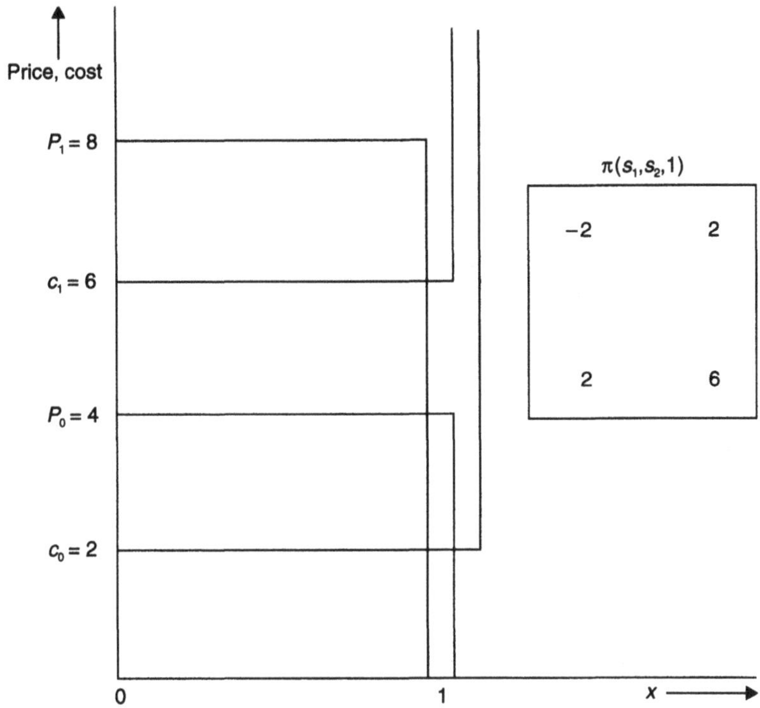

Figure 2.2 Marginal revenue and marginal cost curves: a numerical example

Notes:
Under the assumed conditions
Marginal revenue = Total revenue
Marginal production cost = Total production cost

These values have been chosen to make the problem symmetric, in the sense that the profit impact of a change in demand conditions is the same as the profit impact of a change in supply conditions, i.e. $P_1 - P_0 = c_1 - c_0 = 4$. Both conditions incur the same observation costs, $b_1 = b_2 = 0.25$. Communication costs are ignored, $m = 0$, and the costs to the owner of setting the budget are fairly small, $b_0 = 0.075$.

Restricted solution

The expected net profits for each procedure are given in Table 2.6. Suppose to begin with that the choice is restricted to the regular procedures $k = 0, 1 \ldots, 4$. The optimal procedure for each possible pattern of volatility is indicated in Figure 2.3. It is only in the case where both demand and supply conditions are very uncertain – i.e. for mid-range values of p_1, p_2, which

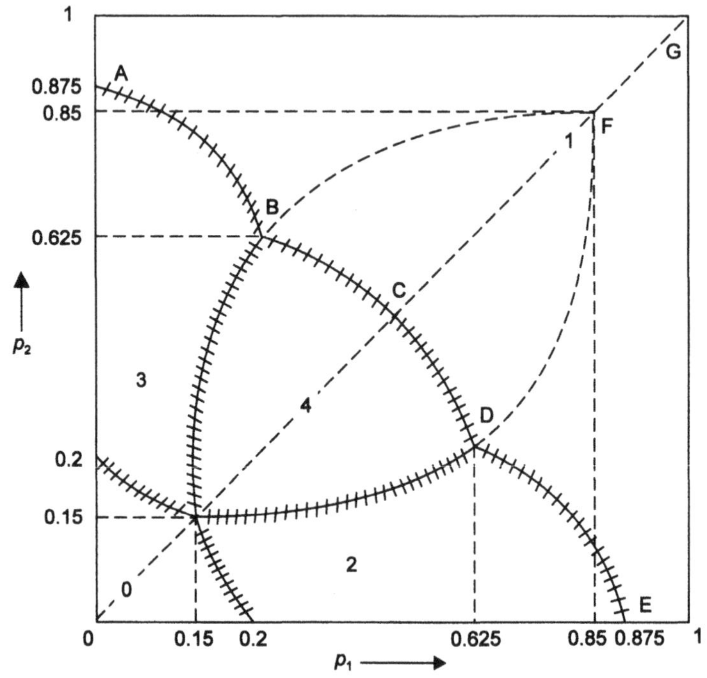

Figure 2.3 Optimisation of regular investigation procedures: the comparative statics of a numerical example

Notes:
The regions defined by the shaded edges represent the regimes that prevail before absolute loss aversion is introduced. The introduction of absolute loss aversion removes the boundary *ABCDE*, and extends regime 4 up to the point *F*. The boundary of regime 2 extends up to *DFG* and the boundary of regime 3 extends up to *BFG*.
The equations of the curves are derived by equalising the values of the procedures which are selected on either side of the line, as given in Table 2.6

correspond to high volatility – that investigation of both conditions is worthwhile (procedure 4). If the owner is subjectively sure that supply conditions will be bad, and the only major uncertainty relates to demand, then only demand conditions are investigated (procedure 2). This generates the marketing-led firm. This firm, though decentralised, is autocratic rather than consultative: the marketing manager is empowered by the owner to fix output on his behalf, but the marketing manager does not consult the production manager before he does so. Conversely, when the owner is subjectively sure that demand conditions will be bad, and the only uncertainty relates to supply, only supply conditions are investigated (procedure 3). The result is the production-led firm, in which the production manager sets the output on the basis of the information he collects and simply instructs the marketing manager what to do.

Table 2.6 Valuation of alternative procedures: the numerical example

k	v
0	$v_0 = 0$
1	$v_1 = 4p_1 + 4p_2 - 2.15$
2	$v_2 = 2p_1(1 + 2p_2) - 0.4$
3	$v_3 = 2p_2(1 + 2p_1) - 0.4$
4	$v_4 = 2(p_1 + p_2 + p_1p_2) - 0.65$
5	$v_5 = 2.25p_1 + 2p_2(1 + p_1) - 0.65$
6	$v_6 = 2.25p_2 + 2p_1(1 + p_2) - 0.65$

Because the firm makes a profit in three of the four possible states of the environment, and a loss in only one, there is a strong bias in favour of the strategy of producing whatever the conditions happen to be (procedure 1), as against not producing at all (procedure 0). This is reflected in the large size of the region in the figure where procedure 1 prevails, and the small size of the region corresponding to rule 0. Procedure 1, however, commits the firm to producing even when both demand and supply conditions are bad. Since $\pi\ (0, 0, 1) = -2 < 0$ this violates condition (6) indicating that procedure 1 is not acceptable to a risk-averse owner. With risk-aversion, therefore, the regimes 2, 3 and 4 extend into the north-east corner of the square, as indicated by the dashed curves in the figure. This confirms the intuition that risk-aversion will encourage the search for additional information before a decision is made. In the region *EDFG* the marketing manager is requested to provide additional information, whilst in the region *ABFG* the production manager is asked instead. Perhaps most remarkable is the fact that when both demand and supply are volatile, in the region *BCDF*, both managers are requested to provide additional information. This shows that a combination of risk aversion and volatility in the business environment can stimulate the demand for information even when the business environment is, on average, quite favourable.

Full solution

The option procedures 5 and 6 are potentially superior to the simultaneous investigation procedure 4 because they only carry out a second investigation when the result of the first investigation indicates that it is necessary to do so. They can therefore obtain the same quality of decision at a lower expected information cost. It is only if there were a cost advantage to simultaneous as opposed to sequential investigation – due, for example, to an economy of scale in observation – that simultaneous investigation might still be preferred. In the present model, different investigations are carried out by different people and so such economies have been excluded from the analysis. The result of including the option strategies is illustrated in Figure 2.4. It

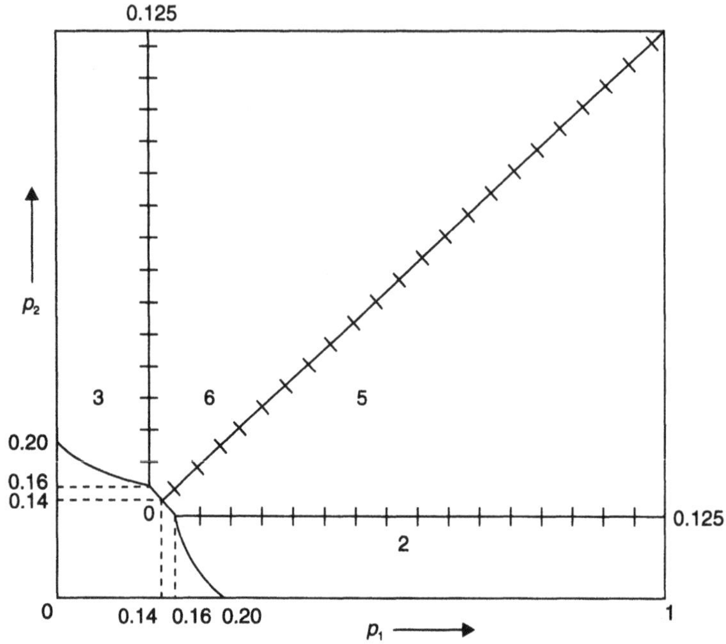

Figure 2.4 Optimisation of firm's investigation procedures when both regular and optimal procedures are available and risk aversion prevails

shows how the option strategies dominate the situation once they are introduced. They make marginal inroads into the use of procedures 2 and 3, but their major impact is to eliminate procedure 4 altogether. The impact is maximised when, as illustrated in the figure, risk aversion prevails. Overall, these results indicate that the exploitation of a *sequential synthesis of information from different sources* is a crucial element in the organisation of the firm.

3. The Market Alternative

The alternative to a firm is an ordinary market. In the present context this signifies an intermediate product market linking an independent producer (formerly manager 2) to an independent distributor (formerly manager 1). In the MNE literature the principal cost of the market alternative to the firm stems from the difficulty of licensing a competitive advantage to independent firms (Buckley and Casson 1976). Another cost arises from contractual default in the intermediate product market – in particular, defective product quality. In each case the problem stems from the difficulty that the purchaser has in assuring the integrity of his supplier. This is due, in turn, to the difficulty of observing the quality of supplies at source: the licensees cannot observe the licensor and the downstream licensee cannot observe the upstream licensee. The emphasis of the present chapter is not on observing quality, however, but on observing the state of the market environment. Quality-related problems are not central to the analysis. The focus is rather on coordination failures caused by imperfect information about the environment. These imperfections are attributed to the process of negotiation in the intermediate product market, in the manner described below.

Consider, therefore, an upstream producer and a downstream distributor, both of whom have licensed the right to participate in the exploitation of the market niche. Competitive bidding for licences ensures that all the rents available from independent exploitation accrue to the licensor. It is assumed that the licence fee is fixed at the outset so that the licensees bear all the risks relating to the state of the market environment.

To preserve the simple binary structure of the model it is assumed that there are just two prices at which the intermediate product can be traded:

$$H_1 = (P_0 + c_1)/2 = 3; \qquad H_2 = (P_1 + c_0)/2 = 7 \tag{8}$$

The quotations h_1, h_2 of the respective parties must take either one or other of these values. The lower price H_1 favours the buyer (individual 1) whilst the high price H_2 favours the seller (individual 2). The basic idea is that when demand conditions are good individual 1 will 'encode' his information in a high price quotation $h_1 = H_2$, whilst when conditions are bad he will encode it in a low price instead $h_1 = H_1$. In each case he pays slightly less than he can sell for, and so makes a small margin (of one unit in the numerical example) on the deal. Conversely, when supply conditions are good, individual 2 is willing to accept a low price, $h_2 = H_1$; it is only when conditions are bad that he will insist on a high price $h_2 = H_2$. He too makes a small margin (of one unit) on each deal.

It is assumed that price quotations can be communicated costlessly. This is because prices constitute explicit rather than tacit information. This assumption is therefore consistent with the earlier assumption that output decisions, which are also explicit, are costless to communicate as well.

Table 2.7 Price and quantity outcomes of one-round negotiations

h_1	h_2	x	h
H_1	H_2	0	–
H_1	H_1	1	H_1
H_2	H_2	1	H_2
H_2	H_1	1	H^*

The rules governing the outcome of the negotiations are set out in Table 2.7. If the seller insists upon a high price whilst the buyer stipulates a low price then no trade will occur. This is quite reasonable, provided that the two quotations both genuinely signal bad conditions. If both parties quote the same price then they close a deal immediately. This is an appropriate outcome when one of the parties faces good conditions and the other faces bad ones. Finally, if the seller quotes low and the buyer offers high then they split the difference and close on the compromise price

$$H^* = (H_1 + H_2)/2 \tag{9}$$

One-round negotiations

For an ordinary market to mimic a firm which uses sequential decision-making, it is necessary that negotiations proceed through several rounds. It is only then that either party can modify their information-gathering strategy in the light of information from the other party signalled to them through the negotiation process. In fact, negotiations of several rounds are very complicated to model, while the results they yield often do not differ materially from those of a single round, as the subsequent discussion makes clear. For expository reasons it is therefore useful to focus on single-round negotiations first.

The problem with the market, as compared to the ordinary firm, is that the buyer and seller do not necessarily have an incentive to match their quotes to their conditions. It may pay them to bluff in order to get a better deal by pretending that their conditions are bad when they are really good. Indeed, it may not be worth their while incurring the observation cost to find out what their conditions really are. Given that they plan to bluff, they may not need to know whether their conditions really are good, unless their bluff is called and they have to decide whether they should concede a better price. But in a single round of negotiations this cannot occur.

The corresponding advantage of the market is that monitoring is not required. Each individual bears full financial responsibility for the consequences of his own decisions, and so has no incentive to waste his budget.

The decision tree facing each party under single-round negotiations is set out in Figure 2.5. Neither individual knows the incentive structure that the other faces, it is assumed. They are locked into a non-cooperative game of incomplete information. Individual 1 believes that individual 2 will quote low (i.e. favourably) with probability θ_2 while individual 2 believes that individual 1 will quote high (i.e. favourably) with probability $\theta_1 (0 \leq \theta_1, \theta_2 \leq 1)$. Under these conditions each party has three dominant strategies – and just two under risk-aversion. These are listed in Table 2.8; they correspond to the solid black lines in Figure 2.5. The values of these strategies, according to the numerical example, are given in Table 2.9. The game is solved by cal-

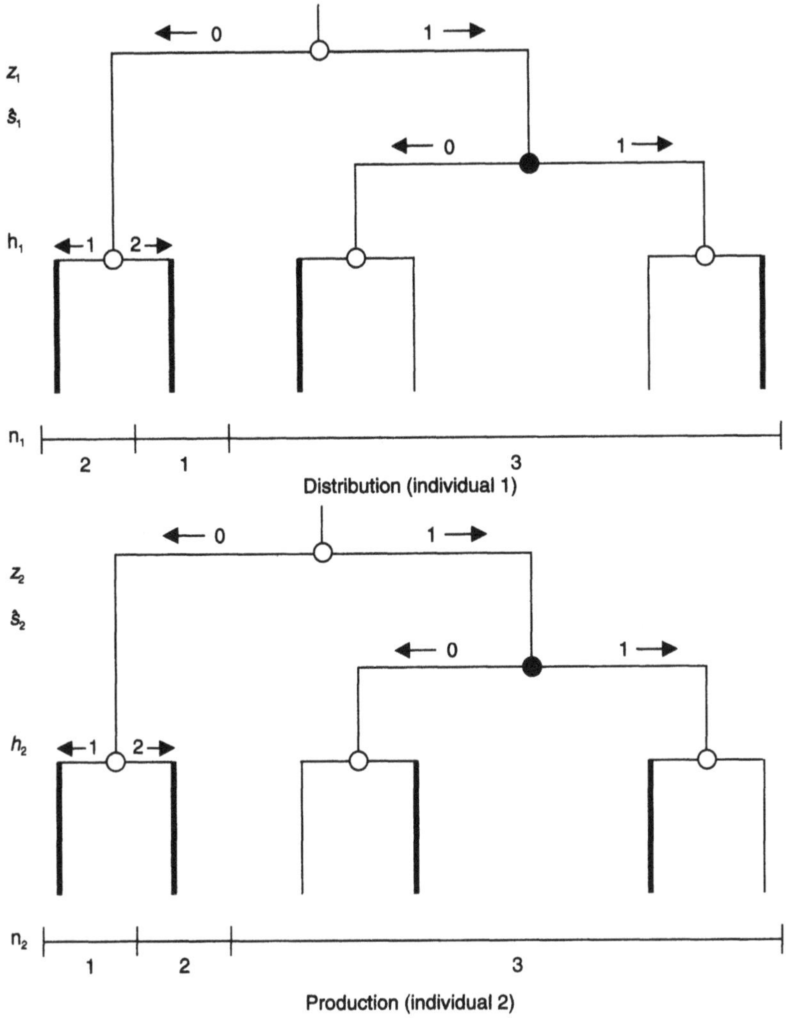

Figure 2.5 Alternative procedures for one-round negotiations

Note:
The solid lines indicate quotation strategies that may be efficient under the assumed conditions.

culating each individual's best response to his own subjective belief about the other party's behaviour. The derivation of individual 1's best response to individual 2 is illustrated in Figure 2.6. The optimal negotiation for any given value of θ_2 and any given p_1 may be read off from the circled numbers which label the three regimes in the figure.

Table 2.8 Dominant one-round negotiation procedures

Strategy	z_1	z_2	h_1	h_2	*Description*	*Acceptability under risk aversion*	*Equilibrium probability*
Manager 1 (marketing)							
$n_1 = 1$	0	–	H_2		Soft line: no investigation	No	$\theta_1 = 1$
$n_1 = 2$	0	–	H_1	–	Hard line: no investigation	Yes	$\theta_1 = 0$
$n_1 = 3$	1	–	$(1 - \hat{s}_1)H_1 + \hat{s}_1 H_2$	–	Investigation: quote a low price if conditions are bad and concede a high price if conditions are good.	Yes	$\theta_1 = p_1$
Manager 2 (production)							
$n_2 = 1$	–	0	–	H_1	Soft line: no investigation	No	$\theta_2 = 1$
$n_2 = 2$	–	0	–	H_2	Hard line: no investigation	Yes	$\theta_2 = 0$
$n_2 = 3$	–	1	–	$\hat{s}_2 H_1 + (1 - \hat{s}_2)H_2$	Investigation: quote a high price if conditions are bad and concede a low price if conditions are good.	Yes	$\theta_2 = p_2$

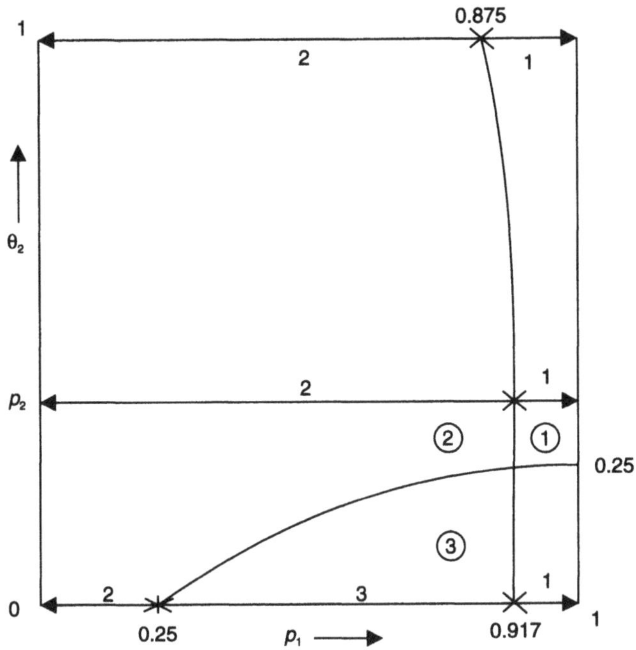

Figure 2.6 Determination of manager 1's best responses to manager 2's investigation procedures

Note:
The numbers in circles identify the three regimes in the figure. The other numbers refer to segments of the three horizontal lines and indicate the range of p_1 values for which the relevant strategy n_1 is the best response to manager 2.

Table 2.9 Values of alternative negotiation procedures: a numerical example

n_1	$v_1\ (n_1)$	n_2	$v_2\ (n_2)$
1	$-3 + 4p_1 + 2\theta_2$	1	$-3 + 4p_2 + 2\theta_1$
2	$(1 + 4p_1)\theta_2$	2	$(1 + 4p_2)\theta_1$
3	$p_1 + (1 + p_1)\theta_2 - 0.25$	3	$p_2 + (1 + p_2)\theta_1 - 0.25$

Note: v is the expected value of the profit accruing to individual *j*.

In equilibrium the probabilities associated with the partner's behaviour must be correct. Thus if individual 2 pursues procedure 1, then the equilibrium belief is $\theta_2 = 1$, as indicated in the right-hand column of Table 2.8. This case corresponds to the top edge of the square in the figure. If individual 2 pursues procedure 2 instead then the equilibrium value is $\theta_2 = 0$, corresponding to the bottom edge of the square, whilst if they pursue procedure 3 then $\theta_2 = p_2$, which is the case indicated by the horizontal line across the

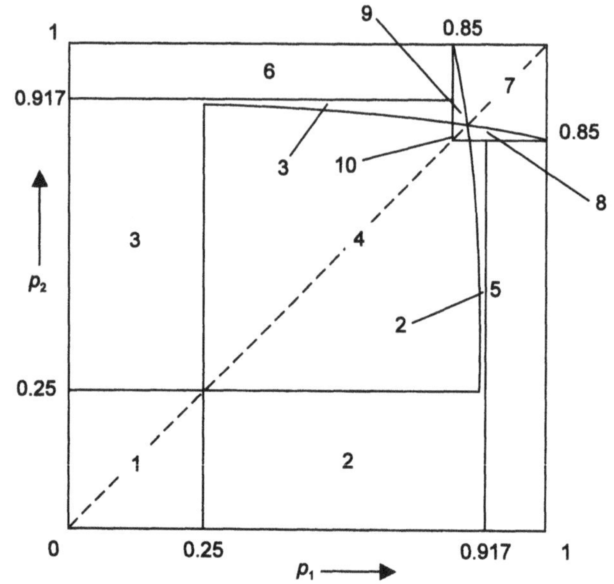

Figure 2.7 Equilibria of one-round negotiation process
Notes:

Regime	(n_1,n_2)	Description
1	(2.2)	No activity
2	(3.2)	Distributor (individual 1) collects information Producer (individual 2) takes a hard line.
3	(2.3)	Producer (individual 2) collects information. Distributor (individual 1) takes hard line.
4	(2.3), (3.2)	Multiple equilibria. Someone collects information and someone does not.
5	(1.2)	No information collected. Distributor adopts a soft line to a hard-line producer.
6	(2.1)	No information collected. Producer adopts a soft line to a hard line distributor.
7	(1.1)	No information collected. Both adopt a soft line. They always produce.
8	(1.1) (3.2)	Multiple equilibria. Either both take a soft line or the producer (individual 2) takes a hard line and the distributor (individual 1) collects information to determine how to respond.
9	(1.1) (2.3)	Multiple equilibria. Either both take a soft line or the distributor (individual 1) takes a hard line and the producer (individual 2) collects information to determine how to respond.
10	(1.1), (2.3), (3.2)	A mixture of (8) and (9).

middle of the square. Because of the symmetry property of the numerical example, noted earlier, individual 2's responses to individual 1 can be derived simply by an interchange of subscripts. Solving for the intersections of the two response functions in $p_1 - p_2$ space gives the equilibrium properties portrayed in Figure 2.7.

It can be seen that there are several cases of multiple equilibria. These arise because the negotiations resemble a game of 'chicken': each would like to bluff the other, but it only pays to bluff if the other person will concede. Bluffing is the best response to a willingness to concede, but concession is the best response to bluffing. Thus in equilibrium one party bluffs and the other does not, but which bluffs and which concedes is sometimes indeterminate.

There is, nevertheless, an underlying logic to the results. Just as in the case of the ordinary firm, information is most likely to be collected on those conditions that are most uncertain. Subjective certainty that conditions are bad encourages an individual to adopt a hard-line strategy, whilst subjective certainty that conditions are good encourages a soft line instead. It is the intermediate case, where conditions may be either good or bad, that encourages investigation.

An important difference from the ordinary firm, though, is that the two parties never collect information on both conditions together. Because of the 'chicken' factor, the combination (3,3), which corresponds to mutual investigation, is never an equilibrium. Thus a regime equivalent to procedure 4 in Figure 2.3 never prevails. The corresponding regime in Figure 2.7 is one in which multiple equilibria involving bluffing prevail instead. This underinvestment in information, and the consequent failure to achieve a satisfactory synthesis, is a major weakness of the market when considered as an alternative to the firm.

As they stand, these results have limited significance because a market cannot fully mimic an option strategy unless the negotiations take place over two rounds rather than one. It is only in a two-round process that one party can provide the other with a price quotation informed by their own investigation which stimulates the other party to respond with an investigation of their own. Suppose that the first round of negotiations takes place exactly as before, but that a no-trade outcome now leads on to the second round, which in terms of procedures is just a replay of the first. From a strategic point of view the second round is not exactly like the first, however, because the parties may enter it either with or without having investigated their conditions first. It is certain that they will both have taken a hard line in the first round, but they may have done so either out of ignorance or as a result of having carried out an investigation and found conditions bad. In the latter case they must still go through the negotiations for a second time around and take a hard line again. In the former case it is possible to carry out the investigation that was omitted in the first round and to make a concession if conditions turn out to be good.

Because the numerical example is symmetric, it is possible to carry out the first steps in the calculations just for individual 1. Individual 1 forms a

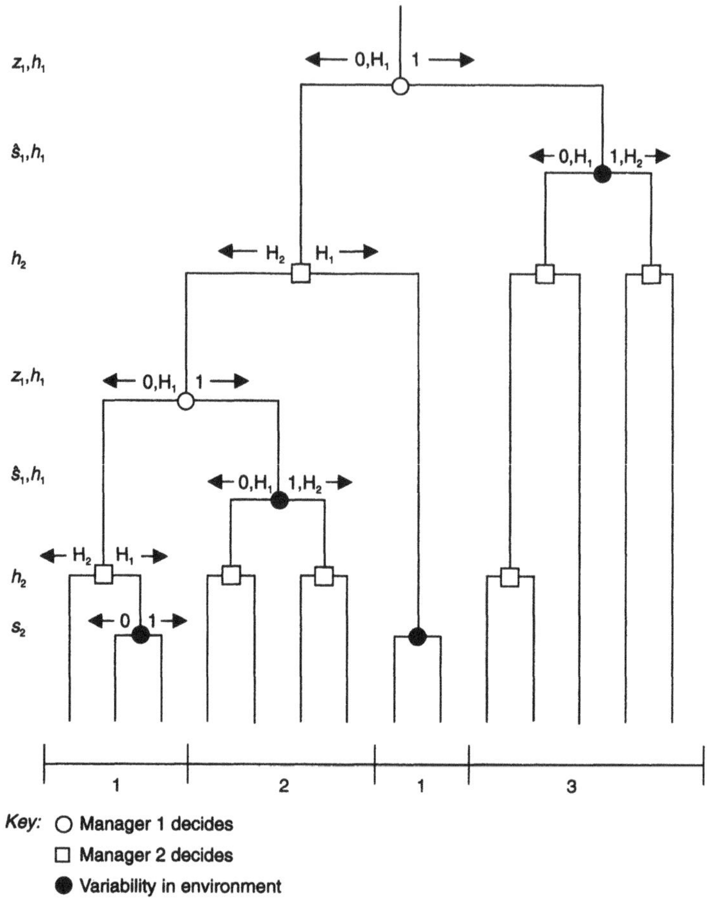

Figure 2.8 Decision tree for manager 1 in two-round negotiations, with absolute loss aversion

subjective belief that individual 2 will concede (i.e. quote H_1) in the first round with probability θ_{21} and that if he does not concede in the first round then he will concede in the second with probability $\theta_{22}(0 \leq \theta_{21}, \theta_{22} \leq 1)$. Risk-aversion is invoked to rule out the possibility that individual 1 may adopt a soft line without investigation. This leaves just three dominant procedures for individual 1, as illustrated by the decision tree in the Figure 2.8. They are:

1 No investigation; take a hard line (i.e. quote H_1) in both rounds;
2 Investigate in the second round if individual 2 takes a hard line in the first round, and concede if conditions are good (i.e. quote H_2); and
3 Investigate initially and concede in round 1 if conditions are good.

Individual 1's response function is derived by maximising expected profit in the same way as before. Individual 2's response function is obtained by an interchange of subscripts. The equilibrium probability values are: for procedure 1, $\theta_{21} = \theta_{22} = 0$; for procedure 2, $\theta_{21} = 0, \theta_{22} = p_2$; and for procedure 3, $\theta_{21} = p_2, \theta_{22} = 0$. Substituting these values into the response functions and computing equilibrium values in $p_1 - p_2$ space gives the remarkable result that the only equilibria are those involving procedures 1 and 2. In the first round both managers quote hard-line prices that are unacceptable to the other. In the second round they replay the earlier one-round process, generating the same pattern of outcome (apart from risk-aversion) as that shown in Figure 2.7. Once again there are multiple equilibria in which only one of the parties investigates, and no equilibrium in which they both do so. Thus the market completely wastes the opportunity for sequential investigation afforded by a two-stage negotiation process. Thus it is only the firm that benefits from the use of option strategies.

4. Comparing Firm and Market

A direct comparison of the economic performance of the firm and the market can be made on the basis of the valuations which underpin Figures 2.3 and 2.7. The valuation of each regime in Figure 2.3 is straightforward, but the valuation of the multiple equilibria in Figure 2.7 is problematic. The selection of an equilibrium can be made determinate by specifying initial conditions for the subjective probabilities θ_1, θ_2 and allowing them to be updated by a learning process (details are given in Casson 1995b). The approach here is simpler, however – each possible equilibrium is just assigned an equal probability of occurrence.

Overlaying Figures 2.3 and 2.7 and invoking this valuation convention gives Figure 2.9. To further simplify the analysis risk-aversion is assumed. In the asymmetric case, where one of the conditions is uncertain and the other is not, the market tends to out-perform the firm. But when a synthesis of information is appropriate the firm tends to out-perform the market instead. This is because of the market's under-investment in information noted above. This is not the only problem for the market, however: the opposite case of over-investment in information can occur as well. This is because even when both conditions are believed to be good, one of the parties may still decide to bluff, thereby forcing the other to investigate defensively whether they should concede.

A wide range of predictions can be extracted from this analysis using comparative static exercises in which the values of the exogenous variables are changed one at a time.

An increase in observation costs favours the market over the firm. This is because the firm tends to make greater use of information than does the market. The advantage of the firm lies chiefly in its recourse to the sequential

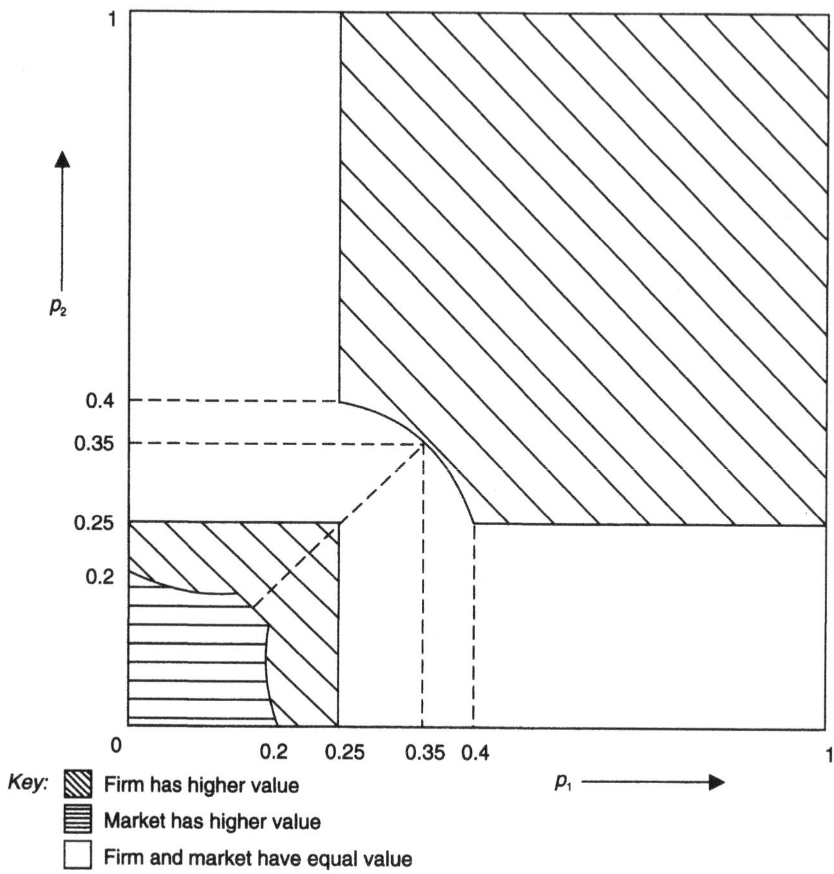

Figure 2.9 Comparison of firm and market when firm has access to option strategies but incurs evidence costs, and market involves two rounds of negotiation

procedures 5 and 6, which synthesise information in an economical way. As the costs of gathering information rise, it pays to economise on information, and to tolerate more mistakes in the output decision as a result. This is done by substituting procedures 2 and 3 for procedures 5 and 6. But procedures 2 and 3 are more likely to be out-performed by the market. Thus instead of switching procedures, the firm may be replaced by the market instead.

An increase in communication costs has much the same effect as an increase in observation costs because under the pattern of consultation assumed here an increase in communication costs impacts selectively on procedures 5 and 6. This is because under these procedures information collected by the managers is always passed on to the owner of the firm. An increase in communication costs therefore favours a switch to procedures 2 and 3, and a switch from firm to market, just as the increase in observation costs did before.

There is one important difference, however, namely that a substantial increase in communication costs may alter the pattern of consultation used for procedures 5 and 6. The owner may decide to economise on communication by delegating the synthesis of information as well as the collection of it. He may, for example, authorise the distribution manager to decide whether the production manager should be consulted, and if so, how the information provided by the production manager should be used. This is a natural extension of the concept of a marketing-led firm described in Table 3.5. Alternatively, the owner may authorise the production manager to decide whether the distribution manager should be consulted. This is a natural extension of the concept of a production-led firm described earlier on. In the context of Table 2.5, these cases generate an organisational structure which is both decentralised and consultative.

An increase in monitoring costs unambiguously favours the market at the expense of the firm. Whether or not the owner consults a manager before the output decision is taken, he needs to check afterwards that the manager has not overspent the budget and pocketed the difference in perks for himself. Such checks are unnecessary in a market context because each negotiator is spending resources of their own. Unlike the previous cases, therefore, an increase in monitoring costs favours the market independently of what decision procedures are used by the firm.

An increase in the volatility of the environment that affects both demand and supply equally favours the firm over the market. In this context an increase in volatility corresponds either to a change in the probability distribution of good and bad states, which makes them more equally probable, or to an increase in the impact that the state of the environment has on the profitability of the firm. An increase in volatility on the first of these two counts means that a procedure that ignores information on either demand or supply conditions is more likely to result in a mistaken output decision, whilst an increase in volatility on the second count means that any mistake that is made is likely to be very expensive. The economic value of information is therefore increased and this favours the adoption of the procedures 5 and 6 which provide a conditional synthesis of all available information. Because the firm is better than the market in effecting a synthesis of this kind, a general increase in volatility favours the firm at the expense of the market.

A change in volatility that affects demand and supply differentially favours the market instead of the firm. When just one factor – whether demand or supply – becomes the dominant source of volatility it is possible to make adequate decisions using information on this factor alone. Information on the other factor is of little economic value. This favours a switch from procedures 5 and 6 to procedures 2 and 3 – a switch which, it was noted earlier, reduces the net advantage of the firm.

By combining these results it is possible to generate other results – for example, to determine the trade-off between volatility and information cost that leaves the owner indifferent to the use of a market or the use of a firm. A fuller investigation of these properties of the model must be deferred to a subsequent discussion, however.

5. Extensions of the Basic Model

The basic simplicity of the model developed in this chapter owes much to the discrete choice approach, and in particular to the binary nature of the decisions. This makes it more versatile than the original theory of teams on which it is based, which uses continuous random variables instead. This versatility can be exploited to extend the model in various ways. For a start, there are a number of minor variations which can be made to investigate the sensitivity of the model to some of the restrictive assumptions made earlier.

It was assumed, for example, that production at the margin would take place if either demand or supply conditions were good; it was not necessary for both conditions to be good. This means that the situation is more promising than it might otherwise be: the lowest price exceeds the lowest cost, and the highest price exceeds the highest cost, and so potential operating profit is quite high. The alternative situation in which both demand and supply conditions have to be good for production to take place is less favourable, and this means that fewer rents are there to be captured by bluffing. This improves the efficiency of the market. Each individual will come to recognise that any attempt at bluffing is self-defeating, because the other individual cannot afford to make a substantial concession even when his circumstances are good. While the incentive for managers to misreport conditions is also reduced, there is still an incentive for them to cheat the owner of the firm when they have not been consulted before the decision was made. The economies in monitoring costs that are available, therefore, tend to be quite small. Thus on balance a reduction of overall rents favours the market at the expense of the firm.

The incentive for negotiators to bluff, and for managers to cheat, is also affected by the existence of intra-marginal units of output. The gains from bluffing or cheating accrue on every unit of output, whether marginal or not. Because the monitoring costs of the firm are independent of the value of output, the existence of substantial intra-marginal output favours the firm. Intra-marginal output is likely to be large when the price elasticities of demand and supply are low. Low elasticities therefore tend to favour co-ordination by the firm. Since low elasticities are often associated with large monopoly and monopsony rents, this reinforces the previous result. It suggests that the existence of low elasticities that support large rents favours the firm, whilst high elasticities that support low rents favour the market instead.

Because of the important role of volatility in the model, it is appropriate to consider what happens when disturbances are permanent rather than transitory and when demand and supply are correlated. If disturbances persist then the model begins to acquire an evolutionary aspect, since the procedures for dealing with the more transitory elements will alter as the more persistent elements intermittently change. Indeed, this approach could be taken further by perceiving the creation of the firm itself as a response to an evolutionary change in the environment. The model would then develop into a far more general theory of organisation in which firms were born and then killed off according to the success of different entrepreneurs in observing and correctly interpreting environmental change.

If disturbances in demand and supply are correlated then the case for observing both demand and supply tends to be undermined. The optimal response for the firm is to replace the observation of correlated variables with the observation of proxies for their principal components. The owner of the firm must look behind the immediate impulses of demand and supply to the fundamental factors – changes in income and changes in social attitudes, for example – which impinge on both demand and supply. This argument suggests that it is generally valid to assume that the firm will observe uncorrelated variables, whether or not it is meaningful to classify them according to demand and supply. The existing statistical formulation is therefore sound, even though the interpretation of the model in terms of supply and demand is just a special case.

The mention of proxies for hidden variables highlights another assumption: that all observations are perfectly accurate. The costs attributable to an observation are not just attributable to the expense involved, but to the risk that errors may be made. In practice almost all economic variables of interest to a decision-maker are hidden variables, and only symptoms of them can be observed. There may be different culturally-specific theories of what hidden variables generate what symptoms, leading different people to offer very different interpretations of similar evidence. The probability of error can be allowed for quite easily in a binary model like the present one, since the familiar statistical distinction between Type I and Type II errors is really all that is required. The calculation of expected net profit becomes more complicated when a procedure involves a risk of observation error, however. The criterion of absolute loss-aversion also needs to be redefined to exclude the unavoidable errors that remain when every reasonable investigation has been made. Subject to these minor qualifications, however, the extension of the model in this direction allows the cultural influence of theory on organisational structure to be taken into account. Different owners, using different theories about the environment, will construct their organisations in different ways in order to respond to what they perceive to be different fundamental factors in volatility.

The culture of an organisation is reflected in other ways as well. It has been assumed that the owner motivates managers to tell the truth by collecting evidence on their reports, but there are alternatives to this 'low trust' approach. Reputation effects can be invoked, social sanctions based on shame can be used, but perhaps most important of all is the way that loyalty and professional ethics can be harnessed to make managers effectively self-monitoring (Casson 1991). Ethics confronts managers with a simple binary choice between honesty and deceit which can be readily incorporated into the model. In conjunction with this, the information communicated by the owner to the managers can be extended from the delegation of rules and the handing down of decisions to encompass the rhetoric by which the rules and decisions are legitimated and the case for integrity set out.

Culture will also be reflected in decisions made about the recruitment of managerial staff. The model assumes that managers are perfectly substitutable from one period to the next. Neither manager has any special talent for their job. Although each manager enjoys certain power once he has made an observation, this power is conferred entirely by the job, and not by any special competence of the manager himself.

An interesting way of extending the model is to evaluate the special competencies that are required for the processing of information and to consider the 'imperfections' in the market for managerial talent which may emerge when only a small number of managers have the aptitudes required (Winter 1988). These aptitudes may relate to symptom interpretation (as discussed above), language skills that aid communication with other managers, or simply a high level of intelligence to facilitate the implementation of a particularly sophisticated decision rule. Aptitudes themselves, however, are only observable through symptoms, so the owner's theoretical view will determine how he screens prospective managers, and hence what qualities he acquires in his management team.

Given the emphasis on volatility, it is appropriate to consider more fully the impact of delays in communication. To some extent the role of delay can be proxied by the cost of communication m introduced earlier; greater delay is equivalent to a higher value of m, in other words. A more sophisticated analysis would recognise, however, that there is a trade-off between the direct cost of communication and the delay involved, which can only be examined properly if the model allows decision-making to be spread over two periods rather than one. Slower decision-making allows cheaper means of communication to be used and permits a wider synthesis of information at an acceptable cost. On the other hand, the information employed is more out of date; the severity of this problem will depend on the persistence (serial correlation) of the shocks to the firm's environment.

Delays in communication are likely to be greatest over long distances, though in this context it is nowadays 'cultural distance' rather than geographical distance that really matters. This factor becomes important when the model is extended over space to encompass multi-plant and multinational firms as indicated in the following section.

6. Applications to the Multinational Enterprise

Previous MNE literature has not integrated the analysis of the boundaries of the firm and the analysis of organisational structure very well. While the boundaries of the firm are analysed by internalisation theory (Buckley and Casson 1976), internal organisation is typically discussed in terms of organisation theory (for example, Bartlett and Ghoshal 1989). Attempts at integration have been made: the discussion of managerial competencies in MNEs by Kogut and Zander (1993) is a welcome step in this direction. But so far no comprehensive framework has emerged which can satisfactorily encompass the two sets of issues. It is suggested that the information cost approach set out in this chapter has the power to effect the requisite synthesis. It may not be the only way of doing it, but it is certainly one way. It has the advantage of formal rigour, and of having already been developed to the point where its methods can be applied with immediate effect.

The simplest approach to the MNE from an information cost perspective is to extend the concept of the intermediate product market from a single linkage between one upstream activity and one downstream activity to a multiplicity of linkages between several upstream activities and several downstream ones. The upstream activities represent production in different countries and the downstream activities represent distribution in different countries. Any production plant can be linked to any distribution facility, provided that necessary transport costs are incurred, and tariff payments made. The set of all possible linkages constitutes a more interesting and realistic concept of a market than the one presented in the simple model in this chapter because it affords a range of substitution possibilities that are missing in the single-linkage case. Each production plant is a substitute for any other plant so far as the sourcing of a given market is concerned – although the plants are not perfect substitutes because some, for example, will be nearer the market than others and so be accessible at lower transport costs. Conversely, each market is a substitute for any other market so far as each production plant is concerned, although again they are not perfect substitutes because of the differential impact of transport costs on market access.

The key to generalising the simple model is to recognise that every local production plant, and every local market, is subject to its own local source of volatility. Local supply shocks impinge on each production plant and local demand shocks impinge on each market. Because different plants are substitutes for each other, as are different markets, each local shock has implications not only for that location but for other locations too. If production costs in one country rise, the efficient response is to switch some or all of the production to other countries instead. If the market grows faster in one country than in another then the efficient response is to divert supplies from other markets, whilst at the same time expanding production around the world to accommodate the overall growth in demand.

Because of the continuing volatility of these local conditions, substitutions of this kind are continuously required. These substitutions necessitate a synthesis of information. Yet it may be uneconomic to synthesise all the information before any decision is made. The information costs of collecting and communicating all the relevant information may be prohibitive. Whether or not a given source of disturbance is kept under observation must depend on its contribution to the overall volatility of the firm's environment, and on the level of information costs faced by the firm. Where disturbances are observed, the information on them will generally be synthesised sequentially to avoid collecting information which is surplus to requirements in any particular case.

The MNE has a range of possible procedures for collecting information. The set of possible procedures encompasses all the subsets of information which could be collected, and all the permutations of the sequence by which a given subset is investigated. Associated with each procedure are alternative managerial divisions of labour which allocate the observation of particular shocks to particular people, and concentrate the responsibility for synthesis on particular people too. The organisational structure of the MNE, and the behavioural responses of its managers to various shocks, are fully determined once the optimal procedure has been chosen and the division of labour by which it is to be implemented has been fixed.

The role of MNE management is to determine the pattern of trade within the internal market. Once the volume of trade along each linkage has been specified the production plan for each plant is set by totalling the trade flows that emanate from that plant. Similarly the sales plan for each market is arrived at by totalling the trade-flows that are destined for that market. Each period the pattern of trade adjusts to changes in local demand and supply conditions. The pattern of trade may be set centrally at global headquarters, or it may be decentralised using procedures which guarantee the mutual consistency of the difference flows decided by different people at a local level.

Just as with the simple firm discussed earlier on, MNEs may be described as centralised or decentralised, autocratic or consultative, and as marketing-led or production-led. The application of these concepts is affected, however, by the greater complexity of the allocation of resources within an MNE. This means that, unlike a simple firm comprising a single-linkage, an MNE may be centralised in one respect but decentralised in another, and so on. In particular, it could be marketing-led in one country (say, a large wealthy country) but production-led in another (such as a small, newly industrialising country used as an export-platform).

It is possible to extend this view of the MNE in various ways. Global shocks may be introduced in addition to local shocks. Global shocks affect all markets rather than just one. Other shocks may impinge at an intermediate level – they may, for example, affect particular elements of the global

Triad (Ohmae 1987). The existence of different types of shock impacting on the firm at different levels of aggregation may be associated with different types of hierarchy within the firm. A preponderance of independent local shocks favours a decentralised consultative organisation of the MNE which emphasises local flexibility and responsiveness. Conversely the dominance of global-level volatility over local volatility favours a more centralised organisation of the MNE with a more powerful headquarters. If a single global shock is dominant, such as the growth of overall demand in the product market niche, then an autocratic style of management may even be appropriate, where the person who observes the key source of volatility fixes the overall corporate strategy.

The message of this approach is that organisational structure needs to adapt to the pattern of volatility in the firm's environment. It is not simply the case that decentralisation and consultation are always best. Current sentiments in favour of decentralisation and consultation can be interpreted as a rational response to the recent integration of global markets induced by lower tariffs and transport costs. This has enhanced the substitution possibilities between different locations and so promoted the demand for a global synthesis of local information. It is no longer the case that global market trends can be predicted from changes in a single leading economy – the United States – and hence it is no longer appropriate that decision-making power in MNEs should be vested in autocratic US managers. In terms of the model presented in this chapter, therefore, recent changes in the internal distribution of power and in the corporate cultures of US MNEs can be understood as a rational response to changing patterns of volatility in the business environment driven by the economic integration of different national markets within the world economy.

These changes also have implications for the boundaries of the MNE. The enhancement of the substitution possibilities within the wholesale product market linking production and distribution means that competitive forces can be used more easily to discipline bluffing in arm's-length negotiations. As the intermediate product market becomes more competitive, therefore, the advantages of internalisation diminish because the potential distortion of prices in the external market is reduced. This encourages the replacement of vertically-integrated MNEs by networks of subcontractors. In some cases the firm retains an intermediating role, buying competitively from independent producers in different countries and selling competitively through independent retail channels. In other cases the MNE disappears altogether, and is replaced by competing national producers in different countries trading directly with competing national distributors.

The integrated approach based on information costs thus has the ability to explain recent changes in both the boundaries of the firm in international business and in the organisational structures of those firms that still remain as MNEs. The analysis suggests that both sets of phenomena have a common cause – namely the growing international integration of wholesale markets. This is driving firms towards increasing reliance on a global synthesis of diverse sources of local information. But unlike the simple model of the single-linkage firm discussed in Figure 2.1, where such reliance on synthesis favoured the firm, the more complex case of the MNE generates an additional countervailing effect. By strengthening substitution possibilities the globalisation of wholesale markets reduces the scope for bluffing and so favours the substitution of the market for the firm instead. The growing integration of the world economy is making final product markets and factor markets for capital and labour more competitive too. This is reducing the monopoly rents available to firms in their home markets, and further reducing the scope for bluffing. This reinforces the tendency to allocate resources through competitive market mechanisms, for the reasons explained in Section 5. These changes are not equally strong in all industries, of course. The model predicts, in line with experience, that changes in organisation are likely to be greatest in those industries which have experienced the greatest amount of fundamental environmental change.

7. Conclusions

Coase began his seminal paper by noting that economists tend to explain both the firm and the market in similar terms – namely, by the need for co-ordination. Considered as a coordination mechanism, the main advantage of the firm, he suggested, was that it avoided the costs of price discovery in the external market.

Prices may be misleading simply because they are based on inadequate information. The possibility of obtaining monopoly rents through bargaining distorts the incentive to collect information. Prices encode information, and if, for strategic reasons, it is known in advance what the information encoded needs to be, then there is little point in discovering whether it is really true. The strategic propensity to lie therefore leads to under-investment in the truth.

The key factor that distinguishes the firm from the market, from this perspective, is that the firm is committed to processing information for decision-making without encoding it in prices first. It does not rely on bargaining opportunities to motivate the collection of information. Its aim instead is to effect, where necessary, a direct synthesis of information which will improve the allocation of resources under its control – for example, by setting an appropriate level of output. To assure the quality of information the firm monitors its managers and penalises them if they do not tell the truth. These penalties are exacted after decisions have been taken – often in the light of the outcome. The market affords no such follow-up. Deals once made are final, whether or not it subsequently emerges that one of the parties was bluffing. The advantage to the market is that it is cheaper to communicate prices rather than ordinary information, because prices are explicit while information is tacit, and that the follow-up costs of collecting evidence are then avoided too.

Although this chapter has emphasised information costs in general, rather than transaction costs in particular, it is still appropriate to see it as a development of the transaction cost approach. Specifically, it invokes the concept of volatility to augment the analysis of where the boundaries of the firm are drawn with an analysis of what goes on inside them. It thereby links the Coasian tradition to the tradition of Hayek (1937), Richardson (1960) and Malmgren (1961), which emphasises the need to synthesise information from different sources when allocation decisions are made. This act of synthesis, effected by the option procedures described above, is, indeed, the core activity within the boundaries of the firm. It is the need to structure this synthesis efficiently (the information cost issue) and to assure the quality of the information provided (the transaction costs issue) that together determine both what goes on inside the boundaries of the firm and where these boundaries are drawn.

Acknowledgements

A preliminary version of this paper was presented to the ESRC Industrial Economics Network at the University of Buckingham, September 1995. I am grateful to the participants, and to Animesh Shrivastava, for their comments.

3

THE ECONOMICS OF BUSINESS PROCESS DESIGN IN MULTINATIONAL FIRMS

Peter J. Buckley and Martin J. Carter

The declared aim of this book is to bring together insights from the work of economists and management theorists on questions of the organisation of the firm. Each approach has much to offer the other. Economists interested in the organisation of international business have tended to focus on questions of the *boundaries* of the organisation, that is of its *external structure*. The analysis of transaction costs has been used, for example, to explicate the decision to export, to license or to manufacture overseas, and also the participation in international joint ventures and alliances (Buckley and Casson 1976, 1985; Buckley and Glaister 1994). However, a good deal of attention in the management literature is applied to the debate about *internal* organisation. Writers on management have promoted new structures and new approaches to organisation, using ideas from many sources. These include studies of Japanese business (Pascale and Athos 1981), of successful American businesses (Peters and Waterman 1982) and the analysis of quality management (Deming 1988). This chapter is an attempt to apply insights from the transaction costs approach to questions of internal organisation of the kind addressed in this management literature.

There are close parallels between the analysis in this chapter and the preceding chapter by Casson. Both use Marschak and Radner's team theory (1972) to explore the role of synthesizing decentralised information in determining the most appropriate form of organisation. Both demonstrate that the costs and the benefits of acquiring information can influence appropriate decision structures of a firm. Interestingly, Casson goes on to demonstrate that information considerations can also influence the comparative performance of internalised and market transactions. Casson's analysis is confined to information concerning a single decision, whereas our concern here is to explore the options within a firm for coordinating multiple actions.

The formal methodologies of the two chapters are complementary. Casson considers discrete, binary choice and state variables, while this chapter illustrates the use of continuous choices and states. Both are important, as firms are faced with both discrete choices (to enter or to exit) and continuous choices (production quantity). The two are closely related if used to examine the marginal decision.

The chapter is divided into five sections. The first section examines a key current concept in the management literature – the 'business process' – and interprets it as a form of team entrepreneurship within the firm. The second section sets out a framework for categorising internal transaction costs and for describing the design of a firm's internal organisation. Section 3 considers the business processes which are characteristic of multinational firms and associated organisation design and transaction costs issues. It is suggested that the problem of business process design is particularly acute for the multinational. This is illustrated in Section 4 using a simple model of a representative business process. The chapter ends with a concluding discussion.

1. Business Processes as Team Entrepreneurship

A common feature of the new approaches to organisation is that the internal activities of firms are seen as a *process* or a set of processes and that the organisation problem of the firm centres round optimising the outcomes of internal processes. Processes take inputs and convert them to outputs on behalf of the 'customers' of a given process. Proponents of the new ideas suggest that key personnel engaged in executing the firm's processes should be 'empowered' to act on behalf of their 'customers', that multilevel hierarchies are replaced by leaner, flatter organisations which concentrate on quality and customer satisfaction and that staff are given both the discretion and especially the information to act on behalf of their customers.

The origins of this process-oriented approach to organisation lie in the central role played by quality management and statistical process control in the development of the new ideas, initially in manufacturing but spreading to services and to all kinds of administrative activity. It has achieved particular currency in the recent strand of literature and practice which has become widely labelled 'Business Process Reengineering' (BPR)[1] (Hammer 1990; Hammer and Champy 1993; Davenport 1993; Champy 1995)[2]. The aim of this chapter is to focus on the first half of the BPR label: to suggest an economic interpretation of the business process concept, to consider economic factors which influence process performance and to propose ideas about how internal organisation might affect performance, particularly in the context of the multinational enterprise. The other part of the label – 're-engineering' – is concerned with restructuring or reorganising business processes within a firm, and an understanding of the economics of business processes is a pre-requisite to an economic view of re-engineering.

What is a Business Process?

According to Hammer and Champy (1993 p. 35[3]) a business process is a collection of activities that takes one or more kinds of input and creates an output that is of value to the customer.
They further go on to suggest that business processes

> correspond to natural business activities, but they are often fragmented and obscured by the organisational structures. Processes are invisible and unnamed because people think about the individual departments, not the process with which all of them are involved. (1993: 118)

Giving examples, they suggest that the name given to a process 'should imply all the work that gets done between the start and the finish', what they also call the 'state-change'. Thus:

Process	*State-change*
Manufacturing	Procurement to shipment
Product development	Concept to prototype
Sales	Prospect to order
Order fulfillment	Order to payment
Service	Inquiry to resolution

(Hammer and Champy 1993: 118)

One good example of the design of a complete business process is the order fulfillment system of a major British multinational. As order fulfillment is the key process within the firm, the process is planned and monitored from the beginning – the number of times the phone rings – through implementation (checking the item in the catalogue, transmitting the order to the computer regulated delivery belt, picking and packing) to delivery.

We wish to offer an economic conception of the term 'business process', focusing on two aspects. First, the term 'process' implies a dynamic character, dealing with the activities and mechanisms by means of which outcomes are achieved rather than solely the outcomes themselves. And second, we highlight the suggestion that business processes are *collections* of activities which are not separable by the normal organisational compartments of firms, but which may be dispersed amongst the functional units of the organisation. Briefly put, we will suggest that just as *internalisation* is an alternative to the market in resource allocation, then the business processes are the *internal* counterpart of the *market process*. And insofar as the market process coincides with the idea of *entrepreneurship* (Kirzner 1979), then we consider that the internal processes of firms are an aspect of entrepreneurship.

Consider the nature of 'activities' within the firm and their relation to the orthodox theory of the firm's choice. The usual marginalist analysis is concerned with the *outcomes* of maximising behaviour, rather than with the processes through which choices are made and implemented. Making choices often entails, as Nelson and Winter have pointed out (1982: 65–71), a *process involving deliberation*. We take it that activities within firms comprise the *deliberations and information processing* that are necessary for firms to decide the actions they will take and also to respond to unfolding events as decisions are implemented. While orthodox analysis provides powerful propositions concerning nature of the choices which maximise a firm's objective function, these are valid only if the deliberative process has successfully discovered and implemented the optimal choice.

The nature of these deliberative activities which enable firms to make and implement decisions are the *generation and synthesis of knowledge* (tacit and explicit) and the collection and transmission of information and data relating to that knowledge for the purpose of making choices and responding to unfolding events as these choices are implemented. According to North

> In fact, the real tasks of management are to devise and discover markets, to evaluate products and product techniques, and to manage actively the actions of employees; these are all tasks in which there is uncertainty and in which investment in information must be acquired
>
> (North 1990: 77)

This process is *entrepreneurial* in character. In effect, entrepreneurship is a process concerned with discovering, developing and exploiting opportunities for gains from trade. As Casson has pointed out:

> The key function of the entrepreneur – the one that may be regarded as defining his role – is to take important decisions that are difficult to make.
>
> (Casson 1985b: 177–8)

By extension, the deliberative processes, those activities which take inputs and 'create' outputs (cf. the quote from Hammer and Champy 1993), are entrepreneurship internalised within the firm.

An important aspect of Hammer and Champy's definition is that business processes comprise a *collection* of activities. While the division of labour within firms has often been described in the context of Adam Smith's pin factory[4], it has been increasingly the case during the current century that there is a division of *managerial* labour. See, for example, Radner (1992). Indeed the division of managerial labour is a primary reason for the organisational problem within the firm (Radner 1992; Carter 1995). Casson has suggested the term 'team entrepreneurship' for the situation in which no single individual possesses the requisite skill or capacity to undertake all the difficult decisions (Casson 1985b: 184–6) and managerial, deliberative activities are shared among several individuals. The problem of organising business processes is, we suggest, the problem of organising an entrepreneurial team.

We have suggested elsewhere (Buckley and Carter 1996) that there are three problems which must be overcome in the organisational design of a business process team. One arises from the *distribution of information*, when one member of the team may have access to knowledge or information that would aid another member. The second is *coordination*, since there is frequently interaction or *complementarity* between actions that are the responsibility of different individuals. That is to say, when the choice made for one action can affect the value to the firm of the choice made for another action. When activities are complementary, it may be important to ensure that the deliberative choices are made *jointly* so as to optimise the overall gains from trade for the firm. The final problem is *motivation*: of ensuring that the individual members of the entrepreneurial team each carry out their individual activities in pursuit of the *shared* interests of the team, rather than in their own individual interests. These organisational problems are particularly acute in a multinational firm, where team members are geographically separated and where they may also have differences in tacit knowledge and cultural background (see Section 3 in this chapter).

In summary, we suggest the following economic conception of a business process: *a set of complementary deliberative (entrepreneurial) choices involving the collection and synthesis of knowledge for the generation of gains from trade*. High complementarity between activities provides a natural definition of the activities which constitute a given process. (Hammer and Champy's 'natural business activities'). When complementarity is *low* between activities, then they are separable into distinct processes, for which coordination is less important.

Categories of team entrepreneurship

The concept of entrepreneurship can encompass the deliberative, judgemental processes undertaken by teams of individuals within firms, as well as the more conventional usage relating to the actions of 'unique' individuals within markets. The key characteristics of entrepreneurship are the synthesis of knowledge and information, and undertaking to act so as to create improved gains from trade. We can distinguish three categories of entrepreneurship, according to the nature of information or knowledge concerned.

1 Dealing with 'fluctuations' in an otherwise stable framework. Knowledge in the sense of capabilities (tacit knowledge) and understanding (explicit knowledge) are fixed, but there are variations in demand conditions and cost conditions which can be observed by an alert and responsive entrepreneurial organisation. These might, for example, be represented by fluctuations in marginal revenue and marginal cost, and information about these may be decentralised with, say, the firm's marketing specialists having the best information on marginal revenue and the production department knowing most about marginal cost. The best output decision would depend on combining the knowledge of separate departments. This situation is accessible to formal modelling (Carter 1995; Buckley and Carter 1996) and Section 4 in this chapter provides an example of such a model for an MNE. We might characterise this category as generating no new 'knowledge', only responding to new *information.*

2 'Incremental development', in which there is a gradual adaptation of existing knowledge and capabilities. For example, much product development work may be in this category. New knowledge is developed within the framework of an existing 'paradigm'. These developments are likely to arise out of 'recombinations' of the knowledge and information acquired by different individuals. Because the process takes place within a maintained paradigm, it may be feasible to plan team structures so as to maximise the expected return. Our approach to modelling can also be used to represent aspects of this kind of process.

3 'Discovery and innovation', encompassing a shift in knowledge to a new 'paradigm' and exploitation of the new knowledge. While novel paradigm-changing discoveries are likely to be dependent on particular creative or insightful individuals, they may also come from combining the ideas from several sources. Furthermore, the whole innovation process has multiple stages (formulated, selection and implementation: Buckley and Casson 1992), each requiring distinct capabilities and which may or may not be separable into distinct, separable sub-processes.

2. Internal Transaction Costs and Organisation Design

In Section 1 we referred to three problems of organisation design: the *information problem* arising from decentralised information, the *coordination problem* arising from complementarity between the actions of separate individuals and the *motivation problem* arising from the pursuit of individual rather than shared goals. We have used these three organisational problems to construct a classification of internal transaction costs (Buckley and Carter 1996). Suppose that there is a set of actions, not initially known to the members of the firm, which would maximise the value of a firm's objective function (say its discounted expected profit stream). The deliberative process of choice will discover the optimal set of actions if:

1 All participants have access to the best decision-relevant knowledge (*perfect information*);
2 All complementary actions are chosen jointly (*perfect coordination*); and
3 All members of the firm shared the firm's objective function (*perfect motivation*).

The expected value of the objective function, given these optimal actions, is the firm's optimal pay-off. We define the following cost measures, being departures from the optimal pay-off:

Information loss	The reduction in pay-off to the firm caused by members not having the best available information
Information cost	The cost of acquiring and transmitting information
Coordination loss	The reduction in pay-off to the firm arising when complementary actions are not chosen jointly
Coordination cost	The cost of communication about complementary actions or of providing for them to be combined
Motivation loss	The reduction in pay-off to the firm caused by members pursuing their own objectives
Motivation cost	The cost of incentive measures taken by the firm. This might include the cost of incentive schemes, or the cost of supervision for monitoring employees' actions, or the cost of training and 'socialisation' designed to induce employees to adopt the firm's values and goals

Information, coordination and motivation losses are, in effect, internal 'externalities' arising from the division of managerial labour within the firm, and the associated *costs* measure the resource deployed in correcting the externalities. The goal of the firm's organisation design problem is to minimise the sum of these six transaction costs.

We also formalise the discussion of organisation design in terms of two design characteristics, the process *architecture* and the *goals of process members*.

Process architecture

The architecture of a process comprises:

- The number of individuals engaged in the process and the allocation of responsibilities amongst them;

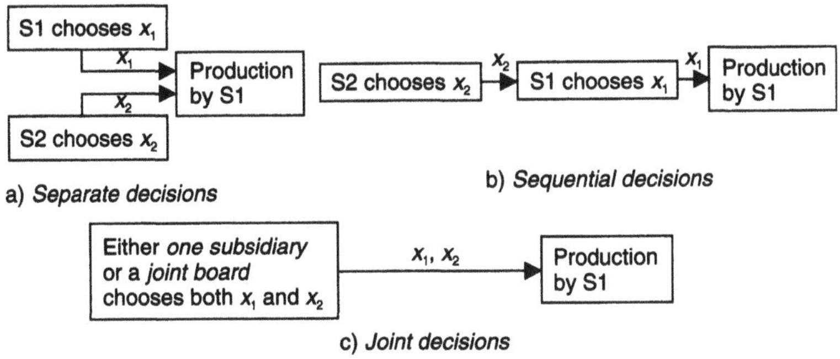

Figure 3.1 Three architectures for two-country output decision process

- The capabilities of the individuals;
- The information and knowledge available to each individual;
- The communication between individuals;
- The time sequence of decisions.

The architecture details how the process uses *information* and *coordination*. For example, consider how an MNE which produces in one country but sells in several might deal with fluctuations in demand conditions and cost conditions in its production-planning process. Suppose its output is produced in Country 1, but it sells in Country 1 and Country 2? Its output choice process must decide production for both Country 1 and Country 2, say x_1 and x_2. The subsidiary in Country 1 (S1) can be expected to have specialised knowledge of production costs and of demand conditions in Country 1, while the subsidiary in Country 2 (S2) has particular knowledge of demand conditions in Country 2, although not of production costs. We might suppose, say, that S2's knowledge of production costs is confined to a standard cost reflecting historical accounting. There are various ways to organise decision-making about output in this MNE, of which three are illustrated in Figure 3.1.
These three architectures are now considered in more detail:

1 *Separate decisions*
Each subsidiary uses its available information to choose the output it would like, which is then duly produced by S1. This minimises information losses concerning market conditions, but because S2 lacks precise knowledge of production costs, there may be some production information loss. More subtly, if the marginal cost changes with output there are also *coordination losses*, since then the value of marginal cost depends on *both* decisions. There is then complementarity between decisions, implying that both actions should be part of the same business process. If the goal of each subsidiary is to maximise *joint* profits independently (see Section 4 in this chapter), then each must implicitly guess the likely

output the other will choose and the resulting level of marginal cost. Coordination losses arise if subsidiaries' expectations of the action the other takes are wrong. The alternative is for some means of coordination to be used.

2 *Sequential decisions*
A degree of coordination is achieved if S2 indicates its level of demand first and the decision is passed on to S1, since S1 no longer has to estimate S2's output when it makes its own decision. But coordination is imperfect, because the first decision might still be based on an erroneous guess about what the second one would be. Each decision-maker can still use their own superior information, but there are information losses, since Subsidiary 2 has imprecise knowledge of costs.

3 *Joint decisions*
In the final case both actions are chosen together, which eliminates coordination losses. The figure indicates two possibilities. First, the decisions might be undertaken by *one* of the two subsidiaries, in which case not all of the best information would be used, or it might be possible for both subsidiaries to act together via a *joint board*. While the last option implies both perfect information and perfect coordination, it is not automatically the best architecture for the firm, as this would depend on the size of potential information and coordination losses compared with the costs of operating a joint board.

Each of these architectures has different potential levels of information loss and coordination loss as well as different costs and performance depends on architecture. We provide a quantitative analysis in Section 4. Of course, the three structures illustrated are not the only possibilities. In these cases, subsidiaries use only their own knowledge in choosing their action, whereas they could communicate some of their knowledge to one another, or they could transmit price signals.

Goals of process members

Architecture describes the use of information and coordination which leaves the question of the motivation of the individuals engaged in deliberative activities of choice. Consider two cases:

1 *Shared objectives: team behaviour*
A 'team' can be defined as a group of individuals with a common goal (Marschak and Radner 1972) and 'teamwork' is one of the most widely advocated ideals in management. For an MNE, such as in Figure 3.1, the individuals in separate subsidiaries can be said to constitute a team if they all work towards a common objective, such as the profit of the MNE as a whole. Whether this behaviour is likely in practice may

depend on 'corporate culture' (Casson 1991) and the extent to which internal social conditions persuade employees to 'internalise employers' values' (Hennart 1986). Factors of geography and national culture may make this more problematic for MNE's than for a single-country organisation. It is worth noting that complementarity between actions, which we suggest is the defining condition for actions which should be grouped together in a business process, implies that the firm's goal is not additively separable into individual goals for each actor. Therefore, for a business process with several members, perfect motivation (see p. 62 where an optimal deliberative process is defined) requires that all members share the same goal.

2 *Different individual goals*
If members (subsidiaries) cannot be induced by cultural measures to adopt the firm's objectives, then the firm must accept that they will pursue individual goals, although the extent to which they do so can be limited by measures the firm chooses to adopt. One possibility is to substitute discretion with fiat, so that a central authority dictates the actions of subsidiaries. There will be resultant information losses, which may be severe as subsidiaries are better informed about their own markets, but coordination and motivation losses are eliminated. Alternatively, the firm can adopt a system of targets and incentives for individual subsidiaries, subject to the inefficiencies which arise in principal–agent problems, such as moral hazard and adverse selection (Radner 1992), corresponding to what we have here called motivation losses.

3. Business Processes and Organisation in MNE

The business processes which are of greatest significance in MNEs are those in which complementary entrepreneurial choices are dispersed across national borders. Some typical examples are mentioned briefly here. Firstly, there are situations such as we discussed earlier, in which the firm must adapt to fluctuations in demand and cost when production and markets are located in different countries. The picture can be further complicated when there are production facilities in more than one country, sharing world production. Decisions about production capacity at each facility must take into account the level of demand in the firm's various markets, and individual market supply decisions must make due allowance for production costs which can be affected by decisions in other markets.

The geographic separation of production from the market can be due purely to economies of scale in production so that it pays to locate factories in only some of the countries served. Internalisation of cross-border marketing may be preferred to simple exporting because specialised sunk investments in marketing knowledge are needed for individual countries.

Alternatively there may be a risk of expropriation of technology. But further, production and market-making are often closely interdependent activities, with aspects which are complementary in the sense defined earlier. Product and service quality, for example, can be particularly important and complementary efforts required by both production in quality control and by marketing and distribution in advertising, promotion, timely delivery, after sales service, warrantee etc. (Casson 1982, 1985a; Carter 1996). Successfully managing established products in the face of unfolding events in production and in increasingly competitive global markets can place significant demands on the firm's responsiveness and capabilities.

Furthermore, the scope for incremental development is comparatively large in MNE's, since there are opportunities and competitive pressures to adapt product designs for individual country markets. Complementary knowledge of market requirements and technological opportunities and constraints are essential if adaptations are to be successful. These considerations apply *a fortiori* to more radical innovation. There are wide sources of market and scientific knowledge available to prompt the formulation of innovative proposals; the good judgement needed in successful selection depends on the synthesis of global knowledge; and implementation calls for complementary capabilities of the kind already discussed in relation to the management of quality.

Transaction costs in MNEs

While the challenges and opportunities to be accommodated in the organisation of MNEs are comparatively large, so are the factors which affect the organisational externalities and costs (information, coordination and motivation) discussed earlier. The simplest set of factors, increasing the costs of communication and the exchange of ideas and knowledge, is the spatial separation of individuals who hold complementary knowledge and who could gain from coordinating their actions, and the likelihood that they have different first languages. These are essentially technical in character, and technology and education can play a large part in overcoming them. For example, the growth of electronic mail and video conferencing at both international and local levels makes it appear that worldwide and intra-office communications will increasingly converge.

While language itself is only a technical obstacle, it may obscure more fundamental differences between national outlooks and routines, which influence communication and coordination in a number of ways. For example, the way in which information and knowledge are constructed in different cultures has been studied by Hedlund and Nonaka (1993). They summarised common perceptions about differences between Japanese and western firms in terms of differences in the extent to which the firm's knowledge is 'tacit' or 'articulated' and differences in whether knowledge is held by individuals or groups. They characterise the western firm by individually-held, articulated knowledge and the Japanese by tacit knowledge held at the level of the group and the organisation. More generally, there are numerous differences in the everyday assumptions (norms) which individuals make about the actions of others in a given situation, about what constitutes acceptable behaviour and about the interpretation of tacit signals such as body language, which play a major part in the successful coordination of the actions of groups. These differences in routines may in themselves imply differences in performance of some kinds of tasks (Buckley and Casson 1992: 228–31), but where related tasks are to be carried out by individuals who hold different social and cultural assumptions, the dangers of misunderstanding and misinformation may detract significantly from the joint effectiveness of the collaboration, unless considerable time is spent in developing mutual understanding.

Finally, as mentioned earlier, it may be particularly difficult to motivate individuals in different countries to pursue diligently the interests of the organisation as a whole. There are two considerations here. In the conventional economic arguments about moral hazard and adverse selection in organisations, the monitoring problem is exacerbated by the geographic and the cultural differences we have just discussed. Opportunistic risks may therefore be higher and the costs of counter-measures may be higher too. In addition, we can depart from purely individualist reasoning, and observe that individuals may also identify with a group or a 'community' within which they behave 'altruistically', or with the shared interests of the community in mind. Insofar as this does occur, it may well be expected that individuals would favour the perceived interests of their national subsidiary over the interests of the firm.

Organisational responses: divisions, matrices, strategic business units, joint ventures

There has been no shortage of organisational prescriptions for solving the problems of organisation in MNEs, of which the business process approach is simply the most recent. Placing these in a stylised historical sequence, they can be seen as progressive responses to the problems of information, coordination and motivation.

The divisional ('M-form') hierarchy makes use of local information in decision-making by devolving operating decisions to specialist divisions, coordinates the application of shared assets via the head office, and motivates divisions through their profit contributions in the firm's internal capital market (Williamson 1975: chapter 8). Internationalisation resulted either in national divisions – with divisions duplicating product marketing and sometimes production – or a product division, with several divisions operating across the same borders. Both forms leave residual opportunities for sharing common resources and knowledge, and the matrix approach is an attempt to provide cross-linked channels for information exchange and coordination of activities. But these channels are a cumbersome way of dealing with information, being bureaucratic and hierarchical in character, and introduce the motivational problem that 'no man can serve two masters'. Divided loyalties can result in motivation losses, and the cost of information and coordination can be a large head office.

The strategic business unit can be seen as a development of the full matrix structure, and has been termed the 'weak matrix' (Lorange 1993). Selected linkages of, say, country and product are combined into identified 'business element' teams charged with achieving specified targets where an opportunity has been identified for capitalising on an improved combination of knowledge and coordinated action. Team performance targets can provide clear motivation for team members. However, competition between groups can reduce the beneficial sharing of complementary knowledge and resources, particularly as the business unit leaders are often engaged on a 'managerial' promotion track and focus on group performance rather than the exploitation of technology (Buckley and Casson 1992).

The advantages of increased flexibility and decentralisation of authority that have been claimed for joint venture networks are not always born out in practice. The advantage is that individual business elements are more free to choose appropriate collaborations, and if they wish it can be possible to participate in several joint ventures together (Buckley and Casson 1995). Knowledge can be exploited as its holders choose, and the motivation comes from their returns on their portfolio of joint ventures. However, the value of JVs can be contingent on the circumstances of the partners, and the risk that they will prove short-lived has often resulted in reduced trust between the partners and less than complete disclosure of the information that the venture is established to share (Buckley and Casson 1988, 1992).

Pros and cons of the business process approach

The business process approach is not necessarily an exclusive alternative to the organisational devices just discussed, but may complement them and be an aid to the designation of, say, strategic business units. What is distinctive is its emphasis on combining those 'natural' collections of actions which are needed for the things that actually happen – the 'state-change' and 'all the work that gets done between the start and the finish' – rather than on preconceived 'functions' or organisational units, reflecting its origins, perhaps, in the methods of work study and industrial engineering (Davenport and Short 1990). We have attempted to express that here in terms of the economics of entrepreneurship, where 'natural' linkages arise from the externalities which arise from dispersed and complementary information. We suggest that the advantage as a method of organisational analysis is that it focuses directly on the underlying economic problems of information, coordination and motivation and on the processes within the firm, and abstracts from a superimposed structural framework.

In a previous discussion it was suggested that an important element in the execution of processes within the firm is the continuity of personal responsibility (Buckley and Casson 1992). The business process approach recasts the responsibility for change from individual entrepreneurship to team entrepreneurship. While the vision of optimal cooperation between team members is attractive, the reality may be more difficult to achieve. The key requirement for the business process approach to be successful is *trust*. Trust is needed both between the members of process teams, and between the team and the firm and the firm and the team. Trust is a commodity that takes both time and skill to build (Axelrod 1984; Buckley and Casson 1988). This is often at odds with the perceptions of employees in firms who introduce the business process approach, where it is seen as another exercise in down-sizing. If the business process approach is to be successful it will be important for firms to spend the necessary time and attention to building trust with and between its employees (Casson 1991).

4. The Impact of Architecture

The promotion of trust and cooperation may be the first requirement of the business process approach to organisation, but if this is achieved the organisation then has to find the most effective allocation of responsibilities among members. It has to choose an architecture. In this section we set out a quantitative model of the impact of architecture on the performance of a firm and illustrate its results by comparing two of the architectures discussed earlier. The model uses team theory (Marschak and Radner 1972) to analyse the two-country output problem discussed earlier.

Set-up of model

The purpose of the output choice process in this case is to deal with fluctuating demand conditions in the firm's markets and cost conditions in its production facility. We represent the varying demands and costs by stochastic revenue and cost functions as follows:

$$\begin{aligned} r_1 &= b_1(s)x_1 - x_1^2 \\ r_2 &= b_2(s)x_2 - x_2^2 \\ v &= c(s)x + Cx^2 \qquad (1) \end{aligned}$$

where r_1 and r_2 are the revenue functions in Country 1 and Country 2 and v is the variable cost function. x_1 and x_2 are the sales volumes in Countries 1 and 2, and $x = x_1 + x_2$ is total output. The coefficients $b_1(s), b_2(s)$ are stochastic 'benefit' coefficients and $c(s)$ is a stochastic cost coefficient. These stochastic variables capture fluctuations in the demand and costs, and are functions of the unknown state of the world, s, drawn at random from the set S of all possible states. C is a positive constant. We assume that the stochastic coefficients are normally and independently distributed with the following means and variances:

Variable	Expected Value	Variance
$b_1(s)$	$\bar{b}_1$	σ^2_{b1}
$b_2(s)$	$\bar{b}_2$	σ^2_{b2}
$c(s)$	$\bar{c}$	σ^2_c

Next, we represent the specialised knowledge of the subsidiaries, S1 and S2. Each subsidiary knows the *true*, fluctuating value of the revenue function in its own market, but only the *expected value* of revenue in the other market. And S1 (the producer) knows the true value of variable costs, but S2 knows only the expected value. These are summarised in Table 3.1.

Table 3.1 Information assumptions

	S1	S2
Knowledge of a_1	True $b_1(s)$	Expected value $\bar{b}_1$
Knowledge of a_2	Expected value $\bar{b}_2$	True $b_2(s)$
Knowledge of c	True $c(s)$	Expected value $\bar{c}$

These assumptions can be used to construct *information structures* of alternative output-choice architectures, that is the values of the information variables employed when choosing the two outputs x_1 and x_2. Consider the architectures in Figure 3.1, labelled 'separate decisions', 'sequential decisions' and 'joint decisions'. Two possibilities were indicated for the 'joint decision' case, one in which both outputs are selected by one of the subsidiaries and the other in which they are chosen by a joint board. Let us say that S1 is the 'parent', since it operates the production facility. We will call a joint decision architecture in which S1 chooses both outputs 'parent choice'. If both subsidiaries participate in the joint decision, we will call the architecture 'joint board'. Therefore we consider the information structures of *four* architectures: 'separate decisions' (*SEP*), 'sequential decisions' (*SEQ*), 'parent choice' (*PC*) and 'joint board' (*JB*). These are shown in Table 3.2. Notice that this approach treats the team entrepreneurial process *parametrically*. We are not modelling the process as such, but are *assuming* variations in individual capabilities (i.e. what individuals are able to observe) and then exploring the consequences of differences in team organisation – represented by different information structures – for the capabilities of the team.

Table 3.2 Information structures

	$\mathbf{I}_{SEP}$ $(A = SEP)$	$\mathbf{I}_{SEQ}$ (A=SEQ)	$\mathbf{I}_{PC}$ (A=PC)	$\mathbf{I}_{JB}$ (A=JB)
Information used in choice of x_1				
$E(b_1 \| A)$	$b_1(s)$	$b_1(s)$	$b_1(s)$	$b_1(s)$
$E(b_2 \| A)$	$\bar{b}_2$	x_2 decision known	$\bar{b}_2$	$b_2(s)$
$E(c \| A)$	$c(s)$	$c(s)$	$c(s)$	$c(s)$
Information used in choice of x_2				
$E(b_1 \| A)$	$\bar{b}_1$	$\bar{b}_1$	$b_1(s)$	$b_1(s)$
$E(b_2 \| A)$	$b_2(s)$	$b_2(s)$	$\bar{b}_2$	$b_2(s)$
$E(c \| A)$	$\bar{c}$	$\bar{c}$	$c(s)$	$c(s)$

Calculating architecture performances

The performance of any given architecture cannot be predicted with certainty, since revenues and costs are stochastic. But we can calculate the *expected* performance and this is done in three stages. First we determine the decision which maximises the objective function for each team architecture as a function of the information structure. Then we put this *decision function* into the firm's gross profit function to calculate the expected gross profit contribution. Finally we must take into account the costs of deliberative decision-making to provide the expected net profit contribution of a given process architecture.

The goal of the output choice team is to choose x_1 and x_2 so as to maximise the *expected gross profit contribution* of the output to the firm, being revenues net of variable costs. Using the definitions in equation (1), the gross profit contribution is:

$$g(x_1, x_2, s) = r_1(x_1, s) + r_2(x_2, s) - v(x_1, x_2, s) \tag{2}$$

and the goal of the process team is:

$$\max_{x_1,\, x_2} E[g(x_1, x_2, s) | \mathbf{I}_A] \tag{3}$$

where $\mathbf{I}_A$ is the information structure of a given architecture as shown in Table 3.1. Solving (3) gives the (stochastic) decision of the process team as a function of the state of nature s and the information structure:

$$\hat{x}_1 = \hat{x}_1(\mathbf{I}_A, s)$$
$$\hat{x}_2 = \hat{x}_2(\mathbf{I}_A, s) \tag{4}$$

The second stage of the calculation is to substitute the decision functions (4) into (2), and take expectations to find the *expected gross profit* contribution, $\hat{G}(A)$.

$$\hat{G}(A) = Eg(\hat{x}_1, \hat{x}_2, s, A) \tag{5}$$

Finally, we allow for the different costs of deliberative (entrepreneurial) choice of each architecture. The expected *net* profit contribution is:

$$\hat{\Pi}(A) = \hat{G}(A) - \kappa_A \tag{6}$$

where κ_A is the cost of deliberative choice, including collecting and exchanging information, and deliberating about the decision. It is convenient to assume here that the costs of choice κ_A are fixed for any given architecture, that is they are independent of both choices x_1 and x_2 and of the state of the world s. In the present context they include the costs we have earlier called *information costs* and *coordination costs*. Since we are assuming team behaviour, we can suppose that motivation costs are separate. We make no attempt here to model the costs of choice κ_A and they will be introduced simply as parameters (say κ_{SEP}, κ_{SEQ}, etc.).

We now carry out the calculations for the information structures detailed in Table 3.2. The team objective function in full is as follows:

$$g(x_1, x_2, s) = b_1(s)x_1 - x_1^2 + b_2(s)x_2 - x_2^2 - c(s)(x_1 + x_2) - C(x_1 + x_2)^2 \tag{7}$$

Equation (7) is concave provided $C \geq -\frac{1}{2}$. The first order conditions for (3) are then

$$\begin{aligned} 2(1+C)x_1 + 2CE(x_2|\mathbf{I}_A) &= E(b_1|\mathbf{I}_A) - E(c|\mathbf{I}_A) \\ 2CE(x_1|\mathbf{I}_A) + 2(1+C)x_2 &= E(b_1|\mathbf{I}_A) - E(c|\mathbf{I}_A) \end{aligned} \tag{8}$$

The solutions of (8) for the various architectures are found indirectly by assuming general linear forms for the decision functions (4), substituting these into (8), taking expectations and rearranging to derive the decision functions. The method is illustrated in Carter (1996). Table 3.3 lists resulting decision functions. Note that the following normalisation (9) is used, so that in effect the functions listed are *deviations* from the choice which would be made without specialised information.

$$\bar{b}_1 = \bar{b}_2 = \bar{c} = 0 \tag{9}$$

This normalisation simplifies the expressions but does not alter the *relative* pay-offs of the architectures.

Table 3.3 Decision functions

Architecture	*Decision function*
Joint board	$\hat{x}_1 = \frac{1}{2(1+C)}[(1+C)b_1(s) - Cb_2(s) - c(s)]$
	$\hat{x}_2 = \frac{1}{2(1+C)}[(1+C)b_2(s) - Cb_1(s) - c(s)]$
Parental choice	$\hat{x}_1 = \frac{1}{2(1-C)}[(1+C)b_1(s) - c(s)]$
	$\hat{x}_2 = \frac{1}{2(1+C)}[-Cb_1(s) - c(s)]$
Separate decisions	$\hat{x}_1 = \frac{1}{2(1+C)}[(1+C)b_1(s) - c(s)]$
	$\hat{x}_2 = \frac{1}{2(1+C)}[(1+C)b_2(s)]$
Sequential decisions	$\hat{x}_1 = \frac{1}{2(1+C)}[b_1(s) - c(s)] - \frac{c}{2(1+C)}b_2(s)$
	$\hat{x}_2 = \frac{1}{2(1+C)}[(1+C)b_2(s)]$

The next step is to substitute from Table 3.3 into (7) and so calculate the expected gross profit of the two architectures. That is:

$$\hat{G}(A) = E\{b_1(s)\hat{x}_1(A) - [\hat{x}_1(A)]^2 + b_2(s)\hat{x}_2(A) - [\hat{x}_2(A)]^2$$
$$-c(s)[\hat{x}_1(A) + \hat{x}_2(A)] - C[\hat{x}_1(A) + \hat{x}_2(A)]^2\} \tag{10}$$

These substitutions and taking expectations yield the expressions in Table 3.4.

Table 3.4 Expected gross profits

Architecture, A	*Expected gross profit,* $\hat{G}(A)$
Joint board ($A = JB$)	$\frac{1}{4(1+2C)}[(1+C)(\sigma_{b1}^2 + \sigma_{b2}^2) + 2\sigma_c^2]$
Parental choice ($A = PC$)	$\frac{1}{4(1+2C)}[(1+C)\sigma_{b1}^2 + 2\sigma_c^2]$
Separate decisions ($A = SEP$)	$\frac{1}{4(1+2C)}\left[(1+C)(1-\frac{C^2}{1-2C})(\sigma_{b1}^2 + \sigma_{b2}^2) + (2 - \frac{1+C}{2(1+2C)}\sigma_c^2\right]$
Sequential decisions ($A = SEQ$)	$\frac{1}{4(1+C)}(\sigma_{b1}^2 + \sigma_c^2) + \frac{1+C}{4(1+2C)}\sigma_{b2}^2$

Interpretation

The expressions in Table 3.4 are for the *expected* gross profit which different architectures would yield in a world in which revenues and costs are fluctuating, written in terms of the basic model parameters. The connection with the transaction costs framework set out earlier is made clearer if we re-express these results using the following quantities. These represent the expected value to the firm of information about the stochastic coefficients in the revenue and cost functions.

Stochastic coefficient	Expected Information Value
$b_1(s)$	$V_{b1} = \frac{1+c}{4(1+2c)}\sigma_{b1}^2$
$b_2(s)$	$V_{b2} = \frac{1+c}{4(1+2c)}\sigma_{b2}^2$
$c(s)$	$V_c = \frac{1+c}{4(1+2c)}\sigma_c^2$

Furthermore, we define the 'complementarity factor' F, a secondary parameter which depends on the second order cost parameter C:

$$F = \frac{C^2}{1+2C} \tag{11}$$

The expressions for $\hat{G}(A)$ in Table 3.4 can be rewritten using these definitions as shown in the second column of Table 3.5. This version of the expressions links the performance of each architecture in terms of the transaction cost concepts defined in section 2.

Table 3.5 Expected gross profits and organisation losses

A	$\hat{G}(A)$	*Expected organisation losses*	
		Information loss	*Coordination loss*
JB	$V_{b1} + V_{b2} + 2V_c$	0	0
PC	$V_{b1} + 2V_c$	V_{b2}	0
SEP	$(1-F)(V_{b1} + V_{b2}) + (1+\frac{F}{c})V_c$	V_c	$F(V_{b1} + V_{b2}) - \frac{F}{C}V_c$
SEQ	$(1-\frac{F}{1+F})V_{b1} + V_{b2} + (1-\frac{F}{1+F})V_c$	V_c	$\frac{F}{1+F}(V_{b1} + V_{b2})$

First, consider the joint board (*JB*) process. This architecture makes both use of the best available information in both decisions (Table 3.2) (perfect information) and chooses actions jointly (perfect coordination). The organisation losses are zero and the expected gross profit is the sum of the information values of all the stochastic benefit and cost coefficients. Notice that V_c contributes twice, since cost information contributes to the output decisions in both countries.

Parental choice (*PC*) differs from *JB* in using the expected value $\bar{b}_2$ for both decisions rather than the true value $b_2(s)$. The expected gross of *PC* profit differs from *JB* by the term V_{b2} and this is therefore the expected information loss which arises in this case. The decisions are made jointly so that there is no coordination loss.

The separate choice (*SEP*) and sequential choice (*SEQ*) cases are more complex as they involve both incomplete information and imperfect coordination. The expected gross profit expressions in Table 3.5 are a combination of information and coordination losses as follows. The information loss concerns costs. In both structures, full cost information is used in the decision about x_1, but x_2 is chosen on the basis of $\bar{c}$ only. Therefore an expected information loss of V_c arises in both.

For *SEP* the coordination loss term is in two parts. The first part, $F(V_{b1} + V_{b2})$, implies that separation of the decisions leads to a reduction in the realised value of the available information about the benefit coefficients in proportion to the complementarity factor, *F*. The value of the second order cost coefficient *C* determines the size of *F*. If *C* were zero, then *F* is also zero, there is no interaction between the decisions and therefore no coordination loss. *C* is the gradient of the firm's marginal cost function, so that a value of zero corresponds to constant marginal costs. There would be no interaction in this case because the decision of one subsidiary has no impact on the costs of the other. But if *C* is non-zero, each subsidiary's costs depends on the choice made independently by the other. A positive value of *C* corresponds to diminishing returns and if these are sufficiently strong ($C > 1 + \sqrt{2}$) then $F > 1$. Interaction would then be so large that the coordination losses exceed the value of the information available to the decision-makers. Clearly separate decision-making should be avoided if marginal costs rise too steeply. Mild economies of scale are also possible (negative value of *C*, provided $C \geq -\frac{1}{2}$), but if $C < 1 - \sqrt{2}$ then once again $F > 1$, and the expected coordination losses would exceed the value of the available information.
The second coordination loss term for *SEP* is $-\frac{F}{C} V_c$, which also vanishes if *C* is zero, but is *negative* if $C > 0$, and so partly *reduces* the size of the loss. However, its lower bound as *C* increases is $-\frac{1}{2} V_c$, so that it can never fully compensate for the expected information loss of V_c. The explanation is that in choosing x_1 the parent not only allows for the true output cost of its own choice, but also compensates for the expected extra costs that the subsidiary will impose from its choice, partly correcting the complementarity effect.

In the case of *SEQ*, the complementarity loss is the single term $\frac{F}{1+F}(V_{b1} + V_{b2})$. This compares favourably with *SEP* because $\frac{F}{1+F} \leq F$, so that $\hat{G}(SEQ) \geq \hat{G}(SEP)$. The two are only equal when $C = 0$ and it appears on the basis of expected gross profit *SEQ* should always be preferred to *SEP*. Furthermore, the upper bound of $\frac{F}{1+F}$ is 1, so that the coordination losses in *SEQ* never exceed the value of the information used by the decision-makers.

However, the preferred architecture depends not on the value of the expected gross profit, but on the *net* profit after taking the decision-making costs into account (equation (6) earlier). For example, the comparison of *SEP* and *SEQ* should not be based on $\hat{G}(SEP)$ and $\hat{G}(SEQ)$, but on the following net profits.

$$\hat{\Pi}(SEP) = \hat{G}(SEP) - \kappa_{SEP}$$
$$\hat{\Pi}(SEQ) = \hat{G}(SEQ) - \kappa_{SEQ} \quad (12)$$

The preferred architecture therefore depends on whether the difference in the two decision-making *costs* (information and coordination costs), κ_{SEP} and κ_{SEQ}, is larger or smaller than the differences in expected gross profit. That is to say, *SEQ* is preferable to the *SEP* if:

$$\hat{G}(SEO) - \hat{G}(SEP) > \kappa_{SEQ} - \kappa_{SEP} \quad (13)$$

We know from above that the left hand side of (13) is positive, so that *SEQ* is better than *SEP* provided the costs of *SEQ* do not exceed those of *SEP* by too much.

Likewise, we can see that while the expected gross profit of *JB* is highest of all, since it entails no information or coordination losses, it only provides the best net profit if its organisation costs are sufficiently low. For example, it would be preferred to *PC* if the difference in organisation costs is smaller than the information loss of *JB*. That is if:

$$\kappa_{JB} - \kappa_{PC} < V_c \quad (14)$$

We can see from this analysis that the architecture adopted by the firm affects its performance. Furthermore, there is no uniquely preferred architecture. The value of any particular $\hat{\Pi}(A)$ depends on several parameters, and there are regions of the parameter space in which each $\hat{\Pi}(A)$ can have the highest value. However, the analysis here goes some way to represent three general factors influencing the best architecture for a firm:

1 The magnitude of the fluctuations in the firm's environment, which contribute to the expected value of the information. In the present model fluctuations are captured by the variance parameters $\sigma_{b1}^2, \sigma_{b2}^2$ and σ_c^2.
2 The firm's technology which, in the case described here, determines the level of interaction between the firm's decision variables via the slope of the marginal cost, *C*.
3 The information acquisition and deliberative decision-making capabilities of individuals within the firm and associated costs, together with

costs of communication between individuals. These are represented here by the information assumptions in Table 3.1, and the organisation costs κ_A.

5. Conclusion

The organisation of the MNE is constantly changing. This may at least in part be due to a lack of founding principles of organisation design. We have tried in this chapter to indicate some features of organisation which such founding principles would need to address.

The first of these is that the actions of firms are the result of deliberative choice, which is the *process* of attempting to discover and implement optimal outcomes. This is not only true for development and innovation processes, but is also important in established markets in which demand, competition, factor supply, statutory conditions and so on can all be turbulent. Optimising (or satisficing) can imply continual adjustment. If such deliberative processes were not required, it is hard to see what continuing function organisations fulfill. A theory of organisation must recognise this dynamic, entrepreneurial character of organised activities.

Second, organisation is a necessary result of the division of managerial labour. The choice processes demand more skills and knowledge than are possessed by a single individual, and successful choice depends on the collaboration of a group of individuals, or on *team entrepreneurship*.

There are three aspects of interaction in team entrepreneurship. The first arises from the *distribution of information*, which implies that successful decisions rely on the transmission of appropriate information. The second is that when there is *complementarity* between decisions, then the process leading to those decisions should ensure that they are coordinated. And there is *motivation*. Collaboration, either in the exchange of information or in coordinating decisions needs collaborators to have some goals in common. A way to think about the effectiveness of organisation is in terms of the *losses* from imperfect interaction (information, coordination, motivation) as well as the *costs* of interacting. All these aspects of organisation are particularly acute in the MNE, for which imperfections and costs of interaction are likely to be substantial.

We think that this framework provides an appropriate economic conception of the *business process* approach to organisation which has become influential in the management literature. Both are concerned with designing the structure of interactions (architecture) on the basis of effectiveness of the process rather than on conventional functional demarcations, and both stress the significance of teams working towards common goals. The analysis of process architecture presented here suggests that the best structure is determined by a combination of the firm's environment, its technology and its deliberative capabilities and costs.

It is worth noting that cross-border, process-oriented organisation is not necessarily the most effective for an MNE. The costs of information, coordination and motivation may be relatively high in MNEs, and it may therefore be the case that close cross-border collaboration is not the most effective approach. The team theory example in the previous section indicates as much, since the architecture in which the parent alone dictates the firm's decisions is to be preferred if the information loss is *smaller* than the cost saving by acting alone (equation (14)).

The ideas in this chapter do not predict the form that organisations should take. Rather they suggest that there are often many possibilities. We have tried to indicate some of the most important factors involved.

Notes

1 Alternative terms which have used are 'Business Reengineering', 'Business Process Management' and 'Business Process Analysis'.

2 Specialised management journals have appeared in this field: for example *Business Change and Re-engineering* (Vol. 1, No. 1, 1993) and *Business Process Re-engineering and Management Journal* (Vol. 1, No. 1, 1995).

3 Page references for Hammer and Champy are for the revised paperback edition, 1995.

4 Including, incidentally, by Hammer and Champy.

4

INCORPORATING THE MULTINATIONAL ENTERPRISE INTO THE THEORY OF INTERNATIONAL TRADE

James R. Markusen

1. Introduction

Literatures on international trade theory and the theory of the multinational enterprise have largely developed separately, with little overlap among either researchers or readers. Trade theory took a general-equilibrium path, with models predominately based on the twin assumptions of constant returns to scale and perfect competition. In such a framework, there is essentially no role for multinational firms since there are no technological or other features to support their existence in equilibrium. Indeed, there is no role for firms at all and authors speak only of 'industries', not firms.

Trade theory was then revitalised in the 1980s, with models based on assumptions of increasing returns to scale, imperfect competition, and product differentiation. These features were incorporated into simple general-equilibrium models with the intention of explaining certain stylised facts, in particular the large volume of trade between similar economies, which were viewed as anomalous from the perspective of traditional Heckscher-Ohlin theory.

Yet the new models are very limited in their treatment of firms. In these models, a firm is generally synonymous with a plant or production facility; that is, a firm is an independent organisation that produces one good in one location. Multi-plant and multi-product production, whether horizontal or vertical, is generally excluded from the analysis. This is potentially troubling. After all, industries characterised by scale economies and imperfect competition are often dominated by multinationals. As a result, the policy and normative analysis that comes out of the new trade theory may be significantly off base. For example, conclusions of the 'strategic trade policy' literature are fundamentally bound up with the notion of clearly defined national firms competing via trade with the national champions of other countries. Substantial foreign ownership of domestic production facilities radically alters the policy implications (Dick 1993).

The theory of the multinational enterprise on the other hand has been predominantly a theory-of-the-firm literature focusing on the characteristics of individual firms that lead to multinationality. This permits a great richness in analysing firms' multiple options for serving markets and their geographic arrangement of activities. But partial-equilibrium analysis of industry structure is somewhat unusual and general-equilibrium considerations are rarely incorporated.

Each literature has strengths, but there is a need to integrate their contributions. Trade theory cannot afford to ignore multinationals given their tremendous empirical importance in international economic activity. The present state of the theory of the multinational enterprise leaves it ill-equipped to answer questions such as why ownership of multinational firms is concentrated in a few countries, and why multinationals are much more important relative to trade among the high income countries than between these countries and lower income countries.

The purpose of this chapter is to survey recent contributions which attempt to integrate the theory of the multinational enterprise into the theory of international trade. The contributions reviewed are primarily by trade economists. The basic models of multinationals are extremely simple such that they can be incorporated into a correspondingly simple general-equilibrium model. There is no expectation on my part that I will teach readers anything new about multinational firms per se and indeed I hope that I do not cause offence by presenting such a simple model.

The next section presents a number of 'stylised facts' on characteristics of multinational firms and characteristics of countries that are sources of and/or hosts to multinational investment. The purpose of the chapter is to reconcile these two sets of facts, and Sections 3 and 4 present a simple model which attempts to do so. Section 5 turns to the question of internalisation and the problem of why a firm, having chosen to produce abroad, will chose direct investment over some alternative mode of serving the foreign market.

2. Some Stylised Facts

Many studies have documented the characteristics of multinational firms and the characteristics of industries dominated by multinationals, comparing the latter to industries in which multinationals play a minor role. Since many of these empirical regularities will be very familiar to readers of this book, I will simply list some of them with little comment.

Extensive empirical evidence offers us a picture of the characteristics of firms and industries that tend to be dominated by multinationals.[1]

Firm and industry characteristics

1 Multinationals are associated with high ratios of R&D relative to sales.
2 Multinationals employ large numbers of scientific, technical, and other 'white collar' workers as a percentage of their work forces.
3 Multinationals tend to have a high value of 'intangible assets'; roughly, market value minus the value of tangible assets such as plant and equipment.
4 Multinationals are associated with new and/or technically complex products.
5 Evidence suggests that multinationality is negatively associated with plant-level scale economies.
6 Multinationals are associated with product-differentiation variables, such as advertising to sales ratios.
7 A minimum or 'threshold' level of firm size seems to be important for a firm to be a multinational, but above that level firm size is of minimal importance.
8 Multinationals tend to be older, more established firms.

These data suggest that multinationals are important in industries in which intangible, firm specific assets are important. These assets can generally be characterised as 'knowledge capital,' ranging from proprietary product or process 'know-how' to reputations and trademarks. Plant-level scale economies are not associated with direct investment.

Other data gives us an understanding of the country characteristics that are associated with source and host countries.

Country characteristics

1 The high-income developed countries are not only the major source of direct investment, they are also the major recipients. Most direct investment seems to be horizontal, in the sense that the bulk of the affiliates output is sold in the host country.
2 High volumes of direct investment are associated with similarities among countries in terms of relative factor endowments and per capita incomes, not differences. But that portion of output which is shipped back to the home country is associated with endowment and income differences.
3 A high volume of outward direct investment is positively related to a country's endowment of skilled labour and insignificantly- or negatively-related to its physical capital endowment.[2]
4 There is little evidence that direct investment is primarily motivated by trade-barrier avoidance; the relative coefficients often have the wrong

sign. Trade barriers seem to discourage both trade and investment, but have a substitution effect toward investment.[3]

5 Direct investment stocks, at least among the high-income countries, have grown significantly faster than trade flows over the last two decades, even though trade barriers have fallen dramatically.

6 There is mixed evidence that tax avoidance and/or risk diversification are important motives for direct investment. Some evidence does suggest that political risk discourages inward investment.[4]

7 Infrastructure, skill levels, and a minimum threshold level of per capita income seem to be very important determinants of direct investment.

8 There is evidence that agglomeration effects are important in direct investment. But it is admittedly difficult to distinguish agglomeration effects from firms being drawn to the same (unobserved) site-specific resources.[5]

In summary, direct investment is concentrated among the high-income countries, and skilled labour in particular is an important determinant of outward direct investment quality. Taxes and trade barriers do not seem to be of first-order importance, but good infrastructure and agglomeration economies do seem to be significant.

3. An Organising Framework

As noted in the previous section, the purpose of this chapter is to connect these firm characteristics with the country characteristics. To do so we first need a very simple model of a multinational firm. Because of the quantitative importance of horizontal direct investment, I will concentrate on that case, but many of the ideas apply equally well to a model of a vertically-integrated multinational.

Many authors begin by noting that there are inherent difficulties and costs to doing business abroad, such that multinationals are assumed to be disadvantaged relative to local firms. Because of these inherent disadvantages and higher costs of foreign production, it is necessary to identify offsetting advantages and conditions under which direct investment will occur. One organising framework was proposed by Dunning (1977, 1981), who suggested that three conditions are necessary for a firm to undertake direct investment (that is, all three factors need to be present for a firm to have a strong motive for direct investment). This has become well known as the OLI framework: ownership, location, and internalisation.

A firm's *ownership advantage* could be a product or a production process to which other firms do not have access, such as a patent, blueprint, or trade secret. It could also be something intangible, like a trademark or reputation for quality. Whatever its form, the ownership advantage confers some valuable market power or cost advantage on the firm sufficient to outweigh the disadvantages of doing business abroad.

In addition, the foreign market must offer a *location advantage* which makes it profitable to produce the product in the foreign country rather than simply produce it at home and export it to the foreign market. Although tariffs, quotas, transport costs and cheap factor prices are the most obvious sources of location advantages, factors such as access to customers can also be important. Indeed, many multinationals are in service industries (for example, hotels) in which on-site provision of the services is an inherent part of the companies' business.[6]

Finally, the multinational enterprise must have an *internalisation advantage*. This condition is the most abstract of the three. If a company has a proprietary product or production process and if, due to tariffs and transport costs, it is advantageous to produce the product abroad rather than export it, it is still not obvious that the company should set up a foreign subsidiary. One of several alternatives is to licence a foreign firm to produce the product or use the production process. Why not just sell the blueprints to a foreign firm rather than go through the costly and difficult process of setting up a foreign production facility? Reasons for wishing to do so are referred to as internalisation advantages; that is, the product or process is exploited internally within the firm rather than arm's length through markets.[7]

Ownership advantages come in many possible forms, and a good approach to identifying them is to seek guidance from the firm-level characteristics about direct foreign investment. Remember, the evidence finds that an industry tends to have a greater proportion of multinational enterprises when the output of that industry is characterised by R&D, marketing expenditures, scientific and technical workers, product newness and complexity, and product differentiation. At a broader level, multinational enterprises are identified with a high ratio of intangible assets of the firm to its total market value. These explanatory variables give rise to the concept of knowledge-based, firm-specific assets. These proprietary assets of the firm are embodied in such things as the human capital of the employees, patents or other exclusive technical knowledge, copyrights or trademarks, or even more intangible assets such as management 'know-how' or the reputation of the firm.

There are two good reasons why these knowledge-based assets are more likely to give rise to direct foreign investment than physical capital assets. First, knowledge-based assets can be transferred easily back and forth across space at low cost. An engineer or manager can visit many separate production facilities at relatively low cost. Second, knowledge often has a joint-input characteristic, like a public good, in that it can be supplied to additional production facilities at very low cost. Blueprints, chemical formulae and pharmaceuticals, and trademarks and other marketing devices all have this characteristic but assets based on physical capital such as machinery usually do not. That is, physical capital usually cannot yield a flow of services in one location without reducing its productivity in others.

In turn, the joint-input characteristic of knowledge-based assets has implications for the efficiency of the firm and for market structure. These implications are encapsulated in the notion of economies of multi-plant production. Such economies arise because a single two-plant firm has a cost efficiency over two independent single-plant firms. The multi-plant firm (that is, the multinational enterprise) need only make a single investment in R&D, for example, while two independent firms must each make the investment. Cost efficiency then dictates that multinational enterprises (multi-plant firms) arise as the equilibrium market structure in industries where firm-specific assets are important, which is consistent with the empirical evidence.[8]

The converse proposition also deserves emphasis. Scale economies based on physical capital intensity do not by themselves lead to foreign direct investment, an argument supported by some evidence (Beaudreau 1986; Brainard 1993c; Ekholm 1995). This type of scale economy implies the cost efficiency of centralised production rather than geographically dispersed production. Of course, some industries with high physical capital intensity may also be industries in which firm-specific assets are important (like automobiles).

What then is being traded when we observe multinational production? Basically, multinational enterprises in this framework are exporters of the services of firm-specific assets. These include management, engineering, marketing and financial services, many of which are based on human capital. They also include the 'services' of patents and trademarks which are other knowledge-based assets. Subsidiaries import these services in exchange for repatriated profits, royalties, fees or output.

4. A Simple General-Equilibrium Model

A small number of authors working from the international trade perspective have constructed models in which multinationals arise endogenously in equilibrium. These authors have combined elements of ownership and location advantages, generally leaving aside the question of internalisation. Early papers by Helpman (1984) and Markusen (1984) allowed for a headquarters or firm-level activity such as R&D which could be separated from production. Helpman's model was constructed such that firms have a single production facility, which could be in a different country than the headquarters. The absence of tariffs or transport costs mean that the firm will never open more than one production facility, so the model is really one of a vertically integrated firm. In Markusen's model, the multinational enterprise would choose production facilities in both countries, becoming a horizontally integrated multinational enterprise. The headquarter's activity is modelled as a joint input (a non-rival input) such that adding additional plants does not reduce the value of the input to existing plants. The respective approaches are extended in Helpman (1985), Helpman and Krugman (1985), and Horstmann and Markusen (1987a).

More recently, Brainard (1993a) and Horstmann and Markusen (1992) have produced models in which horizontal multinationals arise endogenously and in which two-way investment, a characteristic of the North Atlantic economy, can arise in equilibrium. The three key elements of both papers are firm-level activities (like R&D) that are joint inputs across plants, plant-level scale economies, and tariffs or transport costs between countries. Although Brainard models firms as producing differentiated products whereas goods are homogeneous in the Horstmann and Markusen model, the results are strikingly similar. Multinationals are supported in equilibrium when firm-level fixed costs and tariff/transport costs are large relative to plant-level scale economies. Multinationals are more likely to exist in equilibrium when the countries are large (both papers) and when the countries have similar relative factor endowments (Brainard 1993a). These results fit well with the empirical evidence given in note 1 at the end of this chapter.

It may be useful to offer an outline of these newer models. The model sketched here is drawn from Markusen and Venables (1995a). It assumes homogenous goods, but it is clear from Brainard (1993a) that a differentiated-good model generates similar conclusions.

1 Two countries (h and f), producing two goods (X and Y), using the factors 'land' and 'labour' (R and L). Factors are immobile between countries.
2 Y is a homogeneous good produced with constant returns to scale by a competitive industry. Y production uses all of the land (R) and some of the labour (L).[9]
3 X is a homogeneous good produced with increasing returns to scale by Cournot firms. Markets are segmented (arbitrage conditions need not hold). X uses labour as its single factor of production.
4 The costs for producers of X can be measured in units of labour. The costs can be divided into four types:
   firm-specific fixed cost (F);
   plant-specific fixed cost (one G per plant)
   constant marginal cost (c)
   unit shipping cost (t) between markets, assumed symmetric in both directions.

The model employs three firm types, with free entry and exit into and out of firm types. Type m firms are multinationals which maintain plants in both countries.[10] Type h firms are national firms that maintain a single plant in country h. Type h firms may or may not export to country f. Finally, type f firms are national firms that maintain a single plant in country f. Type f firms may or may not export to country h. The term 'regime' denotes the set of firm types active in equilibrium.

In the context of this model, consider first two countries absolutely identical in technologies, preferences and endowments. If transport costs were zero, then there would exist only national firms exporting to each other's markets, since no firm would incur the fixed costs of a second plant. If transport costs were very high, there would exist only multinational (two plant) firms: in this case, a multinational has lower fixed costs per market and therefore out-competes national firms which face prohibitive export costs. At intermediate levels of transport costs, multinational firms exist if firm-specific fixed costs and transport costs are large relative to plant-specific fixed costs (plant-level scale economies).[11] Thus, this model predicts that we should find multinationals concentrated in industries which fit at least one of three conditions: firm-level activities or intangible assets are important; plant scale economies are not particularly important; the overall market is large; and tariffs and transport costs are high but barriers to direct investment relatively are low.

Figures 4.1 and 4.2 present the results of some simulations for this model when the two countries are identical. The shading in the cells give qualitative information on the equilibrium regime. On the horizontal axis is transport costs, measured as a proportion of marginal production costs. The vertical axis of Figure 4.1 measures the absolute factor endowment (economic size) of each of the identical economies (100 is the value used in subsequent simulations). We see the result that national firms dominate when transport costs

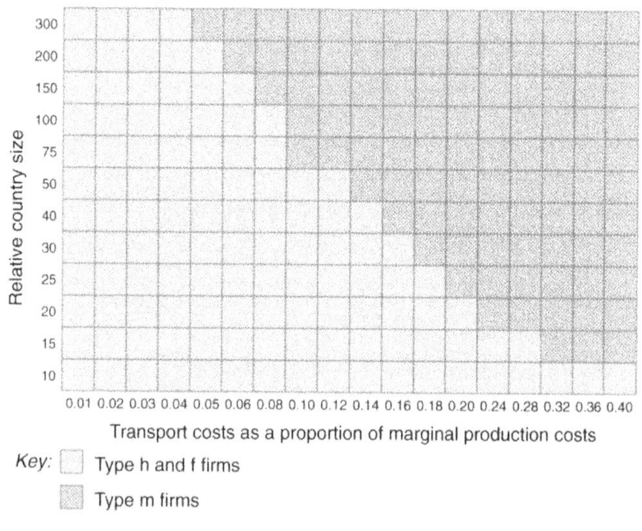

Figure 4.1 Absolute country size (countries identical) – 100 is the value used in other simulations

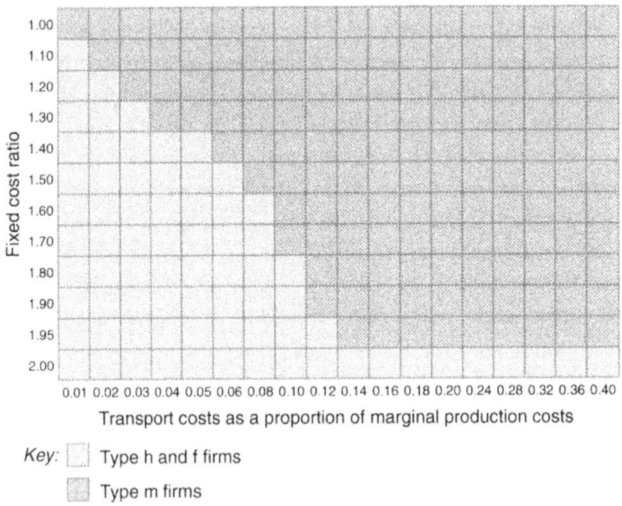

Figure 4.2 Ratio of two-plant to one-plant fixed costs (countries identical) – 1.60 is the value used in other simulations

are low and/or the markets are of modest size: there is intra-industry competition in exports between type-h and type-f national firms, reminiscent of the 'new trade theory' mentioned in the introduction. Multinationals dominate under the opposite circumstances.

The vertical axis of Figure 4.2 gives the ratio of fixed costs for a two-plant multinational to the fixed costs for a one-plant national firm (1.60 is the value used in the other simulations). This value is reduced below 2 by the joint-input nature of knowledge capital discussed above. It is raised above 1 by the physical capital costs of plant construction and by various transaction costs, including foreign investment barriers (assuming the latter fall on fixed costs). National firms dominate in equilibrium when trade costs are low and/or multi-plant economies of scale are weak (or investment barriers are high). Multinationals dominate under the opposite circumstances.

The empirical evidence is consistent with these results, but it also indicates that multinationals are of greater importance between countries that are relatively similar in size, per capita income and relative factor endowments, like western Europe and the United States. It is interesting that the simple model does a good job of capturing the association of direct foreign investment and multinational enterprises with the *similarity* of countries.

Figures 4.3 and 4.4 consider country asymmetries. The horizontal axis of each of these figures is the same as for Figures 4.1 and 4.2. Figure 4.3 considers differences in country size, holding the total world endowment of factors constant. Countries are identical in the top row. Moving down a column, factors are transferred from country f to country h. The numbers on the vertical axis measure country f's factor endowment as a proportion of its initial endowment, with country h's endowment correspondingly larger.

Figure 4.3 shows that national firms dominate at low levels of trade costs (for a given level of the investment cost ratio): there is intra-industry competition in exports by national firms. At higher levels of transport costs, the pattern is more complex. If the countries are of similar size, only multinational firms exist. At a moderate degree of difference, multinational firms compete with national firms located in country h, the large country. When the size difference is very large, only national firms headquartered in country h exist in equilibrium.

In order to grasp the intuition behind these results, consider moving down a column of Figure 4.3, such as $t = .20$. When the countries are very similar, only multinational firms exist in equilibrium. As the countries diverge in size, potential national firms headquartered in country h become more (potentially) profitable. Type-h firms have lower fixed costs than the multinational firms, and have most of their sales concentrated in the large and low-cost (no transport cost) market. Multinationals must make an additional fixed-cost investment to serve an ever shrinking market. Eventually, type-h firms can enter. Conversely, type-f firms cannot enter, because their low-cost domestic market is small and shipping costs would have to be incurred in order to serve market h.

As the difference in market sizes becomes extreme, multinational firms cannot exist at all, and only type-h firms exist in equilibrium. As country f's market becomes very small, no firm can afford a fixed-cost investment in that market (type-m and type-f firms) and all supply is from imports from type-h national firms. Note the contrast between this result and a traditional constant-returns Heckscher-Ohlin model, where differences in country size is not a source of comparative advantage (i.e., at no point in Figure 4.3 would there be any trade or investment).

Figure 4.4 considers differences in relative endowments across the countries, again holding the total world endowment of factors constant as in Figure 3. The countries are identical in the top row of Figure 4.4. Moving down a column of Figure 4.4, we transfer units of labour from country f to country h, and units of the Y-sector specific factor from country h to country f. Moving down a column, we are then creating a Heckscher-Ohlin basis of comparative advantage, in X for country h and in Y for country f. Total incomes of the two countries remain approximately equal as we move down each column. At low levels of trade costs, there is intra-industry competition in exports when the endowment differences are modest, but only inter-industry trade when the endowment differences are large (only type-h firms produce X). The latter region could be termed a 'Heckscher-Ohlin' region whereas the former region could be dubbed the 'New Trade Theory' region as noted earlier (see Figures 4.1 and 4.2).

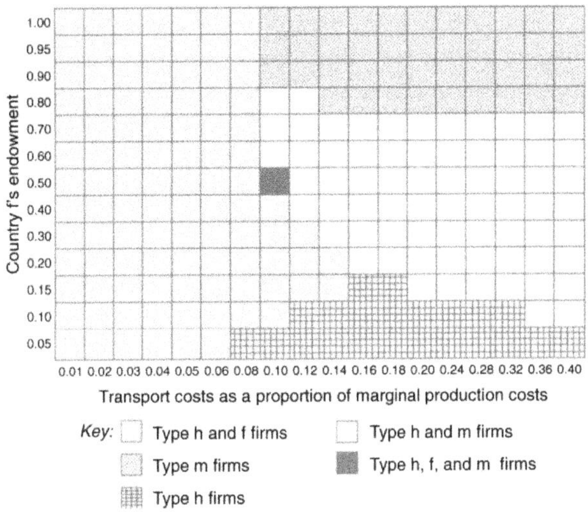

Figure 4.3 Countries differ in size

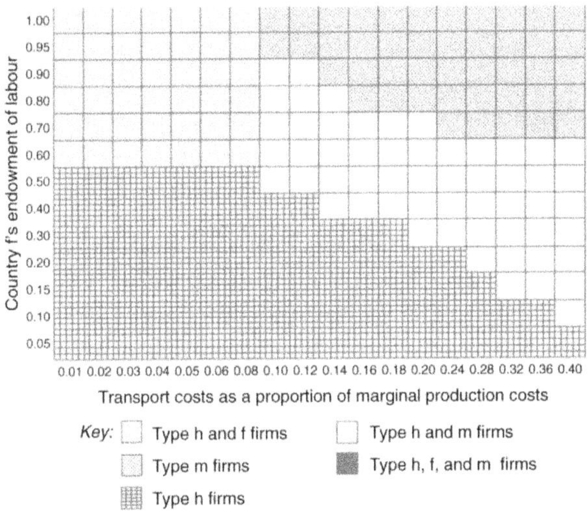

Figure 4.4 Countries differ in relative endowments

At higher levels of trade costs in Figure 4.4, we see a pattern qualitatively similar to that shown in Figure 4.3, where the differences are in relative country sizes. Moving down a column of Figure 4.4 such as $t = .20$, multinationals alone exist when the countries are relatively similar in relative endowments. But as the difference becomes more pronounced, factor prices become unequal across countries, with the price of labour lower in country h, the labour-abundant country. Even though the market sizes are approximately the same, there is now a cost-side advantage for type-h firms which incur all of their fixed costs in country h. Type-m firms must incur fixed costs in both markets, including costs in the high-labour-cost market f. Type-h firms can eventually enter in competition with multinational firms whereas type-f firms cannot. Eventually, these cost factors are sufficiently strong such that only type-h firms exist in equilibrium. Not surprisingly, the endowment difference at which the switch from type-m to types (m,h) and the switch from types (m,h) to type-h occur is increasing in the level of trade costs.

To summarise this section, we see that our very simple model generates outcomes that are at least superficially consistent with many of the stylised facts listed earlier. In particular the model predicts that direct investment will be important relative to trade when (a) countries are large (high income), (b) countries are similar in size, (c) countries are similar in relative factor endowments (crudely proxied by per capita income), and (d) trade costs are modest or high relative to foreign investment costs. Looking at a cross-section of industries between two countries with given characteristics, the model predicts that industries with large levels of multi-plant economies of scale (a low ratio of two-plant to one-plant fixed costs in Figure 4.2) will be more multinationalised. This is also consistent with the stylised facts under the strong suspicion that multi-plant economies are more important for knowledge-intensive industries than for physical-capital intensive industries.

6. Internalisation

Even if foreign production makes economic sense in the terms of the models laid out in the previous section, there is a further question to tackle. A firm might be able to realise many of the advantages of multinational production, while shielding itself from the costs, by signing a licensing agreement with a firm in the foreign country. Thus, a complementary part of the argument must explain why firms choose direct investment, rather than some other mode of foreign entry. Licensing is only one of many such options; others include joint ventures, subcontracting, management contracts, and so forth. Following Dunning's terminology, the question of the mode of foreign entry can be referred to as the 'internalisation' problem.

Much has been written on whether a firm transfers a firm-specific asset (or the services thereof) within that particular firm or through an alternative arm's length arrangement with an independent foreign firm. Other authors in this book figure prominently in this literature, especially Mark Casson. As one might expect, the optimal scope of a firm is determined by factors like the form of corporate governance, the cost of internal transactions versus those in arm's length markets, the specific characteristics of the knowledge and information to be transferred, along with resulting market failures involving concepts like bounded rationality, agent opportunism and asset specificity (Williamson 1975, 1981).

Since many of the readers of this volume may be familiar with the writings of international business economists on internalisation problems, my discussion here will be limited to some fairly specific, formal models produced by international trade economists using the broader notions developed by Williamson (1975, 1981), Casson (1987), Rugman (1986), Teece (1977, 1986) and others. I will also limit myself to a comparison among only three options of serving a foreign market: exports, direct investment and licensing. These three illustrate some of the key trade-offs faced by firms.

As in earlier sections, I am interested in a synthesis between the theory of the multinational and trade theory. Therefore, I will focus on a set of ideas which are quite compatible and complementary with the model developed above, in addition to fitting well with most of the firm-level stylised facts laid out earlier and some of the country-level stylised facts. With respect to the latter, most of the models discussed below generate the empirically relevant prediction that (horizontal) direct investment is more likely to arise between large countries with similar levels of investment.

Many or most of the reasons to transfer assets internally arise from the basic property that knowledge capital can be a joint input to a number of plants; this same property, the reader will recall, was used in the model of Section 5 and is consistent with the association of multinational enterprises with R&D, advertising, and product newness and complexity. A number of papers show quite convincingly that transfers tend to be internal, rather than arms' length, when the products are new, complex, have no prior commercial application, and are produced by R&D-intensive firms (Davidson and McFetridge 1984; Mansfield and Romeo 1980; Teece 1977; Wilson 1977). Thus the same features that create multi-plant economies of scale may be responsible for creating advantages of internalisation.

But although models of internalisation do share an underlying commonality with the ownership-location models discussed in the previous section, internalisation models tend to be somewhat different. Because they focus on characteristics of knowledge capital like non-excludability, asymmetric information, moral hazard, adverse selection and incomplete contracting, the models are often partial-equilibrium in nature and bring to bear quite different tools of analysis. Nevertheless, despite their partial-equilibrium nature, many of the models generate empirically-plausible predictions as noted above. In what follows, I will outline some of the ideas that have been advanced in formal models of internalisation and present a simple analytical example at the end, much the same as I did in Section 3 on ownership and location.

All of the models I discuss below share a common point of departure: firms would like to licence due to the costs of doing business abroad, but licencing carries costs as well. These models can be categorised according to how they draw the link from information issues to difficulties in licencing, and thus why direct foreign investment occurs.

A first problem is that because of the non-excludability property of new knowledge, a firm may not want to reveal (or truthfully reveal) its process or product technology to a potential licensee. After all, the licensee could reject a deal and go and copy the technology at little cost. Conversely, the licensee is not going to deal without knowing exactly what it is getting, which requires revelation on the part of the seller. A complete contract may be costly or infeasible under these circumstances, so the technology is transferred instead to an owned subsidiary (Ethier 1986). More general discussions of buyer uncertainty of this type can be found in Teece (1986) and Rugman (1986).

This asymmetric information problem arises because the firm wants to maintain proprietary control over the results of its research due to the public-goods nature of knowledge capital. But this asymmetric information problem then creates a moral hazard problem as well in the Ethier model. The licencing contract is written before the results of the research are known or even before the research is undertaken (perhaps there could be a string of products). But if the firm is going to maintain secrecy about the results of the research, how can the licensee know that the firm has put forth the contracted amount of research effort? The firm may claim that the results are poor when in fact that is due to a lack of effort (expense) on the firm's part. Of course, there exists the standard mechanism-design arguments to motivate full revelation, but the necessary contingent contracts might be difficult to write, particularly when there are multiple dimensions to the uncertainty. Internalisation may be preferred to costly (rent dissipating) and/or incomplete contracts (Ethier 1986). More general discussions of contracting costs and agent opportunism may be found in the writings of Buckley, Casson, Rugman, Teece and Williamson.

A nice feature of the Ethier model is that it generates some predictions that are consistent with some of the stylised facts discussed earlier. For some rather complicated general-equilibrium reasons that I will not go into, it predicts that direct investment is more likely to arise between similar countries, and for new and/or technically complex products (where the uncertainty of research outcomes is high).

A third informational asymmetry associated with newness focuses on the case where the potential licensee has superior information, usually about how the product will sell in its local market. This is more or less the opposite of Ethier's informational asymmetry. The multinational enterprise is reluctant to build a foreign plant without information about whether sales will be high or low, information that could be provided by the foreign agent. But the agent knows that if it reveals demand to be high, the firm may decide to produce directly, or a large share of the rents will be extracted from the foreign agent in subsequent periods. Thus, agent's incentives can cause sales to be low even when demand is high. The multinational enterprise can avoid having to share informational rents with the licensee by direct investment (Horstmann and Markusen 1996). This model has nice empirical implications in that direct investment is predicted as more likely when the host country is large, and the degree of uncertainty is small (e.g., highly developed host countries). Empirically, many firms do set up foreign wholesale and servicing subsidiaries, possibly to deal with this sort of problem (Nicholas 1982, 1983; Nicholas et. al. 1994; Thompson 1994; Zeile 1993).

A fourth problem is that the same property that makes knowledge easy to transfer internationally may mean that it is easily learned by new employees. If a firm licences a technology to a foreign producer, the managers and workers may learn the technology quickly and be able to 'defect', starting a new domestic firm in competition with the multinational enterprise. While this problem would exist to some extent within a firm as well, it is argued that a firm may more credibly commit than can a licensee to sharing the rents from a string of (uncertain) future products with the employees (Ethier and Markusen 1996). Although many writers have discussed this problem in general terms, Rugman (1985, 1986) in particular, views this as a cornerstone of internalisation theory.

A fifth problem focuses on the costs of transferring technology. Certain aspects of a knowledge-intensive technology are bound up in the human capital of a firm's employees and even in the 'company culture' (Teece 1977, 1986). Such technology is costly to transfer arm's length, which does not contradict the possibility mentioned in the previous paragraph that the technology's value could be easily dissipated once the transfer does take place.

A sixth potential problem for licensing arises when the firm's intangible asset is a reputation for product quality. Product quality may only be observed after the product is purchased and used by the buyer. In this situation, the multinational enterprise cannot extract all rents from a licensee because, if it attempts to do so, the licensee can skimp on quality by producing an inferior substitute product for one period and earn positive single-period rents. To avoid this problem, it may be profitable to produce and sell through an owned subsidiary despite the added direct costs (Horstmann and Markusen 1987b). This problem arises especially in franchising, where the firm wants a uniform level of quality across outlets. Each outlet manager (licensee) has an incentive to free ride on the reputation of the whole (Caves and Murphy 1976). Among other empirically appealing results, the Horstmann and Markusen (1987b) model predicts that direct investment is more likely in larger markets, where the rent-sharing with the licensee necessary to sustain the firm's reputation is larger.

Finally, when a firm employs licensees, it must be concerned about a number of possible forms of moral hazard. For example, licensees may divert selling effort to competing products of other firms or simply shirk (Nicholas 1983; Mathewson and Winter 1985). Of course, these problems can occur within firms as well. Carlos (1994) and Carlos and Nicholas (1990) document how private trading on the part of agents caused difficulties for the Hudson's Bay and Royal African Companies, and how the Hudson's Bay Company was able to create an internal structure and company culture to mitigate the moral hazard and attendant losses. On the other hand, the Royal African Company went bankrupt. Intensive monitoring is one way to deal with licensees, but if a firm is going to monitor licensees with great care, it may be easier simply to own the foreign operation outright.

To add some concreteness to the idea of asset dissipation, we can outline a highly simplified version of Ethier and Markusen (1996). Consider a simple two-period model in which the multinational wishes to exploit a technology in a foreign market by licensing a foreign firm or by setting up a subsidiary (we will ignore exporting in this simple example). Because of the costs of doing business abroad, a licensing arrangement generates the most potential rents. The licensee masters the technology in the first period and can defect to start a rival firm in the second period. Similarly, the multinational can 'defect' by issuing a licence to a second firm in the second period. In other words, we make the strong assumption that no binding contracts can be written to prevent either firm from undertaking such a defection.

We will assume here, with no justification, that defection will not occur from within a subsidiary: that is, a part of a subsidiary will not split off to form another competitor. (This assumption is relaxed in Ethier and Markusen 1996.) A subsidiary is thus (by definition!) costly but 'secure'. An example might be a multinational firm stationing home-country nationals in its foreign-owned plant. While it is costly to keep home-country nationals overseas as opposed to hiring foreign nationals with roughly equivalent qualifications, it is reasonable to conjecture that the home-country nationals are less likely to defect and start a rival firm in the host country (e.g., language, cultural, visa barriers).

At the beginning of the second period, the multinational and the licensee make simultaneous moves, choosing whether to continue their original relationship. If both the multinational and the licensee defect, then the original licensee and the new licensee will compete as duopolists in the second period. For a two-period licencing contract to be self-enforcing, neither the multinational enterprise nor the licensee must wish to defect in the second period.

For the sake of illustration, and with some loss of generality, let us make some assumptions about the rents available in these different scenarios. If the license continues for both periods, let us refer to the total rents as $2R - F$, where R is the rents available in each period and F is the physical capital cost that the licensee (or multinational) must incur to start production. (For simplicity, this example assumes no discounting.) If the multinational sets up a subsidiary, then the rents will be M, where M represents the rents (net of all costs) received when the subsidiary operates on its own. We will assume that $2R - F > M$, which just means that the rents are larger if the licensing agreement continues. This assumption captures the idea discussed earlier that there are costs to establishing a business abroad.

The third situation is where the one-period licence is followed by duopoly. In this case, the rents will be $R + D - 2F$, where D represents the total rents for both members of the duopoly in one period, and the capital costs F must be multiplied by 2 because with two separate producers, the start-up costs must be incurred twice. For the purposes of this example, we posit that the rents from the duopoly option are lowest of these three scenarios; that is, $(2R - F) > M > (R + D - 2F)$.

As one final piece of notation, consider the licensing fee, which we will refer to as L_1 in period 1, and L_2 in period 2.

In this setting, what conditions must hold so that the licensing arrangement continues through both periods? For the licence to continue, it must be better than the alternative both from the point of view of the multinational, and from the point of view of the subsidiary. Let us posit that if one partner defects, that partner must incur the additional costs of F, the non-defecting partner retaining the original F.

For the licensee to not defect and start up production on its own, its second-period earnings ($R - L_2$, with no additional start-up costs) must be at least equal to $(R - F)$, its pay-off from defecting. For the multinational enterprise, its licensing fee L_2 must be at least equal to $(R - F)$ its payoff from defecting.

$R - L_2 \geq R - F$	(incentive compatibility for the agent)
$L_2 \geq R - F$	(incentive compatibility for the firm)

Combining these two inequalities, licensing will be continued in the second period if $R < 2F$; that is, if the rent is no greater than twice the fixed costs.

Furthermore, if the $R < 2F$ condition holds, then the multinational can extract all rents from its licensee. In the second period, the fee $L_2 = F$ is the largest fee that the multinational can charge without causing the licensee to defect, and such a fee will also lead the firm to honour the agreement. The fee $L_2 = F$ leaves the licensee with rents $(R - L_2) = (R - F)$ in the second period. The multinational can extract these with a fee $L_1 = 2R - F$ in the first period. In other words, the fee schedule $L_1 = 2R - F$ and $L_2 = F$ satisfies the (incentive compatibility) condition that neither partner will wish to defect in the second period and the (participation or individual rationality) condition that the licensee earns non-negative profits (exactly zero in this case). Notice that $L_1 + L_2 = 2R$, which is to say that all the rents are collected by the multinational through the licence fees. To sum up, if the condition $R < 2F$ holds, then the multinational will license, and it will earn all of the rents.

If the $R < 2F$ condition fails to hold – that is, if the rents are greater than twice the fixed costs – then both the firm and the licensee will defect in the second period. In this case, a duopoly game will result in the second period between the original and a second licensee. Assume that ownership of the original fixed cost F remains with the multinational. Then, the original licensee, now on its own, generates a net second-period income of $D/2 - F$ while the second licensee generates $D/2$ (using the original capital stock F). Knowing that defection is coming in the second period, the multinational is limited in what it can charge in the first period. All it can do is charge the first licensee a first-period fee of $L1 = R + D/2 - F$, which just means that the most the multinational can demand is the second-period profits of the prospective defector. For the same reason, the multinational can charge the second licensee a second-period fee of $L_2 = D/2$. In this case, the total two-period profit for the multinational is $(L_1 + L_2 - F) = (R + D - 2F)$. Both licensees earn zero profits under this fee schedule, but while the multinational captures all rents, additional fixed costs are incurred and some rents are dissipated by the duopoly competition. Thus, if the licensing condition fails to hold, the multinational will seek to avoid this duopoly outcome and instead sets up a subsidiary. Remember, our earlier assumption was that the rents of a subsidiary arrangement are M, which exceeds the rents of duopoly $R + D - 2F$.

Finally, consider the situation where $F = 0$. This can be interpreted as the case of a 'pure' knowledge-capital technology; that is, when $F = 0$, the licensee can costlessly enter production in the second period after one period of learning-by-doing. Under the assumption that $F = 0$, it is clear that $R < 2F$ will fail to hold and licensing will not sustain itself. As a result, the multinational chooses a costly subsidiary over a rent-dissipating licensing contract. We thus have a result that is consistent with both the theoretical ideas developed here and with some of the micro facts listed earlier. Direct investment in a subsidiary is more likely in cases where the technology has the joint-input characteristic of knowledge capital. The Ethier-Markusen model also predicts that multinationals (long-term relationships covering generations of products) are more likely to occur the more similar the home and host countries in size and in relative factor endowments. While the latter involves subtle general-equilibrium factor-market effects that I will not discuss here, the former (country size) result is easily seen in terms of the much simplified model presented here. A large host-country market is interpreted as a larger R relative to F, generating a larger incentive to defect from a licensing contract. Thus a subsidiary is chosen in a large market.

7. Summary and Conclusions

In some sense, this entire chapter is a summary of a great deal of literature and to provide a summary of the summary seems a bit tedious. Thus let me focus on a few points only.

The purpose of the chapter is to take a small step towards integrating the theory of the multinational enterprise with the theory of international trade and associated empirical evidence. A successful attempt should use a micro-model of the firm as suggested by the former literature, and predict that multinationals arise in situations consistent with actual evidence from the trade literature.

I use a micro-model of the firm based on the notion of knowledge capital, which has a joint-input characteristic across geographically separated production facilities, creating multi-plant economies of scale. Such a model is consistent with extensive firm and industry-level data on multinationals as noted earlier. Multinationals are then high fixed-cost firms competing with high marginal-cost domestic firms. In a general-equilibrium setting, the model predicts that multinationals will dominate in equilibrium between countries that (a) have a high total income, (b) are similar in economic size, and (c) are similar in relative factor endowments. While much formal empirical work needs to be done, these predictions are at least superficially consistent with data that shows two things: (1) direct investment has grown much faster than trade over the last two decades among the similar, high-income countries, and (2) direct investment from developed countries to other developed countries accounts for a larger share of all direct investment than the corresponding statistic for exports.

The knowledge-capital model (for lack of a better term) also fits well with the literature on internationalisation motives for direct investment. The same 'public-goods' property of knowledge capital that allows firms to exploit it in geographically separate production facilities also implies that the assets of the firm can be easily dissipated. Thus the risk of asset dissipation due to various informational difficulties suggests that firms may have a tendency to transfer knowledge-based assets internally rather than through arm's-length arrangements such as licensing.

Notes

1 Much discussion, data and many references are found in Caves (1996). For more recent evidence on the points to follow, see Morck and Yeung (1991, 1992), Brainard (1993b, c), Blomstrom and Lipsey (1991), Grubaugh (1987), Dunning (1993), Ekholm (1995) and Beaudreau (1986). For events in which firms do transfer technology abroad, articles by Davidson and McFetridge (1984), Mansfield and Romeo (1980), Teece (1986) and Wilson (1977) show technology is more likely to be transferred internally within the firm by R&D intensive firms producing new and technically complex products. Blomstrom and Zejan (1991) get similar results

with respect to joint ventures: firms are less likely to seek a foreign partner when intangible assets are important.

2 For points 1, 2 and 3, see Brainard (1993a, b) and Ekholm (1995) in particular.

3 Regression coefficients on tariffs and transport costs or distance have often been insignificant and/or had the wrong sign in equations with some measure of multinationality as the dependent variable; for example, Beaudreau (1986) using extensive firm-specific data. Brainard (1993c) has mixed results for equations explaining the level of affiliate sales abroad. Part of the explanation seems to be that many firms have substantial imported content in their foreign production and export modest amounts (on average as noted above) back to their parent. In these respects tariffs and transport costs discourage affiliate production just like they discourage exports. However, using share equations, the *share* of affiliate sales in the total of affiliate sales and exports is increasing and significant in both freight charges and tariffs.

4 Insignificant effects of host-country taxes on inward direct investment have been found by Brainard (1993a, b), Morck and Yeung (1991), Hackett and Srinivasan (1996), and Wheeler and Mody (1992). Negative effects have been found by Grubert and Mutti (1991) and in a number of articles in Feldstein, Hines and Hubbard (1995). Schneider and Frey (1985) examine the role of political as well as economic variables.

5 See Hackett and Srinivasan (1997) and Wheeler and Mody (1992) for evidence on infrastructure. See Head *et al.* (1995) and Wheeler and Mody (1992) for evidence on agglomeration.

6 Of course, it is possible to think of such services as simply being characterised by very high transport costs.

7 Attachment to the OLI framework is not universal, although it has been very appealing to trade economists. Rugman (1981, 1985, 1986) in particular argues that internalisation is really the only thing that matters to understanding the multinational. OLI is also limited in that it only considers the conditions necessary for direct investment. It has little to offer about the choice between alternatives, such as licensing versus joint venture, versus exporting.

8 R&D, advertising and technical/scientific workers are often used as proxies for firm-specific assets, and hence multinationality is highly correlated with firm-specific assets using these proxies (for citations, see the studies listed in Note 2). Alternatively, firm-specific assets (intangible assets) are proxied as the market value of the firm minus the value of tangible assets (Morck and Yeung 1991). In this case, firm-specific assets are *defined* as a residual and this residual is highly correlated with multinationality. Care needs to be taken less the argument become tautological: multinational enterprises tend to be firms with big residual values (unobserved intangible assets) and these residuals are firm-specific assets by definition.

9 The existence of the specific factor R in Y produces a general-equilibrium effect: the wage rate in terms of Y rises as the X sector expands, drawing more labour from Y. This effect 'convexifies' the model and tends to limit the concentration of the X sector into one country.

10 Assume that multinational firms, when they exist in equilibrium, draw their labour for firm-specific fixed costs evenly between countries, so that we make no attempt in this minimal model to associate multinationals with particular countries.

11 This last statement is what Brainard (1993c) refers to as the 'proximity-concentration hypothesis.'

Part II

INTERFACES AND ORGANISATION

INTRODUCTORY NOTE

Part II is made up of contributions which consider the organisation of linkages at the boundaries of multinational enterprises. The first chapter by Burton brings together insights from Porter's (1980) notion of competitive advantage and Kanter's (1994) notion of collaborative advantage to form the hybrid concept of 'composite' strategy. The pursuit of either extreme is unlikely to be optimal. The critical choice is the appropriate *combination* of competitive and collaborative strategies that are appropriate to the firm's internal and external environments. This formulation is particularly important in the context of international business, where flexibility is an essential element of success. Collaboration with a rival in one market may well be accompanied by fierce competition in another. The multinational firm's optimal strategy fits all these competitive and collaborative sub-strategies together into the overall picture of corporate composite strategy.

The second chapter by Mudambi and Mudambi focuses on the vertical linkage between buyer and supplier. No matter what type of relationship a buyer has with a particular supplier, the buyer faces the decision of whether to stay with the supplier or to switch to another supplier. The chapter introduces a model of the buyer's switching decision that integrates tenets of both transaction cost economics and relationship marketing. The model analyses how the switching decision is affected by parameters such as transaction-specific assets, information quality and the time dimension. The resulting Nash equilibria reflect strategies in which each player makes its optimal decision, taking into account the optimal decision of the other players. A sensitivity analysis of the effects of the parameters on the performance measures of price and profit provides intuitively sound results, and demonstrates how a common ground can be found between two schools of thought on buyer–supplier relations. Finally, the analysis is applied to the specific case of the multinational firm, developing a location-based taxonomy of the buyer–supplier linkages of multinational firms. This is useful in identifying the situations in which the model results are most applicable.

5

THE CONJUNCTION OF COMPETITION AND COLLABORATION IN INTERNATIONAL BUSINESS

John Burton

1. Introduction

Both contemporary micro-economics and strategic management analysis are concerned centrally with questions about the organisation of the firm. These are, however, *different* perspectives, and they are concerned with different sets of questions relating to business organisation. In order to avoid confusion, it is valuable at the beginning to delineate the perspective adopted in, and the concerns of, this chapter.

Over recent decades, a major topic for economists involved with the analysis of international business has been that of defining its inherent 'nature' or, more precisely, its causes and origins.[1] This economics literature follows in the footsteps of the seminal work of Coase (1937) about the nature of the firm, asking such questions as: Why do we observe the *existence* of multinational enterprises (MNEs hereinafter) that produce in more than one country? Why, conversely, is not all production organised under autonomous domestic firms? What explains the inter-industry incidence of the foreign control of production? Moreover, why has the 'global reach' of MNEs extended considerably over the past half-century?

These are all, indubitably, important questions – particularly from the perspective of economic science. Strategic management analysis, however, pushes such matters into the background. The existence of the MNE, and the contemporary globalisation of business are – as it were – taken for granted. Here, the central concern becomes that of the *implications* of the internationalisation of the business environment for the formulation and implementation of company strategy. It is this latter perspective that this essay is primarily concerned with. Nevertheless, as hopefully will be revealed below, contemporary discussions of international business strategy from the perspective of strategic management analysis do raise some questions about the 'nature' of international business today that are of considerable relevance to the economic perspective also.

Section 2 sets out what may be described as the 'orthodox' analysis of international business strategy, which has developed on the basis of the highly influential works of Michael Porter (1980, 1986) and which, in essence, equates the execution of business strategy (including international business strategy) with the conduct of *competitive* strategy. This analysis is of undoubted relevance to the contemporary setting for business, especially given the fact that 'few, if any, industries now have much "natural protection" from international competition, whereas in the past... geographical distance created a strong insulating effect' (Dicken 1992:4).

Whilst the (often intensifying) competitive environment of many businesses is a contemporary reality that cannot be ignored by many firms, it does not necessarily follow that business strategy boils down entirely to *competitive* strategy. Over the past decade in particular, there has emerged an alternative school of strategic thought which highlights the increasing role of cooperative (as against competitive) strategy in the conduct of contemporary business, and as a foundation of superior business performance. This Collaborative Strategy School – as it might be called – is of a more eclectic nature and origin than the Competitive Strategy School (founded in Porter's work), but its most prominent leader is another Harvard scholar, Rosabeth Moss Kanter (1989, 1996).

Proponents of collaborative strategy as a source of sustainable advantage for the firm point to 'the explosion of (corporate) alliances world-wide' (Lynch 1993: 1), and assert that cooperative relationships between firms are usurping old-style competition (Urban and Vendemini 1992). Section 3 of this chapter examines ideas about the role and sources of the contemporary proliferation of collaborative business arrangements (CBAs hereinafter) in the international setting.

Whatever the precise relative dimensions of intensifying competition and increasing collaboration on the international business scene today, a reasonable conclusion can only be that the contemporary MNE prospectively needs to construct a business strategy that involves *both* competitive and collaborative elements. How, however, are these two faces of strategy to be brought together? Cases exist (as we shall later see) whereby the prosecution of a collaborative strategy undermined the MNE's competitive position – and vice versa. There needs, in other words, to be an appropriate *conjunction* of competitive and collaborative strategy in the contemporary international business. This topic – which I have elsewhere described as the terrain of *composite strategy* (Burton 1995a) – is examined in Section 4. The next section then examines some speculations about the future and implications of the

Janus-faced contemporary international business system, and Section 6 offers some brief general conclusions.

2. International Business Strategy–The Porter Framework

The now orthodox framework for analysing business strategy is the competitive strategy paradigm originally advanced by Michael E Porter (1980), an economist who had moved from industrial organisation studies to strategic management analysis: an intellectual transmutation accompanied by his geographical move in Boston, Massachusetts, across the Charles River from the site of MIT to his (current) academic residence at the Harvard Business School.

Porter advanced strategic management analysis greatly by bringing with him, in his 'move' from industrial economics, an explicit framework for analysing the industry environment of the firm that drew upon standard industrial organisation theory – a basic structure/conduct/performance framework of the 'Harvard School' variety[2] – and then provided an analysis of the strategic options for the individual firm in a variety of stylised industry settings (for example, the fragmented industry, the mature industry, emerging industries, industries undergoing decline).

In this Porter framework, the key to the formulation of business strategy – so as to generate a *sustainable competitive advantage* (SCOMA) for the firm over other players in the industry – revolves around relating its internal strengths and weaknesses to its *competitive environment* or the *industry structure* that surrounds it. Porter (1980), however, does not define the relevant industry structure in a narrow fashion – to include only the structure of a competition among present rivals in the particular product field in question.

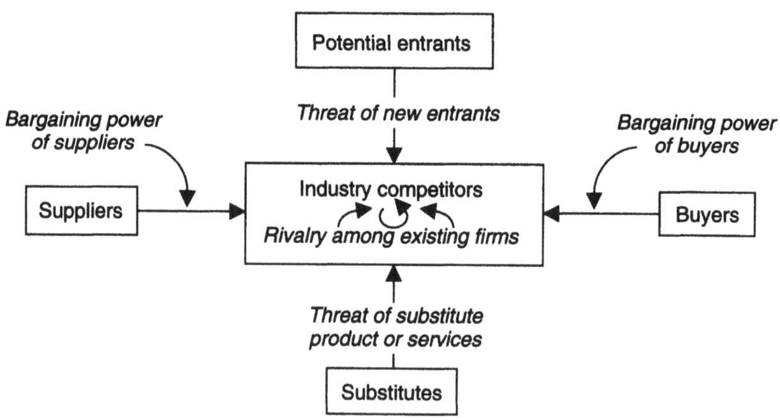

Figure 5.1 Analysing competition: the Five Forces Framework

In the Porter approach, firms are viewed not only as conducting competitive measures (and defences) against their horizontal rivals at the same vertical stage in the process of production, but also against their suppliers, potential entrants to this product market, the firm's customers and distribution channels, and the producers of substitute commodities located in other industries. Thus, in considering/evaluating the competitive environment of the firm, there is not one, but rather five dimensions of competition to consider. This is summarised in Porter's famous 'Five Forces' diagram, replicated here as Figure 5.1.

The essence of Porter's analysis is that the strategising business needs to assess the strengths of these separate five forces in its specific industry context and then to position itself/check them/alter them in its favour so as to optimise its own sustainable competitive advantage (SCOMA) within the (evolving) structure. The basic model for the formulation of business strategy involved is encapsulated in Figure 5.2.

The entire tenor of Porter's (1980) treatment of strategic management analysis is very much in terms of rivalry – *competitive* strategy – and adversarial

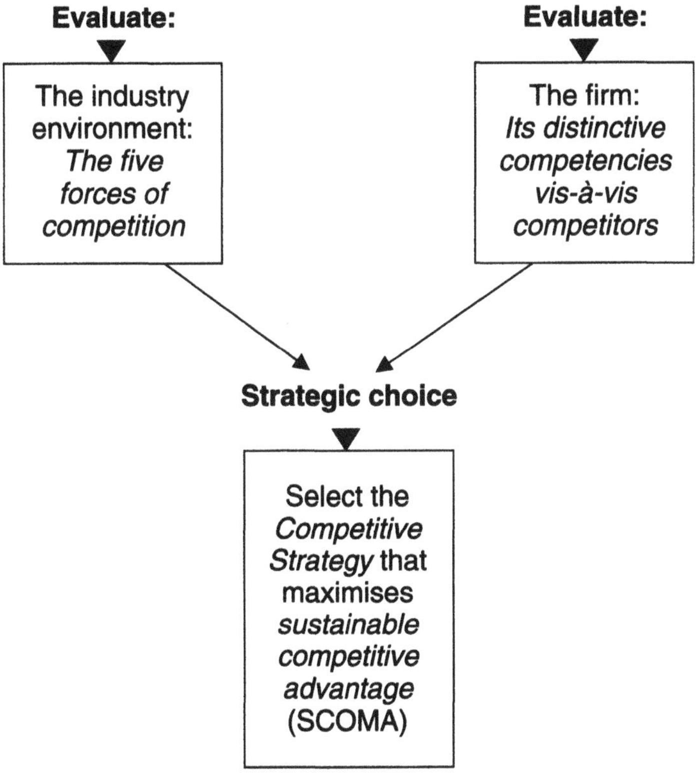

Figure 5.2 Formulating competitive strategy: the Porter approach

moves to maximise bargaining power over suppliers and customers, or to protect the business against counter-endeavours of this sort, or threats from potential competitors and substitutes. In this framework, business strategy is thus viewed as being essentially *adversarial*, in all dimensions. The Porter Framework thus provides an agenda for the individual firm for squeezing the maximum sustainable competitive gain out of the context in which it is located – or, how to avoid/minimise the prospect of being so squeezed by other players, in all of the five dimensions of competition.

Given the competitive environment, Porter (1980, 1985) identifies three *generic competitive strategies* that a company may seek to deploy:[3]

- *Cost leadership*: constructing the firm's value chain around the goal of being the lowest-cost producer of the array of products on offer in the market;
- *Differentiation*: devising of the firm's value chain in a way that yields products to buyers that are perceived as unique compared to those offered by competitors;
- *Focus*: whilst the two foregoing strategies are (by definition) employed on a broad front to the array of products in the industry, those following a focus (or 'niche') strategy apply *either* cost leadership or differentiation policies towards a narrow target in terms of competitive scope (i.e., a particular segment of the overall market).

This triad of strategic options is set out in Figure 5.3. It is implicit in Porter's (1980) account that these three generic strategies apply to *all* firms, irrespective of the geographical scope of their operations. When the international dimension of competitive strategy is explicitly introduced to the analysis – as in Porter (1986) – it is further necessary to distinguish the strategies of international firms according to whether they are:

- *Global*: i.e., the prosecution of a particular generic strategy by the firm across the world (in terms of cost leadership, differentiation, or focus); or
- *Country-centred*: tailoring strategies to separable national markets either due to voluntary strategic choice (a *nationally responsive* or *multi-domestic* strategy) by the firm or due to the fracturing of the potentially global market by differential country legislation (the *protected markets* or *blocked globalisation* category).

Adding this distinction to the triad of generic strategies in the Porter Framework (as in Figure 5.3) we may visualise a general typology of competitive strategic alternatives in international industries, as shown in Figure 5.4 below.

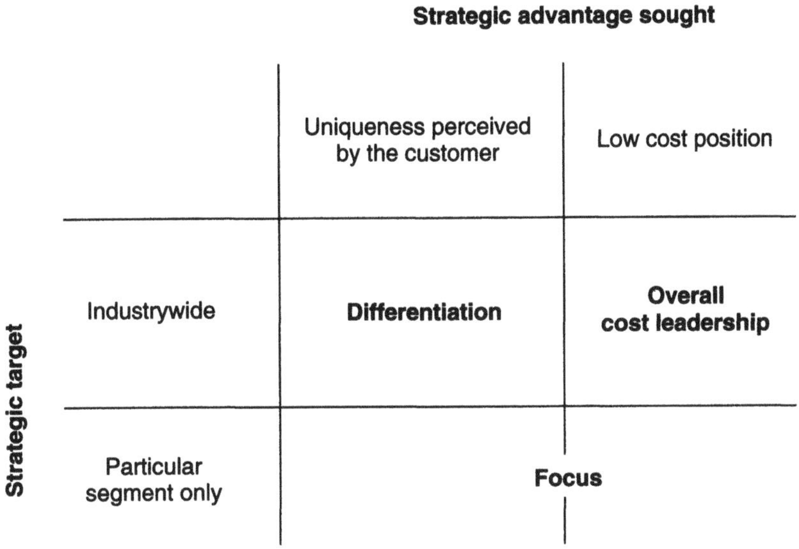

Figure 5.3 Porter's generic strategies

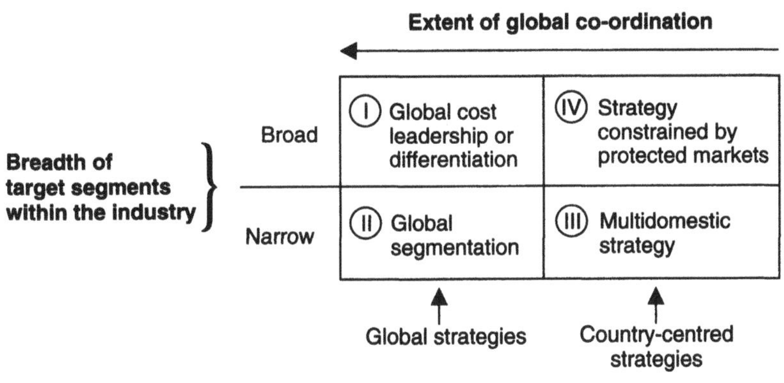

Figure 5.4 Competitive strategies in international industries

Source: Adapted from Chakravarty and Perlmutter (1985)

Different industries offer differential prospects for the success of these alternative international business strategies. *Global* strategies (quadrants I and II in Figure 5.4) are summarily diagnosed by strategic management analysts as being relevant only in those cases where the pressures towards, or need for, local adaptation is low, but where the incentives (for example, economies of scale) in production or marketing for prosecution of a global business are large (for example, computers, consumer electronics, civil aircraft, construction machinery). In other industries, however, local tastes may differ substantially whilst globalisation of business functions offers no decisive competitive advantage, with the result that the international market is highly segmented into different regions/countries each with different customer characteristics. In this latter setting – which may typify processed foodstuffs, cash dispensers, and medical equipment – the overall incentive for the international business is to follow a multidomestic strategy (quadrant III in Figure 5.4). There also remains a considerable number of industries where the pressure towards globalisation might otherwise be strong, but this avenue is blocked by laws or government policies (for example, public procurement policies favouring domestic producers). In this protected market setting – quadrant IV in Figure 5.4 – firms are *constrained* to follow a country-centred strategy (this, for example, would typify much of the telecommunications industry around the world currently).

Thus, a globalised competitive strategy – be it via the cost advantage, differentiation or focus route – is not always a sensible strategy for the international firm. Nevertheless, it is a common contention of many strategic management analysts that 'globalization of industries is on the rise' (Chakravarty and Perlmutter 1985). Commonly cited reasons for this increasing salience of a globalised competitive strategy in many industries include (Henzler and Rall 1986; Chakravarty and Perlmutter 1985):

- *Increasing homogenization of tastes/product needs* around the world;
- *Cheaper and more reliable international transportation;*
- *Better global co-ordination within international businesses due to advances in international communications;*
- *The emergence of global buyers and suppliers;*
- *Reductions in barriers to international business* (for example, elimination of tariff barriers/protectionist policies, privatisation programmes and the deregulation of national markets around the world).

The extended Porter analysis outlined above thus seemingly provides a valuable general framework for the analysis of the strategic management of international businesses in the contemporary era, providing an understanding of the growth of international competition and the emergence of global firms in some industries. Not unsurprisingly, it has been widely adopted in texts on international business as the standard framework for examining strategy formulation in MNEs (for example, Rugman and Hodgetts 1995: 8; Dicken 1992: 5).

This orthodox framework, however, also suffers from an increasingly severe limitation in the contemporary era. It puts the entire emphasis upon *competitive* strategy, and the achievement of sustainable *competitive* advantages for the firm. Yet, as noted in the introduction, the situation in international business today is also one typified by a major growth in *collaboration* as well as competition. It is to this aspect of contemporary international business that the discussion turns in the next section.

3. The Significance and Sources of CBAs in International Business

It is difficult to be dogmatic about the present quantitative extent of 'collaborative business arrangements' (CBAs) between international businesses because the statistics are deficient in various ways. Nevertheless, the evidence overall would seem to support the contention that the 1980s and 1990s have witnessed a mushrooming growth of CBAs in the international domain especially (for example, Hegert and Morris 1988; Perks 1993). This development has been particularly pronounced in industries that are hi-tech; Krubasik and Lautenschlagger (1993) found that recent years have witnessed up to a *fourfold* annual increase in CBAs in international industries such as electronics, computers, aerospace, pharmaceuticals and telecommunications.

In such settings to 'understand what is going on' it is necessary to analyse not *only* the evolution of competitive forces and strategies, but *also* the development of CBAs and collaborative strategies; to focus on the former, whilst ignoring the latter, would provide only a one-sided and distorted picture of the industrial scene.

The Evolution of Competition and Collaboration in the US Car Industry

To bring this general point out sharply, I shall examine briefly the development of competitive and collaborative forces over the past 50 years in an industry setting which – perhaps more than any other – has shaped our impression of business in the 20th century: the US car industry.

Standard accounts of the evolution of the industry over this time period tend to concentrate on changes in the industry's structure and performance as the result of competitive developments. A particularly admirable and succinct account conducted in this 'competitive' vein is provided by Ballew and Schnorbus (1994), on which the content of the following paragraph draws heavily.

In the 'golden age' of American car manufacture, running from 1946 to the late 1960s, the US market was dominated by the Big Three – General Motors (GM), Ford and Chrysler – which together accounted for more than 90 per cent of sales in the US auto market. In the 1970s, however, this rather cosy oligopoly situation was increasingly disturbed by the competitive invasion of the US market by foreign – and, particularly, Japanese – carmakers; the Big Three's combined market share consequently fell as the volume of foreign entry rose. By the 1980s, the Japanese carmakers increasingly set the pace of competition in terms of quality and price (Womack, Jones and Roos 1990). Moreover – as the Porter Five Forces Model indicates – this increasing intensity of rivalry in the US market for cars had feedback effects on suppliers to the Big Three and, particularly, American organised labour and car components manufacturers.

As the standard account by industry experts thus runs, the story of the US car industry from the 1970s onwards is one revolving around a growth in competitive rivalry, as American carmakers tried to gear themselves up to combat the foreign (and predominantly Japanese) challenge. This, undoubtedly, *is* an important part of the story of the evolution of the US car industry over the past 25 years: but it is not the full story. The account above ignores the proliferation of CBAs in the car industry that took place over this time period – and, most significantly, with their major competitors, based in Japan. By the 1990s these had grown into very complex webs of alliances between Japanese autofirms and the American Big Three, which are represented in Figures 5.5(a), (b), and (c) below.[4] Moreover, from the early 1980s onwards the Big Three sought not only to develop CBAs with international competitors, but also with other elements of the Five Forces in their *domestic* scene, most notably their dealers and suppliers – including the United Automobile Workers (UAW).

For example, in its Saturn Project – a new major division for GM, being its first new nameplate since the Chevrolet in 1918 – General Motors strove to forge a new alliance-type arrangement with the UAW. The latter was made a 'full partner' in all Saturn decision-making, with UAW officials placed on both the Strategic Action Council overseeing the development and the Manufacturing Action Council controlling day-to-day operations.[5] Simultaneously, in the Saturn development, GM abandoned arm's-length competitive tendering in supplier selection procedures in favour of supplier relations that

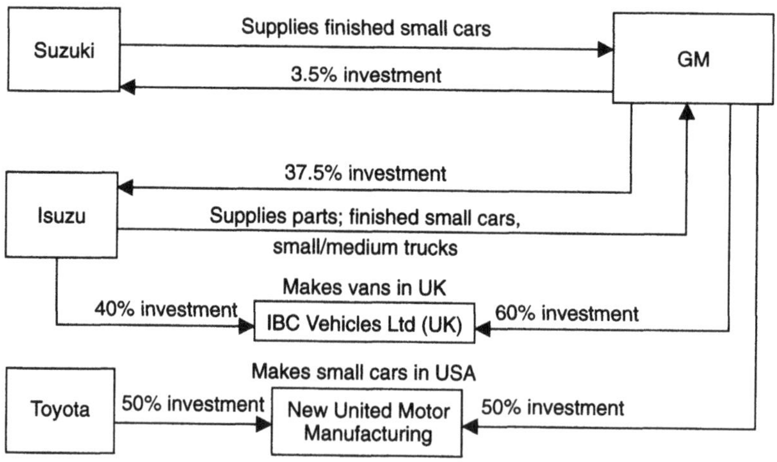

Figure 5.5a GM-Japanese carmaker CBAs

Source: Japan Automobile Manufacturers' Association (March 1993)

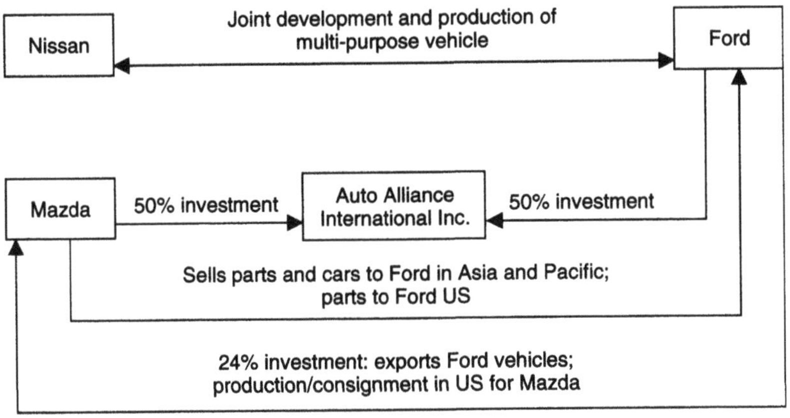

Figure 5.5b Ford-Japanese carmaker CBAs

Source: Japan Automobile Manufacturers' Association (March 1993)

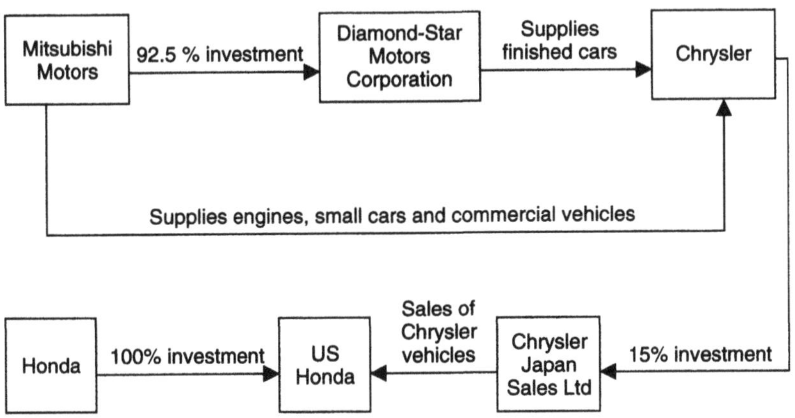

Figure 5.5c Chrysler-Japanese carmaker CBAs

Source: Japan Automobile Manufacturers' Association (March 1993)

were 'far more intimate and collaborative' (Badarocco 1991: 122), whereby those with 'preferred supplier' status were henceforth to work closely with GM on both product and process development. At the same time, through a CBA that GM termed as its Manufacturing Automation Protocol (MAP), GM sought to develop a common communications network via interactive discussions with its strategic web of hardware and software suppliers. Relatedly, GM also took minority equity stakes in a number of small hi-tech firms in the field of advanced automation technology, so as to provide its own engineers with new collaborative avenues for joint design. The Saturn project also involved the creation of a new dealer system based on 'partnership' rather than the traditional arm's-length relations that had previously typified previous GM arrangements with dealers.

In summary, the story of the evolution of the US car industry over the past three decades is not simply one of growing international competition: it is also a history that clearly involves increasing and significant elements of collaboration, both domestically and internationally. The more general point is that this growth of CBAs is not a phenomenon confined to the car industry: similar examples of such an evolutionary development have occurred in many other industries over the past 15 years, ranging from airline services to telecommunications (Burton and Hanlon 1994; Burton 1995a; Faulkner 1995).

Driving forces of CBA growth in contemporary international business

What has caused this contemporary proliferation of CBAs to come about around the world? This is an important question in a scientific sense, from the perspective of economics. It is also an important matter from the perspective of strategic management analysis, as the potential for achieving sustainable advantage via collaborative routes depends upon the identity and strength of the driving forces involved, which are likely to vary greatly from one setting to another.

Some accounts of the growth and proliferation of CBAs in contemporary international business are eclectic as to their origins, pointing to a medley of driving forces possibly involved (for example, Lynch 1993: 5). It is tempting, however, to seek a deeper explanation of the international trend towards inter-firm collaboration, in terms of some underlying causal influence of a pervasive nature. We here examine briefly two prominent analyses of the phenomenon that are of this nature: the *globalisation thesis* of the Japanese business guru Kenichi Ohmae (1985, 1990, 1993, 1995) and the *knowledge link thesis* of the Harvard Business School scholar, Joseph Badarocco (1991).

Ohmae's globalisation thesis

The orthodox analysis of globalisation, outlined in Section 2, generally leads to the presumption of globalising *businesses*: an ever-increasing predominance of large, world-straddling, independent firms in certain industries where the imperatives of globalisation are predominant. Ohmae's analysis rather stands this analysis on its head: according to him, it is the sheer scale of contemporary global industries and markets that requires the organisational format of CBAs, rather than bigger-and-bigger MNEs. In his own words:

> Globalization mandates alliances, makes them absolutely essential to strategy. Uncomfortable, perhaps – but that's the way it is. Like it or not, the simultaneous developments that go under the name of globalization makes alliances – (business) entente – necessary
>
> (Ohmae 1993: 36)

The 'simultaneous developments' that Ohmae presumes to underlie globalisation are:

1 *the increasing convergence of consumer preferences across the world*: a development he refers to as the 'Californialization of Need');
2 *necessary access to critical competencies*: Modern products require the utilization of so many leading-edge capabilities (on both the technological and service side) that most companies (however large and global) cannot maintain a lead in all of them simultaneously;
3 *the need with global products to incur fixed costs: for example, in R&D*; IT; automated/flexible production lines; the building of a global-based reputation and global sales and distribution networks.

It is apparent that there is *some* overlap in Ohmae's account of the trends underlying globalisation in certain industries, and the list of factors involved in more orthodox accounts of globalisation (see Section 2). Yet whilst orthodoxy has lent to the presumption that globalisation of industries means bigger, globally-organised MNEs, Ohmae is in effect arguing that globalisation pressures point instead towards the generation of international CBAs. His argument on this point is that:

> ... the need to bolster contribution points in a single, clear direction: towards the forging of alliances to share fixed costs.
> This is a fundamental change from the competitive world of 15 or even 10 years ago...
> This new logic forces managers to amortize their fixed costs over a much larger market base... this logic mandates entente – alliances that both enable and facilitate global, contribution-based strategies.
>
> (Ohmae 1993:41)

Ohmae's visualisation of the driving forces behind the contemporary growth of international CBAs is summarised in Figure 5.6.

It is valuable, before discussing the general relevance of Ohmae's analysis, to refine it as regards one salient point. As purveyed above, his analysis of international CBA proliferation revolves around the presumed growth of fixed-cost elements in globalising industry settings. The work by industrial economists (for example, Baumol 1982; Baumol *et al.* 1982) on perfectly contestable markets, however, suggests that it is not fixed costs but rather *sunk*

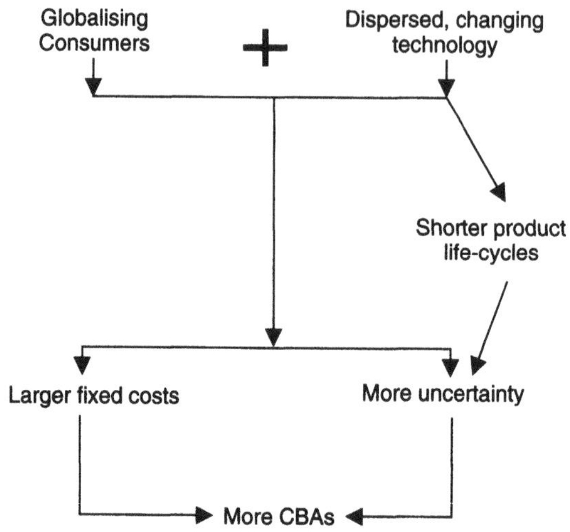

Figure 5.6 Why CBAs grow and grow: Ohmae's analysis

costs which are the critical and relevant cost dimension to be considered.[6] The point here is that if sunk costs are zero – and other incentives to CBA formation, such as governmentally-imposed restrictions preventing 'stand-alone' entry, are also absent – there would seem to be little motive for firms to indulge in international alliances. In such a scenario, any firm could undertake go-it-alone hit-and-run entries to/exits from industries, according to variations in the stream of net returns of being in the industry – without the need to shoulder the costs of forming complex CBAs with other firms. It therefore seems appropriate to restyle Ohmae's analysis in terms of sunk, rather than fixed, costs.

To what extent, however, can the (reformulated) Ohmae hypothesis account generally for the proliferation of international CBAs? It seems to be a plausible explanation of the growth of inter-firm collaboration in some global industry settings where sunk costs are very high (for example, on very specific R&D), yet the demand for the eventual product is uncertain – classic cases including civil aircraft and telecommunications switching devices.

Nevertheless, there are other industry cases in which the hypothesis does not on its own seem to account fully for the phenomenon of transnational CBAs. One such is that of the airline services industry. It has been diagnosed for some time that this industry is in the process of globalising (Gialloreto 1988); and, during the first half of the late 1990s we have also witnessed a profuse growth of international airline alliances (Burton and Hanlon 1994).

The major investment that any airline has to face is the acquisition of its fleet, which are expensive, hi-tech pieces of equipment. But the sunk cost element in such fleets is generally relatively low – airliners can be leased rather than purchased outright; they are also very mobile assets; and there is a well-developed second-hand market in civil aircraft. Consequently, it is generally accepted that the industry is typified by a relatively low ratio of sunk costs to variable costs.

There must therefore remain some question mark as to whether sunk costs alone may reasonably account for CBA growth in the contemporary airline industry. An equally plausible factor involved is that the M&A route to the globalisation of airline businesses is currently blocked by governmental impediments to cross-border airline mergers in a variety of forms (for example, administrative rules favouring national flag-carriers; pervasive elements of state ownership and subsidy; restraints upon foreign acquisition of nationally-based airlines).

The 'Knowledge link' hypothesis

If the Ohmae analysis seems weak as a general explanation of the contemporary growth of transnational CBAs, what of the 'knowledge link' hypothesis? This has been forwarded by Badarocco (1991) and emphasises the role of what he terms as 'embedded knowledge' in the contemporary international economic scene. This he defines as knowledge 'that is not migratory. It moves very slowly, even when its commercial value is high, and firms have strong incentives to gain access to it' (Badarocco 1991: 79).

To overcome these problems, it is argued, firms, from the early 1980s onward, were increasingly led to form new types of CBAs – 'knowledge links' – to exploit their potential complementarities in such types of knowledge. Badarocco cites – as but one of many examples – GM's attempt from 1983 onwards to create with Toyota a North American version of the Toyota production system in the form of a New United Motor Manufacturing (see Figure 5.5(a) on page 110).

Badarocco's insightful analysis cannot be done full justice to here, and it must suffice to note that the embeddedness of certain types of knowledge in businesses cannot explain on its own the contemporary proliferation of CBAs. This is so, for example – and as Badarocco openly accepts – because the mere embeddedness of knowledge does not in itself explain a business preference for a CBA to exploit that knowledge over the alternative of internalising it via a merger or acquisition.

Consider in the latter regard the recent case of BMW, which (as of 1993) did not have the embedded knowledge of the production of either small-car engines or off-the-road sporty vehicles – but which Rover (with its Mini and Metro saloons, and Land Rover range) did so possess. BMW did not, however, spend years wooing Rover into collaboration in these areas: it went for a (successful) acquisition of Rover (in 1994).[7] This case points also to the relevance – noted above – of the absence or presence of impediments to cross-border acquisitions in explaining contemporary transnational CBA growth. Where such impediments are absent or low (as with BMW's acquisition of Rover) embedded knowledge may be obtained via the market in corporate control. Where such impediments are large, however, CBA development may be the only feasible route for obtaining embedded knowledge.[8]

Thus the knowledge link thesis – as with Ohmae's analysis – seems unable to offer on its own a general explanation of the contemporary growth of international CBAs. It nevertheless has much to tantalise about it, not least because the available evidence indicates that CBA profusion has been especially marked over recent years in R&D-intensive industries such as aerospace, telecommunications equipment, pharmaceuticals, computers and electronics (Hegert and Morris 1988).

One factor, however, that is not addressed in Badarocco's (1991) treatment is that much of the knowledge generated in such hi-tech industries is not only very expensive – much of it also represents a sunk cost. For example, by the late 1980s the development of a new aero-engine typically cost at least $1.5 billion, and a new generation of computerised digital switches (for use in telecommunications) around $1 billion (Hladik 1988). The expense of such developments, however, is not necessarily a problem – it is, rather, that if no-one wants the new aero-engine or switches, the knowledge created to produce them may not be redeployable to other uses, such as the production of electric toasters. Businesses in these industry settings thus typically face making highly risky investments in very specific types of knowledge, and which may have little or no alternative uses: a new drug development that has to be dropped due to the discovery of damaging side-effects has, simply, to be dropped.

This points to the suggestion that it is not simply the *embeddedness* of certain types of knowledge, in Badarocco's sense, that is crucial to explaining CBA proliferation in such settings but, rather, the combination of heavy sunk costs and high risks that typifies the R&D process in them. CBAs are a means of spreading the risks of becoming over-committed to a large and expensive flop that has no alternative uses.

Conclusion on the driving forces of international CBA growth

Enough has perhaps been said so far to indicate that whilst we may be getting a little closer to comprehending the causes underlying the contemporary proliferation of international CBAs, it would be most unwise to pronounce that we have as yet anything like an adequate general explanation of the phenomenon. It is possible – and, indeed, not at all unlikely – that the phenomenon has multi-causal origins.

But perhaps enough has also been said to indicate some of the possible identities of the underlying driving forces of international CBA growth in the contemporary era. Amongst these it would seem necessary to include the role of sunk costs, high risks, impediments to other forms of cross-border market entry (for example, those against outright acquisition), especially in those industry contexts where the imperatives of global operation are increasing strongly in the present era.

4. Competitive and Collaborative Strategy for the MNE

Whatever the underlying sources of the contemporary growth of international CBAs (as discussed above), it is apparent that the 'typical' MNE today needs to develop its business strategies on two fronts: not just the competitive front – as singled out in the orthodox, Porter Framework (reviewed in Section 2) – but also as regards international collaboration with other firms. How does this alter our general visualisation of strategy formulation for contemporary international business?

A primary implication is that in an international business setting in which collaboration – in addition to competition – is both extensive and (often) a major means by which firms seek to acquire sustainable advantage, the Five Forces Framework (depicted in Figure 5.1 above) becomes inadequate as a general framework for assessing the firm's overall industry environment, and the opportunities and threats embedded therein. In the contemporary setting of increasing international business collaboration, the standard Porter analysis, with its entire focus upon competitive strategy, suffers from increasingly severe limitations, as it ignores collaborative potentialities that exist in the industry environment of the MNE. Taken on its own, the Five Forces Framework may thus only provide a one-sided or distorted perspective on strategy options that need to be considered by an international business in the contemporary setting (indeed, on its own it might provide a quite erroneous guide to international business strategy).

A second, and more positive, implication is that the typical MNE today needs to assess not *only* the Five Forces of Competition in its industry environment, but *also* what I have elsewhere termed as the Five Sources of Collaboration in its environment. Space is not available here to explore in detail this Five Sources Framework (see Burton 1995a), but the general point is that this provides a sister framework (to the competitive strategy model), and which itemises the potential sources of collaborative advantage for the international firm. The basic dimensions of this Five Sources Framework are set out in Figure 5.7. As with the competitive strategy model, this Five Sources Framework implies a two-stage procedure for assessing the collaborative strategies that may be possible for the MNE, given its international industry environment. As a first step, the MNE must comprehend and evaluate the potentials for developing collaborative advantage along each dimension of the Five Sources (given its own competencies and those of its potential collaborators). The second step is for the firm to choose how to position itself in respect of

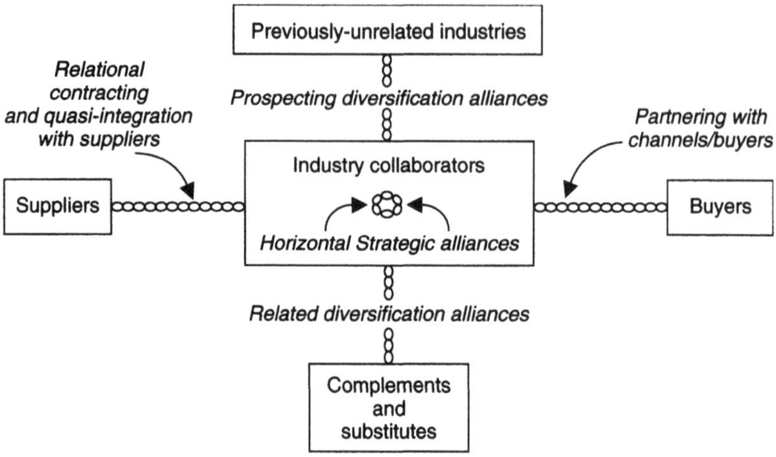

Figure 5.7 Analysing collaboration: the Five Sources Framework

these collaborative possibilities, in order to optimise on its sustainable collaborative advantage (SCOLA for short). The required process for strategy formulation on the collaborative front is itemised in Figure 5.8 below.

The general point is that Porter's (1980) recipe for formulating (competitive) business strategy needs to be complemented in contemporary international businesses by a like procedure for assessing *collaborative* strategy, as suggested above. In today's world of international business, to concentrate upon the former perspective alone might be one-sided and deficient.

The Need for Composite Strategy in International Business

The typical MNE today needs not only to formulate both competitive and collaborative strategies: it also needs to bring these two faces of strategy together, in order to avoid potential clashes and inconsistencies between them. This conjunction of collaborative and competitive business policies I have elsewhere (Burton 1995a) termed as *composite strategy* which involves:

- Choosing the mix of competitive and collaborative strategies that are appropriate in the various dimensions of the industry environment of the firm;
- Blending these two elements of strategy in such a way that they are mutually supportive rather than counter-productive, with the aim of optimising the firm's overall advantage in terms of SCOMA and SCOLA.

In other words, the typical MNE today needs a composite strategy that involves a careful evaluation of when to compete (and how vigorously) and

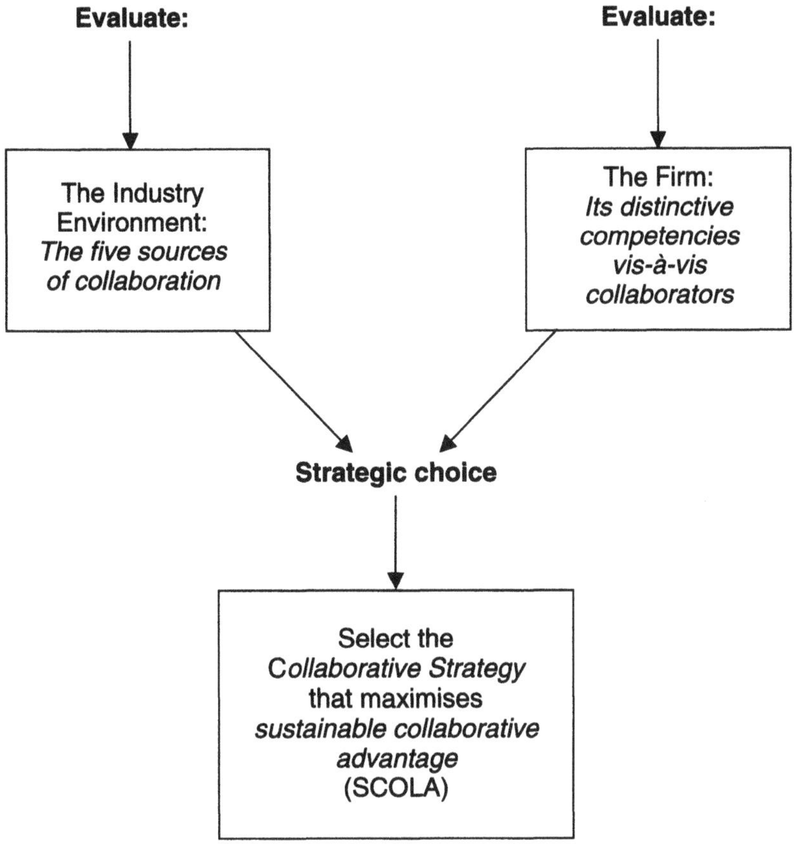

Figure 5.8 Formulating collaborative strategy

when to collaborate (and to what extent). Moreover, these two faces of business strategy need to be tied together carefully into a consistent and mutually-reinforcing whole.

When this crucial strategic task of bringing the two faces of strategy together is not undertaken (or is botched) the likelihood is of a 'schizoidal' outcome whereby the MNE's competitive strategy undermines its collaborative strategy (or conversely). There are numerous cases of such clashes in MNE strategy; two well-known ones are:

1 *Warner-Lambert in Japan*: This company had entered the Japanese market to sell various of its brands of chewing gum, including Trident and Chiclets. It felt, however, that the local Japanese wholesalers that they had chosen were not promoting its products as aggressively as desired. It therefore decided to try to bypass the wholesalers and (in effect) compete with them in that function. Its sales, however slumped, for not only

did this create opposition from its Japanese wholesalers – it also faced a reaction from Japanese retailers, 'who often consider companies unreliable if they switch tactics' (Ricks 1993: 106).

2 *Gillette and the Stainless Steel Blade*: Gillette was the first company to develop a stainless steel blade. It already had, however, a premier position globally with its *existing* razor blades, which required many (rather than fewer) replacement blades by the shaver. It therefore decided to collaborate with a company operating in a different market to utilise its new technology – the British firm Wilkinson, then primarily a garden tool manufacturer. Gillette sold the technology to Wilkinson, *assuming* that the latter would only use it for garden implements; and it failed to restrict Wilkinson to this line in the agreement drawn up. Very soon, Wilkinson Sword Razor Blades were introduced in the UK and US (and then worldwide), demand outstripping supply, and with Gillette's global market share being badly dented.

Both of the companies cited eventually recovered from these costly blunders in international business strategy, but the scenarios do illustrate the pitfalls of combining competitive and collaborative business strategies into an overall and effective composite strategy. In case (1) we see a newly-adopted competitive strategy undermining collaborative advantages, to the detriment of the company's overall position in this foreign market. In case (2), by contrast, the corporation's attempt to protect its competitive dominance via an international arrangement with another company almost undermined that very dominance.

As these cases suggest, in an international environment characterised by both competition and collaboration, firms need to formulate their competitive and collaborative strategies *together*, and in the light of each other, rather than independently. The appropriate framework for formulating business strategy is therefore typically *neither* as shown in Figures 5.2 or 5.8, but rather that as depicted in Figure 5.9.

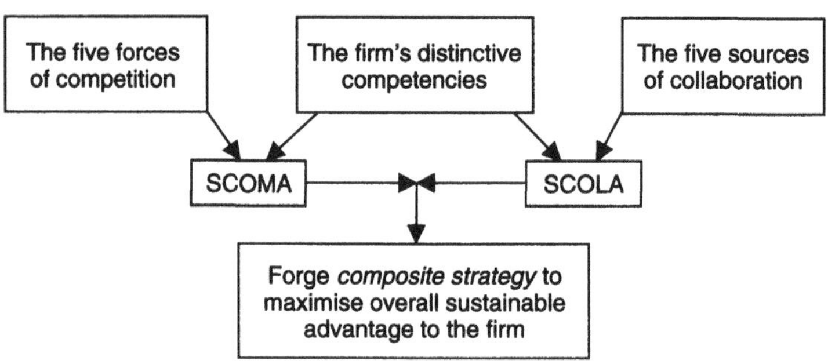

Figure 5.9 The two faces of business strategy: formulating composite strategy

The necessary procedure for constructing business strategy in an international environment involving sources of both competitive and collaborative advantage may appear simple from Figure 5.9. The reality, however, is that this often involves considerable complexity, as elaborated elsewhere (Burton 1995a).

5. The Future Shape of International Business

Standard contemporary accounts of the development of the international business system (for example, Dicken 1992) emphasise the globalisation of many industries. An underlying presumption of much literature on contemporary international business is also that this ongoing globalisation of industry will lead to the increasing predominance of *global firms*, on the basis of the argument that 'global industries require a firm to compete on a worldwide, coordinated basis or face strategic disadvantages' (Porter 1980: 275).

We have reviewed (in Section 3), however, the alternative thesis of Ohmae that contemporary globalisation of industry mandates the growth of global CBAs, rather than 'unitary' global firms. This alternative diagnosis raises the general question of how the international business system might evolve in the future – will it be towards more competition or more collaboration? And what might be the relative role of global firms and global CBAs in the evolving international business system? These are, inevitably, highly speculative matters. In order to anchor the discussion it is useful to base it around a specific prognosis. The one chosen here is that of Freidheim (1993) – a Vice-Chairman of the international consulting firm Booz, Allen and Hamilton – which is interesting because it projects the Ohmae thesis into the far future, whilst adding in a perspective on divergent international economic and political developments, and the consequences of these developments for the future shape of international business.

According to Freidheim, we are witnessing divergent trends in terms of international business/economics on the one hand, and of national politics on the other. On the business/economic front, many industries – ranging from finance to aerospace – are becoming increasingly global in nature, due to underlying economic forces. On the political front, however, it seems that many nation states/previous blocs are polarising or splitting – witness the breakup of the former Soviet Union, and the continuing tensions in Canada.

International firms set in this scenario are thus experiencing two contrary pulls or pushes. Where they are located in a globalising industry setting, the business/economic imperative is to operate on a global scale with a global product-line. Yet this means that they will need to have a presence in all/most local markets – which are fragmenting in terms of national/regional political identity. The 'global' firm – which is inevitably tied to one home base (Hu 1992), however global its production and sales – cannot achieve this double act, according to Freidheim. There is thus an imperative to develop global CBAs with multiple home bases (those of the constituent partners).

Freidheim's analysis is that we are as yet witnessing only 'Stage 1' of this evolving scenario, involving the growth of single-purpose CBAs. In 'Stage 2' of this prospective evolution, according to him – see Figure 5.10 – there will be a strengthening of bonds across networks of partnering firms as trust is built, and global CBAs will start to share common standards and staff. As an existing example, he notes that the development of the B-777 airliner involved the cooperation of the Boeing Corporation of the US and five Japanese partner firms, linked together via a trans-Pacific telecommunications system whereby 500 workstations involved in the design/development process had the same CAD and software.

He also speculates about a 'Stage 3' in which partners in these global CBAs will eventually be able 'to recognise their potential power and begin to act together in broad business areas as a single company'.

These 'Trillion Dollar' CBAs, as Freidheim terms them, that he foresees as evolving in Stage 3 might not obtain, he posits, until one decade from now. Are we headed, then, for a future of a new sort of 'global monopoly capital-

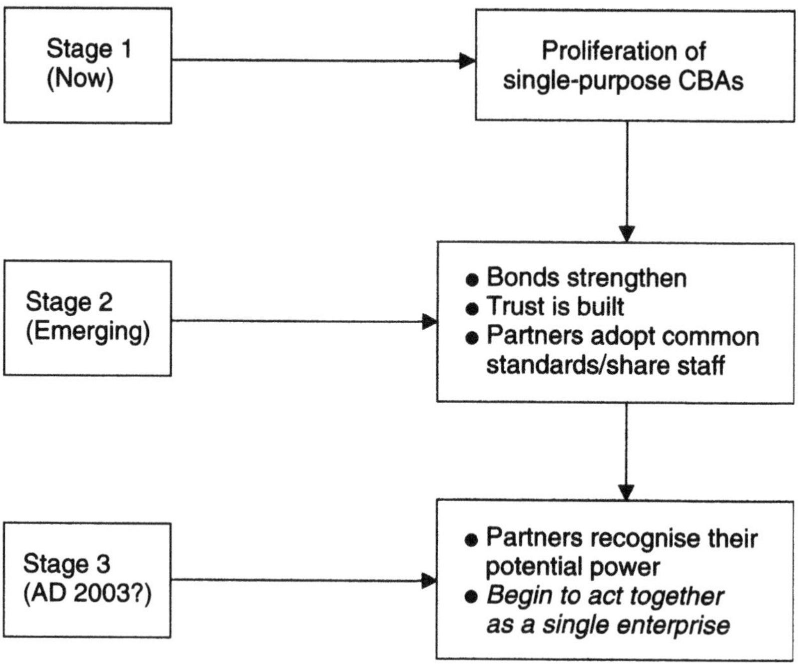

Figure 5.10 The 'deepening alliances' scenario

Source: C. Freidheim, 'The Global Corporation – Obsolete So Soon?', *World Economic Forum*, Davos, 1993.

ism' involving transnational CBAs? Freidheim himself propounds that these posited alliances will be in a position to 'limit competition', and would be 'able to avoid antitrust barriers' which are applied at the level of the nation-state.

That there could be something to these worries, in certain industries, should not be denied. Consider prospective developments in the civilian aircraft industry over the horizon to the year 2000. Currently, Boeing has about 60 per cent of this market worldwide – but its dominance is not without dispute, for over the past 20 years it has had to face increasing competition from Airbus Industry (which is itself a European CBA). In the big projects being considered for the next century by these two manufacturers, however – for example, superjumbos able to carry 600–800 people; supersonic aircraft with thrice the seating of the Concorde, but a longer range – they are already involved in *collaborative* discussions (also with such potential partners as McDonnel Douglas, Mitsubishi, Fuji and Kawasaki). Such vast projects, some conclude, may be too risky for any one firm to undertake alone. But a transnational CBA that does successfully undertake them could then 'enjoy an unassailable (global) monopoly' (Economist 1993:85).

It is thus likely – as the above case indicates – that the current and prospective growth of international CBAs will pose some new problems for competition authorities (and which – with exceptions such as the European Commission's Directorate IV – are largely the offspring of national governments). Nevertheless, it seems unlikely that this will degenerate into a system of cosy transnational business alliances with great monopoly power. There are a number of reasons for maintaining this view.

First, any growth of market power in one part of the international economic system is likely to be countervailed by other developments in many industry settings. Consider the fact that the size of transnational food manufacturers – for example, Unilever, Danon, Phillip Morris – are today enormous compared to the 'small and hapless' individual consumer. The ability of the former to exploit the latter, however, has been greatly offset by the rise and role of large retailers (who, moreover, now often enter into own-label competition with food manufacturers). In the same way, new global CBAs may find any hoped-for market power is offset or checked by the formation of others, or by unforeseen 'countervailing' developments.

Second, international business collaboration is not a costless or riskless activity. In particular, CBAs need to be based on a degree of trust between the partners – which is a scarce and fragile commodity. Moreover, as the ultimate control of CBAs is divided between the parent firms, all of the difficulties inherent in strategic decision-making are likely to be magnified in them compared to a unitary organisation. There are temptations to opportunistic behaviour for each partner, and enhanced frustrations due to difficulties of control and the absence of fully-binding contractual obligations. For such reasons, some (for example, Doz *et al.* 1990) have been led to conclude that many transnational CBAs may be 'intrinsically unstable'.

The evidence is indeed clear that many international CBAs suffer from such fissiparous forces. Bleeke and Ernst (1993) looked at 49 CBAs undertaken by the top 150 companies (ranked by market value) in the US, Europe and Japan (50 apiece). They find that two-thirds of these CBAs 'ran into trouble' within just the first two years of their operation, that only 51 per cent of them were deemed 'successful' by both partners, and that the mean duration of CBA 'life' in their sample was only seven years (with three-quarters of such terminations ending in a sole acquisition by one of the partners).

It has long been understood by economists that collusive arrangements between firms exhibit a tendency to collapse due to the corrosive force of the incentive to 'chisel' (Stigler 1968). It is evident from elementary observation that international CBAs formed for quite other reasons – for example, collaboration in order to compete on the world scene – also suffer from other centrifugal tendencies and difficulties. Moreover, elementary games theory demonstrates that the incentive to opportunistic behaviour within CBAs becomes the stronger as the balance of partner motivations moves towards collusion (Kay 1993: Chapter 10).

In short, whilst the contemporary growth of collaboration in international business poses new questions and problems, the development is most unlikely in general to end in a new scenario of 'global monopoly capitalism' via the backdoor of transnational business alliances.

6. Some General Conclusions

This chapter has sought to examine contemporary international business primarily from the perspective of strategic management analysis. A central conclusion is that, given the context of the present-day growth of international business collaboration, the orthodox analysis of MNE business policy – which concentrates on competitive strategy – is, on its own, deficient. In the contemporary business environment, it is necessary for international firms to think rather in terms of a *composite* strategy that conjoins their competitive and collaborative thrusts in a harmonious fashion.

As regards the future shape of international business, however, some foresee collaboration as becoming even more pronounced than now; and in one extreme variant of this prognosis it is postulated that global firms will become obsolete, to be replaced by international CBAs. It is certainly not impossible that in certain industries the particular conjuncture of economic and political driving forces obtaining will make CBAs the main avenue forward towards globalisation in the foreseeable future (for example, in airlines and telecom services). It would be decidedly unwise, however, to write the obituary for the global firm in all industry settings. Moreover, for the reasons discussed in Section 5, the international business system of the future is likely to continue to involve generally strong elements of competition.

The conduct of international businesses, in all historical epochs, has always involved a complex and evolving admixture of cross-border collaboration and competition. In this basic sense, what we see happening to international business today is no different from the past. Perhaps all that is different now is that the pace of economic evolution in international business is faster than previously. As more and more firms experiment with new conjunctions of transnational collaboration and competition, the need for them to formulate an effective composite strategy is likely to become ever more central to the effective conduct of their international business.

Notes

1 Pitelis and Sugden (1991) contains a number of surveys of this now large literature.

2 For a general description of the Harvard School, in relation to other schools of industrial organisation analysis, see Burton (1994).

3 Porter (1980) argues strongly that these three generic strategies are mutually exclusive: a company that tries to straddle them is likely to get both its strategy and organisational culture confused, leading to low returns from being 'stuck in the middle'. This postulate remains a controversial one; see for example Cranshaw, Davies and Kay (1994).

4 The wider picture of alliances in this global industry is explored in Burgers, Hill and Kim (1993).

5 All 'work units' – of 6–15 employees – on the Saturn project were also to be led not by a management person, but a UAW 'councillor'. GM's current strategy is to transfer this consultative/cooperative working approach to its other divisions (starting with Oldsmobile) – a process that has been dubbed as the 'Saturnisation' of GM (Simonian 1996).

6 Fixed costs refer to any cost elements that are fixed for a given duration of time (for example, the rent specified in a lease agreement), after which they become potentially variable. A sunk cost, on the other hand, is one which is fixed for all time and thus cannot be avoided or changed, whatever the firm's actions in the future.

7 For further details, see Burton (1995b).

8 Licensing may also be a possibility, but this may also not be feasible if the knowledge is 'deeply embedded', and thus not easily transferrable by licence.

6

A MODEL OF BUYER–SUPPLIER RELATIONS WITH IMPLICATIONS FOR THE MULTINATIONAL FIRM

Ram Mudambi
and
Susan McDowell Mudambi

1. Introduction

The wide range of current buyer–supplier relationships defies simple explanation. At one end of the spectrum, single sourcing has been identified as an ingredient of Japanese manufacturing success, yet has not been universally adopted, even in Japan. Relatively few firms truly follow W. Edwards Deming's call for a 'long-term relationship of loyalty and trust' (Deming 1988). Source reduction practices and dual sourcing (Ramasesh *et al.*, 1991) have been advocated as alternatives to single sourcing, with an emphasis on the stability of the supplier base (Morgan and Dowst 1988). Single sourcing with a well-qualified backup supplier is another realistic option (Galt and Dale 1991).

At the other end of the spectrum lie the adversarial relationships of buyers with multiple suppliers for each key component (Landeros and Monczka 1989). Yet empirical evidence suggests that relationships between Western buyers and suppliers are changing (Bergman 1991; Helper 1991). Current buyer–supplier relations in the West can be described as 'close but adversarial' (Helper and Mudambi 1994), in recognition of increases in formal commitment, but not of informal commitment.

No matter what type of relationship a buyer has with a particular supplier, at some point the buyer must decide to either stay with the supplier or to switch. This chapter examines the situation in which a buyer utilises a single source for a particular production input, but recognises another supplier as a backup supplier. Often, the backup is the incumbent supplier for a related input (a cross source), as is the case with Nissan (UK) in its QFD supplier development programme (Rich 1995). At issue is how the buyer decides whether to continue with the incumbent supplier or to switch to the backup. As a number of authors (for example, Ford 1980) have discussed, this decision has strategic and operational implications.

The decision becomes considerably more complex when it is placed in a multinational context. To all the issues involved in the domestic buyer–supplier interface must be added the organisational and logistical considerations of multinational enterprise. For the multinational buyer, by definition, both trade with suppliers and intra-firm movement of goods and services are often picked up in international trade accounts. The mercantilist tendencies of many governments mean that supplier selection is subject to a host of restrictive considerations like tariffs, domestic content laws and import-based re-export requirements. Thus, the dyadic buyer–supplier interface must be analysed in the home country – host country context of multinational operations.

Analyses of buyer–supplier relations generally fall into one of two camps, transaction costs economics (TCE) or the more amorphous camp consisting of advocates of relationship marketing, the IMP model, Japanese management, obligational relational contracting (Sako 1992) and others. For the purposes of this chapter, this second school of thought is called relationship marketing. Relatively few analyses have tried to bridge the divide between these camps, with the work of Nooteboom (1993, 1994a, 1994b), Berger *et al.* (1993), Heide and John (1992) and Pilling *et al.* (1994) providing notable exceptions. To supplement these efforts, this chapter presents a model of the switching decision with parameters that operationalise concepts of both transaction costs economics and relationship marketing.

We first provide a brief overview of the two schools of thought in the context of buyer–supplier relations. We then introduce a model of the switching decision, and carry out sensitivity analysis to assess the effect of various parameters on the Nash equilibrium values. In the final section, we discuss the implications of the model.

2. Transaction Costs Economics and Marketing

Analysing buyer–supplier relationships within a transaction costs framework emphasises two realities: markets are not perfectly competitive, and there is more to selecting a supplier than locating the lowest bid. Market exchanges between buyers and sellers, across technologically separable interfaces, generate frictional losses, or transaction costs, for both parties. Transaction costs were first analysed by Coase (1937), and were further developed by Williamson (1975). Transaction costs are wide and varied in nature, and borne by both buyers and suppliers (see for example, Sheridan 1990;

Cusumano and Takeishi 1991; Sriram and Mummalaneni 1991; Newman and Rhee 1990).

Transaction-specific assets (TSAs) are investments with little value outside the particular buyer–supplier relationship, and consist of multiple types and dimensions (Lohtia *et al.* 1994). TSAs encourage supplier reduction, and thereby generate both risks and opportunities, depending on the level of safeguards built into the relationship, and on the relevant norm of exchange (Heide and John 1992). A buyer that has created important TSAs can find itself at the supplier's mercy. In contrast, to a single source supplier, TSAs may imply a shrinking customer base, a high degree of customer dependency, a great volatility and uncertainty of contract awards, foregone opportunities, and a loss of supplier identity (Newman 1989; Barclift 1991).

Switching to a new supplier increases transaction costs, due to the presence of TSAs. Set-up costs and economies of scale are also important, especially in relatively hi-tech products (Newman 1989; Segal 1989), as well as the costs of re-tooling and training. Switching costs generally relate to the degree of substitutability of the potential entrant's output for the incumbent's, but even if the entrant produces the same product as the incumbent, the buyer may incur expenses in time and money for monitoring the entrant (Ricketts 1994: 7).

Transaction costs analysis treats these issues as instances that can lead to market failure. When the costs of market transaction become high enough, the suggested remedy is vertical integration (hierarchy). This serves to structurally ally the interests of the buyer and supplier.

In contrast, advocates of a more relational perspective view TSAs as investments in a relationship that generates trust, a stronger, lasting bond, and greater competency. This view emphasises how, over time, a well-maintained buyer–supplier relationship decreases many transaction costs. In effect, it offers a low cost means of effecting the same type of control that hierarchy accomplishes by fiat.

Buyers can work closely with a supplier to improve specific areas of performance, leading to savings in quality inspection costs, better integration of design efforts (Newman 1989; Ellram 1990), increased stability of supply, reduction in paperwork and administrative costs, improved quantity discounts due to economies of scale, and savings due to an 'external economy of learning' (Nooteboom 1993). The new relationships also reflect the widening acceptance of just-in-time (JIT) manufacturing and total quality control (TQC) techniques (Turnbull *et al.* 1992), and the adoption of EDI links.

Many of these investments in the relationship serve to improve the quality of information available to buyers and suppliers. The quality of communication affects the role TSAs play by offering partial protection against opportunistic behaviour. Despite difficulties in measuring information exchange, the influence of the quality of communication is well recognised (Metcalf *et al.* 1992).

Some of the disagreement over the role of TSAs also stems from discrepancies in the time dimension. For example, buyer investment in transaction-specific information technology encourages supplier reduction only until the adoption rates of information technology standards increase and firms' investments in information exchange become more generalised (Bakos and Brynjolfsson 1993). In addition, a buyer may take a longer term perspective than do its suppliers, or vice versa, thereby affecting the relationship.

Yet, the dynamics of the relationship are complex and difficult to model (Mudambi and Dobson 1993). The incumbent supplier may well be suspicious of any overture the buyer makes to a backup, just as a faithful husband may incur the wrath of his wife if he so much as looks at another woman. In a different type of environment, developing a harem of suppliers may be possible. The buyer can consider its present suppliers of related products as potential backup suppliers, as part of a cross-sourcing strategy. Buyers may encourage incumbent suppliers to expand their capability to provide one or more products currently provided by another incumbent supplier. Cross sourcing serves to minimise the total number of suppliers, and has been shown to be an effective risk reduction technique (Newman 1989). It may provide a compensating opportunity for an incumbent who has lost out to a backup. The form of cross sourcing used by the Japanese car industry, called parallel sourcing, combines the competitive benefits of multiple sourcing with the relational benefits of sole sourcing (Richardson 1993).

This strategy fits very well into the current efforts by multinationals to reap the benefits of specialisation (including localisation advantages) and volume (including globalisation advantages). Within multinational firms, this often works through the designation of particular national operations as 'world sources' for particular parts or sub-assemblies. This has even carried over into buying where particular suppliers are sometimes named as 'world sources'.

Whatever the relationship, the buyer realises that there may come a day when the primary supplier is no longer the clear choice. Switching costs alone does not tell the whole story. As Noordewier *et al.* (1990) concluded, 'managers should not focus exclusively on transaction cost minimisation given the multidimensional nature of performance.' Performance indicators of price and profit also guide the buyer. If, after taking all these factors into consideration, the buyer feels they can get a better deal elsewhere, they may well dump the supplier and respond to a new, more tempting offer from a rival supplier.

The following section introduces a model of the switching decision that incorporates ideas and assumptions of both the general approaches to buyer–supplier relations.

3. A Model of the Switching Decision

This model describes the bidding competition between an incumbent supplier and a potential entrant, or backup supplier. The model is a stylised game, with the buyer and the suppliers acting in their own self-interest, but also in awareness of the decisions the other players are likely to make.

The model examines the price-setting behaviour of the suppliers and the buyer's decision-making process. Unlike previous models, it operationalises three parameters at the heart of the disagreement between TCE and relationship marketing, and determines their effects on the switching decision.

The first parameter, the level of *transaction-specific assets*, is the product of the total amount spent on the relational investments and the proportion that is specific to the relationship. The second parameter, *quality of communication*, is the variance of the supplier's expectations of the buyer's switching costs. And third, the *time dimension* is a time discount factor which recognises that switching costs are incurred in a different period than the benefits received.

Given these parameters, the model is solved to find the Nash equilibrium strategies, i.e., the strategies in which each player has made its optimal decision, taking into account the optimal decision of the other players. Then, using sensitivity analysis, the changes in equilibrium values of price and profit are related to perturbations in the underlying parameters. Such an examination of equilibrium is frequently absent in models of buyer–supplier relationships.

In the model, the buyer re-evaluates the relationship with its suppliers each period for each major input. This evaluation process can range from cursory to comprehensive. The buyer reviews the performance of the incumbent and the overall quality and strategic fit of the two suppliers. This evaluation may take place either from the perspective of the entire operation of the buying firm or merely the particular perspective of the national unit that is directly involved. Global versus local sourcing considerations become relevant here.

Both suppliers arrive at their bid prices by utilising available information on their own costs, their estimates of the buyer's switching costs, and the contract size. The buyer scrutinises the bid prices, applying the principles of supplier price analysis (SPA), as detailed by Miller (1987) and Newman (1992). Buyers want to ensure that the bid is a viable one and not a 'low-ball' bid solely to win the contract, under the expectation that future contracts will recoup any losses.

In the end, the buyer must choose whether to continue with the incumbent supplier, or to switch to the backup, and must decide on its purchased quantity. The buyer will switch to the backup if purchasing from the backup yields greater profits for the buyer, net of switching costs, than continuing to purchase from the incumbent. The model recognises that buyers generally prefer to stay with the incumbent supplier and further develop the relationship, yet want to avoid becoming over-dependent on the supplier.

Modelling a common ground

In operationalising the key parameters, the model tries to find a common ground between TCE and relationship marketing. In the case of transaction-specific assets, both the incumbent and buyer have invested in TSAs, and the buyer's cost of switching to the backup plays an important role in the decision. In addition, the incumbent has made supplier relational investments with some degree of transaction specificity, while the backup's investments are not transaction-specific.

Specific investments by the incumbent are assumed to generally lower the incumbent's operating costs below those of the backup. The buyer derives benefits from the incumbent's TSAs, such as increased staff productivity from dealing with designated supplier personnel, and gains in terms of lower design and production time through better coordination. Yet, the incumbent does not pass on all the benefits of its TSAs to the buyer. The incumbent naturally seeks a return on its investment and thus retains some control over the buyer's switching costs. In fact, incumbent TSAs generally increase the buyer's switching costs.

The model also addresses the issue of the quality of communication. The model is one of incomplete and asymmetric information. The incumbent and backup do not observe the switching decision and the actual level of the buyer's switching costs, although they do realise the importance of switching costs to the buyer. Therefore, the suppliers form an expectation of these costs based on a probabilistic assessment of the buyer's situation; there is a common knowledge prior probability distribution over the buyer's unknown switching costs. By this we mean that neither supplier has an informational advantage over the other. The incorporation of differential quality of communication is not a major technical difficulty. However, it is unclear as to why the buyer should impose *ex ante* handicaps on either supplier. Indeed, Mudambi and Schründer (1995), in a study of buyer–supplier partnerships, find no evidence of *ex ante* informational discrimination against backups even where considerable investments in TSAs have been made.

The buyer, too, often does not know its switching costs until they are incurred. Nonetheless, it is reasonable to assume that the buyer has an informational advantage over its suppliers in estimating the true value of the switching costs, since it has data on previous supplier switches. The buyer can calculate its switching costs with reasonable accuracy and weigh these against any expected cost savings from the switch. The model addresses the issue of how much information about its switching costs the buyer chooses to reveal to its suppliers. In this context, the quality of communication can serve as a proxy for relationship commitment or trust.

Third, the model recognises the different perspectives on the relationship's time dimension. Since switching costs are incurred at a different point in time than the profits from the switching decision are realised, the profits must be discounted into present value. A shorter time horizon implies that future returns are valued less by the buyer. This translates into a smaller present value of future funds and therefore to a higher rate of time discount. In addition, the discount rate can proxy the pattern in which switching costs are incurred. In this sense, a high value indicates a front-loading of switching costs, while a smaller value indicates that the costs are spread over the period. If switching costs and profits are realised simultaneously, the discount factor is zero. The model recognises that the rates of time discount of buyers and suppliers may differ, depending on the nature of the relationship.

The model depicts a buyer–supplier relationship with at least the trappings of formal commitment, in the form of TSAs and binding agreements. However, this formal commitment is placed within a non-cooperative environment, in which the parties each act to better their own self-interest, not the relationship as a whole. Also, information about key aspects of the relationship is incomplete. The key aspects of the relationship (asset specificity, quality of communication and the time horizon) indicate the level of informal commitment, and indirectly determine the measurable outcomes of the relationship. Some level of informal commitment is present in most buyer–supplier relationships. Yet, whether this informal commitment is truly evidence of lasting and mutual trust and confidence is better explored by other models (Morgan and Hunt 1994; Metcalf *et al.* 1992; Heide and John 1992).

One final point needs to be made in the context of model specification. An important aspect of transaction costs economics, namely environmental uncertainty, is not explicitly introduced into the model. However, it does appear implicitly. As environmental uncertainty rises, the current value of any fixed sum of future return declines. Thus, a more uncertain environment is similar to one where the future is discounted more heavily. The incumbent and backup are modelled as having differential rates of future time discount and this can be used to pick up different degrees of environmental uncertainty. Since the buyer is a multinational firm, it is quite possible, and even likely, that the two suppliers operate in different countries (or ever continents!).

Specifying the model

We now present the model in a descriptive manner. The results are derived in a formal manner in the appendix to this chapter. The root decision is the buyer's choice of supplier. It is assumed, of course, that at least one supplier with roughly similar production capabilities to the incumbent exists. The buyer decides to switch to the backup if purchasing from the backup yields greater profits, net of switching costs, than continuing to purchase from the incumbent.

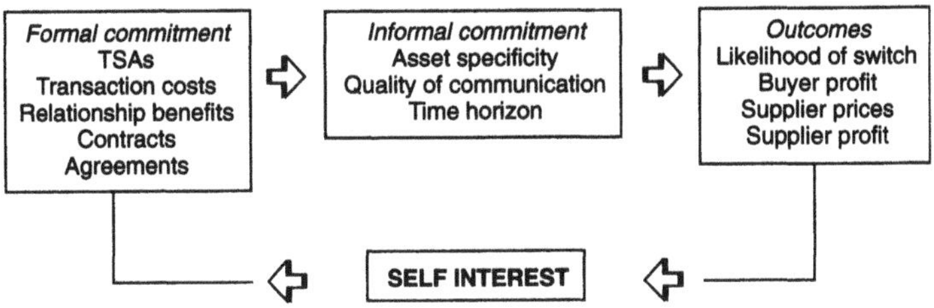

Figure 6.1 Model of buyer–supplier relations

The incumbent supplier's ability to raise the buyer's switching costs by investing in TSAs is introduced in a simple linear manner. The linearity assumption is not a critical one, but does considerably simplify the notation. The perceived probability of switch to the backup emerges from the fact that the suppliers do not observe the true value of the switching costs. We assume that they can bound the true value within an interval. In the absence of any further information, they assume that the true value of switching costs can occur anywhere in this interval with equal likelihood. The probability of a switch to the backup may then be computed. The underlying conceptual model is depicted in Figure 6.1.

Each supplier seeks to offer a winning bid, but one which maximises expected profit. In the model, the suppliers' prices are determined simultaneously given their costs, their expectations regarding the size of switching costs, the quality of their information about switching costs, and the contract size.

Maximising the incumbent supplier's expected profits with respect to its decision variable (its price bid) yields its best response function. Similarly, maximising the backup's expected profits with respect to its price bid yields its best response function. It is well recognised that the simultaneous solution to the two best response functions is the Nash equilibrium.

In a Nash equilibrium, each player has made its optimal decision, taking into account the optimal decisions of the other players. Explicitly, both the Nash equilibrium price bids are functions of the level of buyer's and incumbent supplier's TSAs, the buyer's and incumbent supplier's time horizons, the quality of communication between the buyer and the suppliers and all the other underlying production parameters. (Mudambi (1990) provides a comparative analysis of Nash and other game theoretic equilibria in a buyer–supplier relationship.)

Utilising these bid prices, the suppliers can evaluate the probability that the buyer will actually switch to the backup in response to their equilibrium decisions. The analytic solution to the suppliers' perceived probability of a switch to the backup in response to equilibrium bids is a function of the same parameters as the Nash equilibrium price bids.

In sum, this model of switching behaviour yields closed form (computable) solutions for the performance indicators of a buyer–supplier relationship. This makes it possible to analyse the effects of a number of parameters on the equilibria. In the next section, these effects are assessed using numerical sensitivity analysis.

4. Sensitivity Analysis

To draw out the implications of the model, a sensitivity analysis is carried out on the Nash equilibria developed in the previous section. The Nash strategies followed by the suppliers lead to a computable equilibrium by setting numerical values for the parameters specified. The suppliers' optimal price bids and their perceived probability of a switch can then be computed. The specific values are intended to illustrate the general principles involved. A wide range of other values were utilised, with little or no disparity in the pattern of results.

The standard level of per unit production costs in the suppliers' industry is ten. The incumbent's TSAs reduce unit costs at the rate of 10 pence for every £1 of investment. Thus, the backup's costs disadvantage depends on the level of the incumbent's TSA. Expected switching costs are set at 25. The sensitivity of the performance indicators is analysed with respect to the incumbent's TSA, quality of information available to suppliers, and the time dimension.

The effects of transaction specific assets

In Tables 6.1, 6.2 and 6.3 S_I represents the incumbent's level of transaction related investments, while ΘS_I represents the level of TSA. The model analyses the influence of both the level of general supplier relational investments, and the level of TSA expenditure. The level of specificity is allowed to vary.

The role of Θ merits explanation. When it is zero, the incumbent supplier has no TSA; the acquired assets may be disposed without loss in the event that a switch occurs. At the other extreme, when $\Theta = 1$, the incumbent's incurred expenditure is completely specific to the relationship with the buyer. In the event of a switch, nothing can be recovered. In this case, both the level of these expenses and the incumbent's time horizon are irrelevant to the determination of the equilibrium bids and the expected probability of a switch. This is because the incumbent's TSA are in effect 'sunk' costs, and it is well known that sunk costs do not enter into optimal decision-making.

Result 1: *The benefits of the incumbent supplier's relational investment depend on the specificity of the investment.*

Table 6.1 Numerical sensitivity analysis – the effects of relational investments and TSA

S_I	Θ	P_I	P_B	p	*Profit* (I)	*Profit* (B)
15	0.5	12.29	10.46	0.172	8.906	0.709
20	0.5	12.31	10.46	0.174	6.334	0.724
25	0.5	12.33	10.47	0.176	3.762	0.739
30	0.5	12.35	10.47	0.178	1.191	0.755
35	0.5	12.38	10.48	0.179	−1.380	0.770
25	0.3	13.03	10.83	0.311	3.851	2.321
25	0.4	12.68	10.65	0.244	3.696	1.420
25	0.5	12.33	10.47	0.176	3.762	0.739
25	0.6	11.98	10.29	0.108	4.048	0.279
25	0.7	11.64	10.11	0.040	4.554	0.039

As seen in the example in Table 6.1, increasing relational investment, S_I, with a given specificity level, Θ, increases both suppliers' equilibrium prices and the backup's expected profit, but decreases the incumbent's expected profit and increases the probability of switch. Increasing the transaction-specificity of the incumbent's relational investment reduces equilibrium prices, the probability of switch, and the backup's expected profits. The incumbent's expected profits initially decline through the increased losses incurred in the event of a switch. However, the positive effects of Θ in reducing costs eventually dominate and increase the incumbent's expected profit.

The effects of quality of communication

The buyer has considerable control over how much information to reveal to the suppliers about its estimated switching costs (S). Suppliers often have reason to be sceptical about the accuracy of the buyer's announcements of switching costs, as they may be understated. If the buyer claims a lower level of switching costs, the incentive for entry increases, thereby weakening the incumbent's position, and lowering the equilibrium price for the buyer, and lowering profits for all the suppliers.

The model examines the question of whether it is in the buyer's interest to provide good quality, believable information to the suppliers. This question is answered by examining the two components of switching costs: the suppliers' perceived mean switching costs (A), and the variance of perceived switching costs (V). The higher the variance, the lower the quality of communication between the buyer and its suppliers.

Result 2: *Withholding information about switching costs works against the buyer's interests.*

Poor quality communication leads to higher optimal bid prices from both the incumbent and the backup. Because poor information acts as a cost to the suppliers, the suppliers offer higher bids. The worse the communication, the higher the optimal bids. An increase in V leads to a higher probability of switch and higher expected profits for both suppliers.

Table 6.2 Numerical sensitivity analysis – the effects of quality of communication

A	V	P_I	P_B	p	*Profit (I)*	*Profit (B)*
25	5	11.27	9.40	0	−2.340	0
25	10	11.53	9.67	0	0.049	0
25	15	11.80	9.93	0	2.442	0
25	20	12.07	10.20	0.095	3.195	0.172
25	25	12.33	10.47	0.176	3.762	0.739

This effect of poor communication operates regardless of the relative costs of the suppliers, the size of the switching costs, or the contract quantity. Table 6.2 presents one example. These results show that the avoidance of higher bids gives the buyer an incentive to maintain high quality communication channels with its suppliers. In order to be credible, the buyer must offer the suppliers evidence of its switching costs.

The effects of the time dimension

The model recognises that the decision time horizon of buyers and suppliers may differ. A longer horizon implies greater patience in waiting for future benefits, and must indicate, *ceteris paribus*, that the future is discounted at a lower rate. In the example given in Table 6.3, the supplier has a higher discount rate than does the buyer. In other words, the supplier has a shorter decision time frame, and is less willing to wait patiently for profits to be realised from the relationship.

Table 6.3 Numerical sensitivity analysis – the effects of the time discount factors

δ	δ_I	P_I	P_B	p	*Profit (I)*	*Profit (B)*
0.06	0.05	12.28	10.44	0.166	5.049	0.664
0.06	0.10	12.33	10.47	0.176	3.762	0.739
0.06	0.15	12.39	10.49	0.186	2.480	0.828
0.06	0.20	12.45	10.53	0.197	1.202	0.934
0.06	0.25	12.52	10.56	0.211	−0.070	1.061
0.04	0.10	12.28	10.46	0.176	3.409	0.727
0.06	0.10	12.33	10.47	0.176	3.762	0.739
0.08	0.10	12.38	10.48	0.175	4.131	0.752
0.10	0.10	12.43	10.49	0.175	4.516	0.766
0.15	0.10	12.57	10.51	0.174	5.557	0.802

	Probability of switch	*Incumbent profit*
Incumbent specificity of investment	–	+
Incumbent time frame	–	+

	Supplier price	*Buyer profit*
Quality of communication	–	+
Buyer time frame	–	+

Figure 6.2 Summary of resultant effects

Result 3: *Incumbent suppliers benefit by placing the buyer–supplier relationship within a longer time frame.*

A fall in the incumbent's rate of time discount, relative to a given rate for the backup, leads to decreases in equilibrium prices and backup profit. More importantly for the incumbent, it also leads to a decrease in the probability of switch, and an increase in incumbent profit.

The results provide theoretical support to relationship marketing. The results are summarised in Figure 6.2, but the implications merit further discussion.

One tenet of relationship marketing is that suppliers should continue to invest in their relationship with the buyer, and that transaction-specific assets are beneficial. As shown in Table 6.1, increases in the incumbent's specificity of investment eventually cause the probability of switch to fall and the incumbent's expected profits to rise. A timid venture into installing TSA may prove counter-productive, as fears of switch reduce expected profits. However, a bold move is likely to produce desirable results as the probability of a switch itself is made to fall rapidly.

Another tenet is that suppliers should place the buyer–supplier relationship within a longer time frame. The results indicate that a longer time frame does benefit incumbents by lowering the probability of switch and increasing the incumbent's expected profits.

From the buyer's perspective, relationship marketing suggests that buyers should maintain a high level of communication with their suppliers. The results indicate that better communication about switching costs leads to lower supplier prices and an increase in the buyer's expected profits. In practice, buyers provide this information in return for cost information from suppliers. A buyer using the principles of supplier price analysis expects suppliers to present documented evidence of their cost structures, in order to ensure that the suppliers are not creating an unstable situation by underbidding.

Ultimately, the decision on how much information the buyer should reveal hinges on whether or not it expects to remain with the incumbent. If the buyer expects to remain, it is unambiguously beneficial to correct a supplier overestimate of switching costs. However, if the suppliers have underestimated switching costs, then correcting this estimate can cause the incumbent's optimal bid to rise. This is because the incumbent's increased confidence in its incumbency may outweigh the lowered uncertainty through better information. The reverse is true if the buyer expects to make a switch.

Finally, buyers, too, have been encouraged to think beyond the short term when dealing with suppliers. The results suggest that a longer time frame benefits buyers through a decrease in supplier prices and increase in the buyer's expected profits.

5. Implications for Multinational Buyers

The linkages between multinational firms are many and varied and often hinge on the relationships between buying units and suppliers. Many issues are complicated by location, specifically, situations where buyers and suppliers are separated by political boundaries. A taxonomy of buyer–supplier relations in the dimension of location can serve to simplify the complexity of these locational issues.

In the taxonomy (Figure 6.3), two components of the buying firm are treated separately – the headquarters, where top management resides and the buying unit, which generally is associated with production and other operational activities. The location of the headquarters is considered to be the 'home country'. The actual buying unit may be located either in the home country or in another country, which is called the 'host' country. The incumbent supplier and the backrup supplier may be located in the home country, the host country or in a third country.

Domestic relationship

In this situation both the buying unit and the supplier operate in the home country. The buying firm's multinationality is of marginal relevance here, except in the sense that it may have lower switching costs to an overseas backup supplier. Thus, the bargaining power of the buyer may be enhanced by its multinationality. This will be true to a greater or lesser extent for all the relationships considered here.

<table>
<tr><td colspan="2" rowspan="2"></td><th colspan="2">BUYING UNIT</th></tr>
<tr><th>Home country</th><th>Host country</th></tr>
<tr><td rowspan="3">SUPPLIER</td><td>Home country</td><td>Domestic relationship</td><td>Offshore assembly</td></tr>
<tr><td>Host country</td><td rowspan="2">Offshore sourcing</td><td>Locally integrated subsidiary</td></tr>
<tr><td>3rd country</td><td>Strategically independent subsidiary</td></tr>
</table>

Figure 6.3 A location-based taxonomy of buyer-supplier linkages

Offshore assembly

In this situation, the buying unit is not located in the home country, but chooses to buy from suppliers in the home country. This type of relationship is often found when the buying firm is a subsidiary established to surmount tariff or other trade barriers. Thus, the suppliers may be long term suppliers to the buyer's parent firm, or firms in which the parent has an equity interest. In the latter case, the supply may be in the form of major sub-assemblies or even knock-down kits, and the buying unit may be little more than a screw-driver assembly operation. Early Japanese plants in the US and Western Europe had such relationships with *keiretsu* suppliers back in Japan.

Under these conditions, the incumbent supplier is likely to make substantial investment in TSAs and the information flow between the buyer and supplier is likely to be good. If the supplier has a good working relationship with the parent company, it is likely to place the relationship within a long time frame. All these factors indicate that the incumbent is likely to be well-entrenched.

Offshore sourcing

Alternatively, the buying unit may be located in the home country, while the supplier is located overseas. Such offshore sourcing has been increasing substantially over the last two decades as firms try to gain competitive advantage through reduced costs, especially since economic liberalisation has allowed the development of competent suppliers in low-cost developing countries. Often, the buying unit acts as little more than a packager and distributor, trading on its brand name in the developed home country. This is particularly likely in the case of relatively low technology products. Since the driving force here is cost reduction, the quality of communication between the buyer and supplier is likely to be poor. Furthermore, the buyer is likely to be considering ever lower-cost offshore sources, as the location of its current source develops and becomes a higher-cost economy. Thus, US multinationals which dealt with suppliers in Taiwan and Singapore two decades ago, moved on to suppliers in the Philippines, Thailand and Malaysia; Vietnam and Bangladesh may become important in the future. The inexorable forces of the market are likely to undermine the development of most buyer–supplier relations of this type.

Locally integrated subsidiary

This case is the converse of a domestic relationship, with both the buying unit and the supplier in the host country. It typically comes about as the subsidiary matures. The subsidiary may develop relationships with local suppliers, become well-integrated into the local economy and even become a local exporter. This has occurred with subsidiaries of several European multinationals like Unilever and British American Tobacco. A second scenario is the development of offshore assembly, where the buying unit is followed overseas by many suppliers from its home country, who set up overseas subsidiaries of their own. The buying unit then progresses to more sophisticated operations, but its integration is a function of the local adaptation of its suppliers. This has occurred with many Japanese multinationals like Sony and Toyota.

Strategically independent subsidiary

There are two basic requirements for this situation to arise. First, the subsidiary must be mature and, second, the overall strategy of the multinational firm must allow for a non-centralised organisational structure. In light of the current moves of many multinationals towards so-called 'transnational' (Bartlett and Ghoshal 1989) or 'matrix' (Czinkota *et al.* 1996) organisations, which seek to reap the benefits of globalisation and localisation simultaneously, these requirements are being met in an ever-growing number of cases (Mudambi and Ricketts 1997). The subsidiary is now charged with making strategic sourcing decisions which affect the operations of the multinational in many countries. This has been the case, for example, with Vauxhall, GM's UK subsidiary, which has operational and purchasing responsibilities for some products which are sold across Europe and sometimes globally (Larkin 1995). Similar structures are found at the US multinational 3M, as well as the European multinational, Philips.

Such buying units are very likely to find themselves in 'close but adversarial' situations with their suppliers, since they may inherit suppliers from national subsidiaries which have been superseded by the new organisational structure. They may therefore find it particularly useful to start with a clean slate and attempt to implement good communication and a long-term perspective to encourage the suppliers to invest in TSAs. Such actions will certainly increase the benefits of the new organisational structure.

These five types of locational patterns represent a simplification of real world complexities. Not all buyer–supplier relations fit neatly into one of the boxes, yet the taxonomy helps to focus on the key strategies and issues involved. In particular, the messages of the 'close but adversarial' model are especially relevant for all multinational buyers, with the possible exception of those considered to be offshore assemblers.

6. Concluding Remarks

This chapter has attempted to model buyer–supplier relationships as 'close but adversarial', using elements of both relationship marketing and transaction costs economics. The trappings of formal commitment are represented by an investment in transaction specific assets by both the buyer and the incumbent supplier. The lack of fully developed informal links and trust is represented by the non-cooperative solution methodology used in finding the equilibria of the game.

The results generally support the argument for closer relationships between buyers and suppliers. What is particularly interesting is that these results are generated in a *non-cooperative game*. Even in a relationship where trust and informal commitment are lacking, formal commitment reduces the incentive to engage in short term prisoners' dilemma-type opportunism. The resulting Nash equilibria accurately reflect real-world strategies in which each player makes its optimal decision, taking into account the optimal decision of the other players. The power of the results are seen from the fact that an unambiguous improvement in the performance of both the buyer and the supplier is gained without requiring either to do anything other than to pursue their own objectives selfishly.

Although some proponents of transaction costs economics and relationship marketing may not want to admit it, the two schools of thought need not be in opposition to each other. Indeed, a synthesis of several key tenets supports the development of closer buyer–supplier relationships as a rational strategy. Even in a 'close but adversarial' relationship, short term opportunism is usually not optimal.

How might these results be tested? The various measures associated with a buyer–supplier relationship are obtainable from survey data, but the switching probability presents some problems. One approach would be to elicit subjective responses, with all the associated drawbacks. An alternative approach, adopted by Helper and Mudambi (1995), is to generate proxy variables based on quantifiable measures that may be related to the suppliers' perceived probability of a switch. Indeed, preliminary findings reported in that study provide some support for the model presented here.

It is clearly impossible to deal with all the factors which impinge on a 'close but adversarial' buyer–supplier relationship within a simple model.

An interesting extension would be the inclusion of transaction frequency. As pointed out by Nooteboom (1994a), this introduces relationship-specific 'learning' into the model. Another extension would be to extend the location-based taxonomy to incorporate cases explicitly where the multinationality of the supplier equals or exceeds that of the buyer. This would bring into focus the complex sourcing decisions involved when the supplier itself sources from units in several different countries. These and other unresolved issues highlight the continuing importance of buyer–supplier relations to the organisation of the firm in international business.

Appendix

The model uses the following notation:

$P_I \equiv$ the incumbent's announced price or bid

$P_B \equiv$ the backup supplier's announced price

$C_I \equiv$ the incumbent's average costs

$C_B \equiv$ the backup's average costs

$Q \equiv$ the contracted quantity

$F(Q) \equiv$ buyer's output, or its production function

$A \equiv$ the suppliers' expectation of the buyer's switching costs; i.e., the mean of the common knowledge prior distribution

$V \equiv$ the quality of the suppliers' information about the buyer's switching costs, a measure of the variance of the common knowledge prior to distribution;

$S_I \equiv$ the amount of the incumbent's relational assets;

$\Theta \equiv$ the proportion of the expenditure on relational investment that is not recoverable when disposed of on the open market; $0 \leq \Theta \leq 1$;

$S = S_0 + n\Theta S_I \equiv$ actual value of the buyer's switching costs, which increase linearly as the incumbent's TSAs increase; $n \geq 0$;

$\delta \equiv$ the buyer's time discount factor, a measure of its decision time horizon; $0 \leq \delta \leq 1$

$\delta_I \equiv$ the incumbent's time discount factor, a measure of its decision time horizon; $0 \leq \delta_I \leq 1$;

$p \equiv$ the suppliers' perceived probability of a switch to the backup.

$C_B = c \equiv$ backup's marginal cost of operation;

$C_I = c - m\Theta S_I \equiv$ incumbent's marginal cost of operation, which declines linearly as its TSAs increase.

The buyer makes a switch if profits obtainable from dealing with the backup exceed those obtainable by dealing with the incumbent,

$$(1-\delta)[F(Q) - P_B Q] - S > (1-\delta)[F(Q) - P_I Q] \tag{1}$$

or,

$$S_0 < Q\times(1-\delta)\times(P_I - P_B) - n\Theta S_I \equiv v \quad (2)$$

We assume that the suppliers' incompleteness of information is the same and that they can both bound the true value of S within the interval, $[A-\frac{1}{2}V, A+\frac{1}{2}V]$. They assume that S_0 is uniformly distributed over this interval. The probability of a switch to the backup is then computed as:

$$p = P(S_0 < v) = [v - (A - 1/2V)]/V \quad (3)$$

Using (2), the incumbent's expected profit is:

$$E(\Pi_I) = (1-p)[(1-\delta_I)(P_I - C_I)Q - S_I] + p[-\Theta S_I] \quad (4)$$

Similarly, with δ_B as the backup's rate of time discount, the backup's expected profit may be computed as:

$$E(\Pi_B) = p(1-\delta_B)(P_B - C_B)Q \quad (5)$$

In this chapter the incumbent's investment in supplier relational investments acts to ensure that $C_I < C_B$. For simplicity, it is assumed that this is a linear relationship. Again the assumption of linearity is not critical.

Maximising (3) with respect to the incumbent's decision variable (P_I) yields its best response function. Similarly maximising (4) with respect to P_B yields the backup's best response function. The simultaneous solution to the two best response functions yields the Nash equilibrium price bids. Explicitly, the Nash equilibrium price bids are:

$$P_I^* = c + (1/3)\{\frac{2S_I(1-\ )}{Q(1-\delta_I)} + \frac{A + (3/2)V + nS_I}{Q(1-\delta)} - 2mS_I\} \quad (6)$$

$$P_B^* = c + (1/3)\{\frac{S_I(1-\Theta)}{Q(1-\delta_I)} - \frac{A - (3/2)V + n\Theta S_I}{Q(1-\delta)} - m\Theta S_I\} \quad (7)$$

Utilising these prices, the analytic solution to the suppliers' perceived probability of a switch to the backup in response to equilibrium bids is:

$$p^* = (1/2) + \frac{S_I(1-\Theta)(1-\delta)}{3V(1-\delta_I)} - \frac{A + [Q(1-\delta)m + n]\Theta S_I}{3V} \quad (8)$$

The numerical sensitivity analysis in the chapter is based on these analytic solutions.

Part III

CURRENT APPLICATIONS

INTRODUCTORY NOTE

Part III consists of contributions which address applied issues of multinational organisation in specific industries. The first chapter by Hartley deals with the European defence industry. It focuses on the various ways in which the single European market might be extended to include the procurement of defence equipment. Issues considered are: (1) the organisation of EU collaborative defence projects, (2) the development of the EU defence industrial base and how it might be brought about, i.e., decision-making rules, (3) issues of resource re-allocation by firms forced out of defence and into other businesses by rationalisation, for example, the 'peace dividend', tanks to tractors, etc. These issues of re-organisation are particularly important in the context of the recent consolidation of the defence industry in the US. The issues discussed in the chapter therefore concern the very survival of European defence multinationals.

The second chapter by Alcock examines the legal aspects of corporate governance under emerging EU institutions, focusing particularly on the draft European Fifth Directive on Company Law. This Directive has made no progress in recent years not least because of the resistance of the UK Government to interference in the internal organisation of public companies. The recent change of government could resurrect the proposals and advance the cause of two-tier boards and employee participation. Such structures have strong academic support, but the chapter suggests that there are arguments in favour of the *status quo*.

Finally, the third chapter by Sako, Lamming and Helper deals with the world automobile industry. Using a comprehensive data set generated by the MIT International Motor Vehicle Program supplier surveys in North America, Japan and Europe, the authors compare the organisation of supplier relationships in these different regions. They find that the organisation does vary in several dimensions and that multinationals tend to attempt to reproduce the supplier relations prevalent in their home countries in foreign subsidiaries.

7

A SINGLE EUROPEAN MARKET FOR DEFENCE EQUIPMENT

Organisation and collaboration

Keith Hartley

1. Introduction: The Policy Issues[1]

A significant proportion of public sector procurement in the European Union (EU) is undertaken by national defence ministries, but defence procurement is excluded from the directives on public procurement in the Single Market. What are the costs of non-Europe in defence procurement; and what are the likely economic benefits and costs of extending the Single Market to defence procurement? This chapter starts with an analysis of the European defence market; it identifies the costs of non-Europe and estimates the benefits of various scenarios for creating a Single European Defence Market, including proposals for greater collaboration; and it concludes by reviewing the costs of change.

2. The European Defence Market

The European defence market is a misleading description since it comprises a set of independent national markets each with a variety of demand and supply arrangements. Nations differ in their defence procurement policies, with some European countries (for example, the UK) favouring a competitive procurement policy characterised by competition and fixed price contracts, whilst others have favoured preferential purchasing from national champions (for example, France). Even those nations which have been willing to open up their national markets to foreign firms have usually required some form of work-sharing for their domestic industry as part of the price of importing. Examples include licensed and co-production (for example, Belgium, Denmark, The Netherlands and Norway purchase of US F-16 aircraft) and offset agreements (for example, Spain's purchase of US F-18 aircraft: Sandler and Hartley 1995; Martin 1996). Typically, a nation's procurement policy will be partly constrained by the extent of its national defence industrial base

(DIB) and its desire and willingness to pay for independence, security of supply and the wider economic benefits which are believed to be associated with a national DIB (for example, jobs, technology and spin-offs).

European defence spending is highly concentrated in a small number of countries with France, Germany, Italy and the UK accounting for about 80 per cent of total EU defence and equipment expenditure. Even so, aggregate EU defence equipment spending was only some 55 per cent of the equivalent US expenditure; but, in the absence of a Single European Market, it is misleading to refer to an EU total. Instead, comparisons should be made between individual European nations and the USA. On this basis, equipment expenditure in the UK was almost 20 per cent of US equipment spending in 1994 and the corresponding figure for France was 11 per cent. Such differences in the magnitude of equipment spending suggest that Europe's fragmented national defence industries are at a scale disadvantage compared with their US rivals (Table 7.1).

Table 7.1 Defence expenditure

		Defence expenditure (US $ million, 1990 prices)	*Defence share (%)*	*Equipment expenditure (US $ million, 1990 prices)*
France	1990	42,589	3.6	6,098
	1994	41,235	3.4	5,742
Germany	1990	42,320	2.8	7,491
	1994	31,258	2.1	3,407
Italy	1990	23,376	2.1	4,091
	1994	23,492	2.1	4,064
UK	1990	39,776	4.0	7,120
	1994	35,055	3.6	9,149
Spain	1990	9,053	1.8	1,150
	1994	8,141	1.7	1,083
Netherlands	1990	7,421	2.6	1,328
	1994	6,263	2.3	952
Sweden	1990	5,909	2.6	786
	1994	5,260	2.5	739
Total EU	1990	187,827	2.4	30,483
	1994	166,990	2.1	27,437
USA	1990	306,170	5.5	75,930
	1994	252,358	4.7	50,219

Notes

i. Equipment expenditure data based on NATO definitions.

ii. Defence burdens for EU are medians.

iii. Equipment expenditures: French data for 1990 uses 1989 data; Sweden's data estimated on basis of average for NATO Europe.

iv. EU is based on 15 countries.

Source: SIPRI (1995).

Table 7.2 EU defence industries

	Employment ('000s)		*Arms exports (US $ million 1990 prices)*		*Arms imports (US $ million 1990 prices)*	
	1995	1990	1994	1990–94	1994	1990–94
UK	288.6	400.0	1,593	6,557	52	2,193
France	250.0	255.0	705	6,287	66	1,612
Germany	117.1	241.0	3,162	10,536	629	5,836
Italy	38.6	80.0	357	1,997	171	698
Spain	28.6	100.0	116	363	964	2,834
Sweden	28.6	30.0	91	646	(90)	(356)
Greece	14.3	14.0	(10)	(53)	973	6,375
Netherlands	14.3	20.0	558	2,065	273	1,092
Finland	8.6	10.0	(0)	(16)	143	1,495
Portugal	8.6	10.0	(5)	(42)	491	1,998
Belgium	8.6	25.0	(50)	(721)	55	694
Denmark	4.3	7.0	(10)	(74)	(50)	(209)
Austria	2.9	20.0	(0)	(267)	(10)	(147)
Total EU	813.1	1,212.0	6,548	28,064	3,766	23,050
USA	1,178.0	2,750.0	11,959	62,354	509	2,147
Total World	na	< 15,000.0	21,725	127,414	21,725	127,414

Notes
i. 1995 employment figures are from Brzoska (1996); 1990 employment data are from Wulf (1993). Problems can arise where different studies use different definitions of the DIB – for example, whether the employment figures are for equipment expenditure only, whether exports are included and whether the numbers include indirect and induced multiplier effects (Hartley, 1996). US 1995 employment data are for 1992.
ii. Figures in brackets are for 1993 and 1990–93 in US $ millions, 1993 constant prices from a different source: ACDA (1995).
Sources: SIPRI (1995); Brzoska (1996); Wulf (1993); ACDA (1995).

The European nations differ in the size, structure, technical capabilities, ownership and performance of their defence industries. Four groups can be distinguished. First, France and the UK have relatively large defence industries with the capability of developing nuclear and conventional weapons and a complete range of advanced air, land and sea systems (for example, combat aircraft, nuclear-powered submarines, aircraft carriers). Second, Germany and Italy: the former has a sizeable DIB, and both nations have independent technical capabilities in some land and sea systems and an involvement in a range of collaborative aerospace projects (combat aircraft, helicopters and missiles). Third, Spain and Sweden with similar-sized defence industries: Spain with a developing DIB and Sweden with its traditional policy of neutrality and independence, including an independent capability in modern combat aircraft (Saab Gripen). Fourth, there is a group of nations with small defence industries with some capabilities in low technology areas (for example, ammunition, small arms and small warships) and in sub-contracting (for example, SABCA, Belgium as aerospace sub-contractor). This fourth group comprises The Netherlands, Belgium, Finland, Portugal, Denmark and Austria (Ireland and Luxembourg have no defence firms). In total, the EU's defence industries employed over 800,000 people in 1995, with France, Germany and the UK accounting for 80 per cent of the total. Table 7.2 also shows the magnitude of job losses following the end of the Cold War: between 1990 and 1995 employment in the EU's defence industries fell by some 30 per cent.

Ownership differs between nation states. British and German defence companies are privately-owned whilst state ownership has been dominant in France, Italy and Spain. Differences in ownership inevitably mean problems for creating a 'level playing field' in any future extension of the Single Market to embrace defence equipment: private firms will claim that state-owned companies with access to subsidies and other forms of state support represent 'unfair competition' (Hartley 1995).

The performance of Europe's defence industries is reflected in their international competitiveness as measured by import penetration ratios and export shares. For example, even though the UK has a relatively open defence market, imports represented under 10 per cent of its defence equipment expenditure for the period 1990–95 compared with some 25 per cent for the UK economy. France, Germany and the UK are Europe's leading arms exporters accounting for 25 per cent of the world's arms exports in 1994 compared with the USA which achieved a 55 per cent share of the world market (SIPRI 1995). Europe's leading arms importers were Greece, Germany, Spain and Portugal, accounting for over 70 per cent of total EU arms imports over the period 1990–94 (Table 7.2).

Differences in the scale of equipment expenditure between individual European nations and the USA are reflected in firm size where firm size is important for economies of scale and scope. In 1993, American companies formed the top five and accounted for 15 of the world's top 20 largest arms-producing companies. At that time the average size of US firms in the top five was almost twice the average size of the top five EU firms (Table 7.3). Interestingly, most of the top five American and EU defence companies were in the aerospace industry (an R&D intensive and hi-tech sector). A comparison of the size of the leading firms in the air, land and sea sectors showed that in 1993 only in ordnance and shipbuilding were the leading European companies larger than their US rivals (Table 7.3).

Further evidence of the scale differences between EU nations and the USA are reflected in the figures for national output and the number of different types of equipment. In 1993 when most NATO nations were adjusting to reduced defence spending, the US national procurement of major conventional defence equipment varied between 1.6 (missiles) and some 10 (combat aircraft) times the national procurement levels for the largest single European nation (usually the UK). Exports further increase output levels and the associated economies of scale and learning; and the relative scale difference

Table 7.3 Leading defence companies, 1993

USA Company	Arms sales ($ million)	*European Union* Company	Arms sales ($ million)
Top 5 Arms Producers		**Top 5 Arms Producers**	
Lockheed (Ac)	10,070	British Aerospace (Ac, A, El, Mi, O)	5,950
McDonnell Douglas (Ac)	9,050	Thomson-CSF (El, Mi)	4,240
General Motors (El, Eng, Mi)	6,900	Daimler Benz (Ac, El, Eng, Mi)	3,450
Martin Marietta (El, Mi)	6,500	DCN (Sh)	3,440
GM Hughes Electronics (El, Mi)	6,110	GEC (El)	3,210
Aircraft & Helicopters: Top 3		**Aircraft & Helicopters: Top 3**	
Lockheed	10,070	British Aerospace (UK)	5,950
McDonnell Douglas	9,500	DASA (G)	3,250
Northrop	4,480	Aerospatiale (F)	2,860
Aero-engines: Top 2		**Aero-engines: Top 2**	
General Electric	2,400	Rolls-Royce (UK)	1,580
Pratt and Whitney (UTC)	1,600	SNECMA (F)	1,060
Military Electronics: Top 2		**Military Electronics: Top 2**	
Raytheon	4,500	Thomson-CSF (F)	4,240
Loral	3,750	GEC (UK)	3,210
Military Vehicles: Top 2		**Military Vehicles: Top 2**	
General Dynamics	3,000	GIAT (F)	1,300
Textron	1,600	VSEL (UK)	690
Ordnance: Top 2		**Ordnance: Top 2**	
Alliant Tech Systems	700	GIAT (F)	1,300
Thiokol	520	Diehl (G)	810
Warships: Top 3		**Warships: Top 3**	
Litton Industries	3,170	DCN (F)	3,440
General Dynamics	3,000	Bremer Vulkan (G)	860
Newport News	1,860	VSEL (UK)	690

Notes
i. A = artillery; Ac = aircraft; El = electronics; Eng = engines; Mi = missiles; O = ordnance; Sh = ships.
ii. F = France; G = Germany; UK = United Kingdom
Source: SIPRI (1995).

Table 7.4a National procurement, 1993

	Tanks	*ACVs*	*Artillery*	*Combat aircraft*	*Attack helicopters*	*Warships*	*Missiles*
France	4	–	42	20	2	4	779
Germany	–	–	30	–	–	–	6,180
Italy	132	–	–	10	6	–	–
UK	–	192	91	5	–	5	9,016
USA	–	340	256	199	140	16	14,084

Table 7.4b National procurement and exports

	Combat aircraft			*Attack helicopters*			*Tanks*			*Warships*		
	National	*Exports*	*Total*	*National*	*Exports*	*Total*	*National*	*Exports*	*Total*	*National*	*Exports*	*Total*
France	20	3	23	2	13	15	4	0	4	4	0	4
Germany	0	82	82	0	0	0	0	215	215	0	26	26
Italy	10	10	20	6	31	37	132	0	132	0	0	0
UK	5	56	61	0	0	0	0	22	22	5	0	5
USA	199	128	327	140	75	215	0	1,816	1,816	16	5	21

Notes
i. Exports include cascading for CFE purposes.
ii. National = national procurement.
iii. Data are Volume figures.
Source: Chalmers and Greene (1995).

between the USA and the major EU defence producers remains substantial. The US competitive advantage is increased further when it is recognised that the EU nations are developing and producing a much larger number of different types of costly defence equipment (Tables 7.4 and 7.5).

Table 7.5 Number of different types of defence equipment: Europe v USA, 1993

Equipment	*Number of types*	
	Europe	*USA*
Land Systems		
Main battle tank	4	1
Armoured Infantry Fighting Vehicle	16	3
155mm howitzer	3	1
Air Systems		
Fighter-strike	7	5
Ground attack – trainer	6	1
Attack helicopter	7	5
Anti-ship missile	9	3
Air-air missile	8	4
Sea Systems		
Frigate	11	1
Anti-submarine torpedo	9	2
Diesel submarine	7	0
Nuclear-powered submarine	2	1

Note
Data at June (1993).
Source: De Vestel (1995).

3. The Costs of Non-Europe

The absence of a Single European Market for defence equipment is costly and inefficient. In a number of nations, inefficiency is reflected in domestic monopolies (for example, aerospace; tanks; warships), government-protected markets with barriers to entry and exit (support for national champions), non-competitive cost-based contracts, state ownership, subsidies and government regulation of profits (with firms pursuing non-profit objectives). Within the EU, independence through supporting a domestic DIB is costly. Each member state's support for its national defence industry has resulted in the duplication of costly R&D programmes and relatively short production runs reflecting small national orders so that there is a failure to obtain economies of scale and learning. For example, in the mid-1990s, six European nations were developing three different types of advanced combat aircraft with production orders for some 1,200 units divided between the three different types (four-nation Eurofighter 2000; French Rafale and Sweden's Gripen).

Nor can nations ignore the need for difficult defence choices resulting from the twin pressures of falling defence budgets and rising equipment costs. For example, between 1990 and 1996, UK defence spending and expenditure on equipment each fell by over 20 per cent in real terms. At the same time, equipment which is already costly has been experiencing real-cost increases of some 10 per cent per annum resulting in a doubling in weapons costs every 7.25 years (Kirkpatrick 1995; Pugh 1993). Rising costs lead to falling numbers being bought and forecasts of long-run trends towards a single ship navy and a one aircraft air force (Starship Enterprise). In these circumstances, nations need to re-appraise their traditional methods of procurement with the Single Market option offering potential efficiency improvements.

4. Economic Benefits of a Single Market

Article 223 of the Treaty of Rome means that defence procurement is excluded from the Single Market's Public Procurement Directives so allowing member states to support their national defence industries. However, if non-Europe and fragmented national markets were replaced by a Single European Market for defence equipment, it is predicted that the resulting economic benefits would lead to substantial budget savings. The expected benefits comprise increased competition, especially between nations; less duplication and hence savings in R&D; economies of scale and learning resulting from longer production runs; and possible dynamic benefits from innovations due to competition and the Single Market.

The European Commission has studied four scenarios for creating a Single European Market for defence equipment (Hartley and Cox 1992; EC 1995). The scenarios were designed to provide information on the costs of the current procurement arrangements in the EU (non-Europe) and the estimated benefits of various Single Market solutions. Each scenario assumed a liberalised competitive market either restricted to member states of the EU or open to the rest of the world. *Scenario I* assumed *limited* liberalisation with certain equipment (for example, nuclear systems; cryptographic equipment) excluded from an open market. *Scenario II* assumed complete liberalisation with an open market for *all* defence equipment and procurement by national defence ministries. *Scenario III* assumed a twin-track approach involving a mixture of competition and collaboration. Under the twin-track scenario, competition would be restricted to small and medium-sized equipment where purchasing would be undertaken by national defence ministries (for example, small arms; some missiles); whilst large projects would be undertaken on a collaborative basis with joint procurement by participating defence ministries (for example, aerospace projects; nuclear systems). *Scenario IV* made more radical assumptions about procurement: it assumed the procurement of common and standardised equipment by a centralised procurement agency which would replace national defence ministries (Table 7.6).

A two-stage methodology was used to estimate the benefits of the four scenarios for creating a Single European Market for defence equipment. First, a series of case studies were undertaken of the estimated savings from standardisation and long production runs. For example, if, instead of the separate development of the Gripen, Rafale and EF2000 combat aircraft, one type were selected, there would be the saving of two R&D bills and the economies of producing a combined output of some 1,200 units compared with a national output of about 300 units. Learning economies suggest a reduction in unit production costs of about 10 per cent for each doubling in cumulative output; hence, an increase in output from 300 to 1,200 units will lead to a reduction in unit production costs of about 20 per cent (Sandler and Hartley 1995: 124).

The second part of the methodology involved estimating competition and scale effects using the simple analytical framework shown in Figure 7.1. Before the opening-up of the market, a nation buys Q_1 at price P_3 with profits Π_1. Opening up the market to lower cost suppliers (AC_0) means that competition based on lower costs and reduced profit margins (Π_0) leads to lower prices (P_3 to P_2). The successful firm then obtains a larger share of the market and obtains scale economies leading to lower costs and lower prices (P_2 to P_1). Company interview studies were used to obtain estimates of the competition and scale effects. The results suggested a minimum-bound competition effect of 10 per cent for the EU market only and 15 per cent for the EU market opened to the world (for example, the effect of competition on equipment prices). Typically, defence industries are decreasing-cost

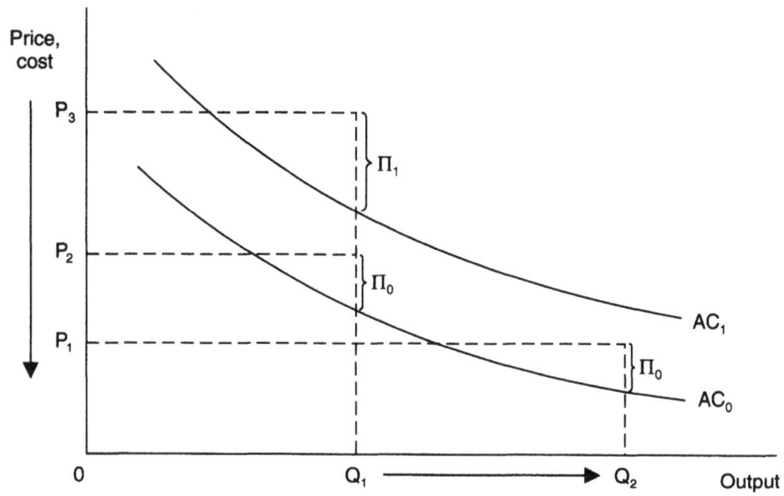

Figure 7.1 Competition and scale effects

industries, especially for major equipment. For substantial increases in output (doubling or more), scale effects were estimated at 12 per cent. In addition, sensitivity tests were undertaken using alternative scale and learning factors. The estimates of scale and competition effects were then applied to various estimates of the EU's total defence equipment spending, so providing broad orders of magnitude of aggregate savings under the various scenarios.

In 1990, total EC defence procurement spending was estimated at some £46 billion, of which 62 per cent was spent on Article 223 items (EC 1995). The estimates of the aggregate savings under the four scenarios were subject to various sensitivity tests, including allowances for nations such as the UK where markets were already open and competitive. Also, because of the difficulties and uncertainties involved in the estimation process (for example, in aggregating across all defence equipment), the focus was on lower-bound estimates. It was also recognised that disarmament since 1990 will have reduced the size of the annual EU equipment budget and that budget cuts will, in the short run, increase the intensity of competition resulting in a larger percentage competition effect than assumed in the study. For 1990, all four Single Market scenarios offered efficiency improvements ranging from almost £4 billion per annum to almost £8 billion per annum (1990 prices). The results are summarised in Table 7.6, where it can be seen that *scenario IV* offers the greatest annual savings. However, politically, and in the short run, *scenario IV* is the most difficult to achieve, so that *scenario III* becomes the second best option.

Table 7.6 The four scenarios

	£billion: annual savings
I Limited liberalisation	3.8–4.7
II Liberalisation	3.9–5.0
III Twin Track: model A	4.6–5.4
: model B	5.3–6.6
IV Centralised procurement	6.7–7.8

Notes
i. The range of estimates are lower bound estimates based on an EU market (lower figure) or a market open to the world (higher figure).
ii. Model A assumed a doubling of collaboration with work allocated on the basis of *juste retour*. Model B assumed collaborative work allocated on the basis of competition.
Source: EC (1995).

The four scenarios outlined in Table 7.6 can be viewed as options for the European Armaments Agency. Such an Agency might aim to create a Single European Market by pursuing the liberalisation options (*scenarios I* and *II*). Or, the Agency could pursue the twin-track approach, with the emphasis on promoting and managing collaborative projects. Or, such an Agency might eventually develop into a European procurement agency buying common and standardised equipment for a single European army, navy and air force (for example, a Federal EU). Whichever option is preferred, there will be continued economic pressures for EU nations to collaborate. For example, in 1996, the UK Government confirmed that 'cost-effective collaboration usually within Europe, is likely to be increasingly important in future' (HCP 209, 210, 1996: iii).

5. The Economics of Collaboration: The UK Experience

International collaboration involving two or more nations in the development and production of defence equipment provides opportunities for cost savings in both R&D and production. In the ideal case, costly development programmes are shared between two or more partner nations and a pooling of production orders enables economies of scale and learning to result in lower unit production costs and output levels which are more competitive with the USA. Table 7.7 shows a simple example of perfect collaboration. The upper part of the table shows two nations pursuing the independent development of similar aircraft, each purchasing 200 units; the lower half of the table shows the results of both nations collaborating equally on the development and production of one type of aircraft.

Table 7.7 Perfect collaboration

		Development cost (£ billions)		*Production cost*	
Independent Venture	*Number purchased*	*Total*	*Each nation*	*Total (£ billion)*	*Unit production cost (£ million)*
Nation A	200	10	10	2	10
Nation B	200	10	10	2	10
Collaboration (2 nations, A&B)	400	10	5	3.6	9
Collaborative savings	—	10	5	0.4	1

Table 7.8 shows some of the stylised facts, characteristics and performance indicators for UK collaborative defence equipment projects. Over the period 1985–1995, the *number* of collaborative projects involving the UK increased from 26 to 46. However, whilst the share of collaborative projects in UK defence equipment expenditure remained relatively constant at 15–16 per cent in the 1980s, between 1990 and 1995, the share declined to 12 per cent, representing a reduction of almost 40 per cent in UK real expenditure on collaborative ventures.

France and Germany have been involved in 50 per cent or more of UK collaborative programmes and the USA became more involved in these programmes on a bilateral and multilateral basis. Also, over the period 1985–95, the number of different European nations involved in UK collaborative ventures increased from eight to twelve. Aerospace equipment dominates UK collaborative projects (aircraft, helicopters and missiles), although its share in the total number declined from some 60 per cent in 1985 to 43 per cent in 1995. There were small increases in the share of both land and naval equipment in the total number of UK collaborative projects; but with naval equipment accounting for only 15 per cent of the total by 1995. Presumably, these share figures reflect the fact that compared with the costs of independence, European collaboration has not been sufficiently worthwhile for land and naval equipment.

The number and proportion of collaborative projects entering production or service are further performance indicators. Over the period 1985–95, some 40–50 per cent of UK collaborative ventures were in production or service. Usually, the attractiveness or otherwise of collaborative ventures becomes apparent during the study phase of the programme: hence, cancellations often occur at this stage in a project's life cycle.

Table 7.8 UK collaboration

	1985	*1990*	*1995*
Number of collaborative projects involving the UK	26	40	46
Number of UK collaborative projects with:			
i. Other European nations only	17	18	24
ii. USA and other European nations	8	13	12
iii. USA only	1	6	7
Number of UK collaborative projects involving:			
i. France only	5	6	8
ii. France and Germany	4	5	4
iii. France and/or Germany and other nations	4	9	19
Number of UK collaborative projects in:			
i. Production or service	12	17	22
ii. Development	14	23	9
iii. Study phase			15
Number and percentage of UK collaborative projects which are:			
i. Naval equipment	3 (11.5%)	5 (12.5%)	7 (15.2%)
ii. Land equipment	5 (19.2%)	8 (20.0%)	11 (23.9%)
iii. Air systems	8 (30.7%)	13 (32.5%)	15 (32.6%)
iv. Missiles	8 (30.7%)	6 (15.0%)	5 (10.9%)
v. Other equipment	2 (7.7%)	8 (20.0%)	8 (17.4%)

Table 7.8 Continued

Allocation of UK equipment expenditure between:			
i. Collaborative projects	15%	16%	12%
ii. UK industry	80%	75%	79%
iii. Imports	5%	9%	9%
Estimated UK expenditure on collaborative projects (£ millions, 1993–94 prices)	1918	1656	1033

Notes
i. 1995 figures are at end-1995; other data for March.
ii. Other equipment includes Midge Drone, satellite communications and identification systems.
iii. Data for UK equipment expenditures based on average of previous five years.
Sources: Cmnd 9430–2, (1985); Cmnd 1022–2, (1990); Cmnd 2800, (1995).

European collaboration has resulted in the creation of a number of international organisations, mostly in the aerospace industry and typically involving national champions from France, Germany, Italy, Spain and the UK. The major EU international companies could form the basis for the creation of a European aerospace industry and they provide a model for the extension of collaboration to land and sea systems. Examples of the major international organisations are shown in Table 7.9. A number of these organisations have associated international companies for aero-engines and avionics (for example, EJ 200 is the international company building the engine for EF2000).

Table 7.9 EU international companies

Joint company	*Project*	*Participants*	*Workshares* (%)
Panavia	Tornado (CA)	B.Ae (UK)	42.5
		DB/DASA (G)	42.5
		Alenia (It)	15
Eurofighter	EF2000 (CA)	B.Ae (UK)	33
		DB/DASA (G)	33
		Alenia (It)	21
		CASA (Sp)	13
Eurocopter	Tiger (AH)	Aerospatiale (F)	50
		DB/DASA (G)	50
EH Industries	EH 101 (MRH)	Agusta (It)	50
		Westland (UK)	50
NH 90	NH 90 (MRH)	Eurocopter (F, G)	67 (F = 43%)
		Agusta (It)	26
		Fokker (N)	7
Euroflag	FLA (TA)	Aerospatiale (F)	To be determined
		Alenia (It)	
		B.Ae (UK)	
		CASA (Sp)	
		DB/DASA (G)	

Table 7.9 Continued

Joint Company	*Project*	*Participants*	*Workshares (%)*
Euromissile	TRIGAT (ATM)	Aerospatiale (F)	33
		B.Ae (UK)	33
		DB/DASA (G)	33
AIRBUS	Civil jet airliners	Aerospatiale (F)	37.9
		B.Ae (UK)	20
		CASA (Sp)	4.2
		DB/DASA (G)	37.9
European Space Agency (ESA)	Civil space research and satellites	13 member states	Member states contribute to mandatory budgets based on national income

Notes
i. F = France; G = Germany; It = Italy; Sp = Spain; UK = United Kingdom.
ii. AH = attack helicopter; ATM = anti-tank missile; CA = combat aircraft; MRH = multi-role helicopter; TA = transport aircraft.
iii. B.Ae = British Aerospace; DB/DASA = Daimler Benz/Deutsche Aerospace.

International collaboration is not without its problems, all of which lead to departures from the 'ideal model'. The governments, military staff, scientists and industrialists in each partner nation form interest groups which will pursue their own self-interest concerned with leadership, design requirements, technology and work shares. Compromise is inevitable and nations will join the collaborative club and remain members so long as membership is expected to be worthwhile (compared with the alternatives of a national programme or imports). Within the collaborative club, nations will reach agreement about the project's military specifications, the delivery dates for each partner's armed forces, work shares and the arrangements for project management. Reaching agreement on such a complex international contract involves substantial transaction costs in specifying, negotiating, agreeing and monitoring where there are information asymmetries and opportunities for strategic behaviour. Typically, such contracts involve specific break or withdrawal points at which the partner nations can withdraw from the collaborative programme: these points are usually the feasibility and design study stages, full-scale development and full-scale production, each of which involves increasing resource commitments. Separate contracts are usually negotiated for development and production. For example, on Eurofighter 2000, development costs for the UK are estimated at £3.9 billion (33 per cent share) and production costs at £10.6 billion (1993–94 prices, with a UK production of 250 aircraft: HCP 724 1995).

The international agreement reflected in a collaborative programme specifies the broad terms under which trading takes place. Given the political, economic and technological uncertainties involved in two or more nations developing and purchasing advanced defence equipment over long-time horizons (ten or more years), the international contract for collaboration is necessarily incomplete but it will specify broad parameters concerned with payments for specific assets (technology and production) and governance structures for the transactions. Nations might be expected to learn from previous experience with collaboration, but such learning benefits might be reduced if new partners are added to the club. Nonetheless, one rule has dominated collaboration, namely, *juste retour*, where the emphasis is on a 'fair share' of the work between partner nations, which usually means work allocated on the basis of each nation's planned production orders (where planned production can change between the development and production phases of the programme). For example, on collaborative aircraft development work, *juste retour* means that each nation will demand its fair share of hi-tech work on the airframe, engine and avionics as well as demanding its own flight-testing centre. Similarly, with collaborative production work, each nation demands a final assembly line. Thus, work is allocated on the basis of equity and political bargaining rather than on the basis of efficiency criteria (competition and comparative advantage).

Nor are the partner governments models of efficient decision-making. Governments and their officials create elaborate and complex committee structures which seek consensus at every level and require unanimity for key decisions: some decisions can only be made by the most senior committees or by ministers. For example, on the EF2000 project there is a four-level hierarchy of committees (originally 39 committees were established), with a steering committee providing overall guidance and meetings attended by national officials and other interested parties (up to 60 people can be present at a meeting). Programme management is further complicated by the need for extensive monitoring arrangements as partner nations seek to 'police' costs and progress on incomplete contracts for costly and complex projects. An international agency is usually created for the day-to-day management of a collaborative programme (for example, NEFMA is the NATO EF2000 Management Agency). However, such agencies often lack a clear mandate; they might duplicate the work of national project management offices; and staff posts are filled by each nation in line with the cost sharing arrangements on the programme (HCP 724, 1995: 33). The result of the government programme arrangements is excessive bureaucracy and slow decision-making which can be a further source of delays and inefficiency in collaboration. Of course, politicians and officials might enjoy international travel, the glamour of meeting in foreign locations and the prestige of inter-governmental conferences.

A simple representation of the choice between efficiency criteria and *juste retour* in allocating work on collaborative programmes is shown in Table 7.10. Each of two nations in a collaborative programme has two strategies and the matrix shows the perceived pay-offs for the four strategy combinations (pay-offs reflect the government's beliefs about the benefits of a national DIB, including its contribution to strategic trade policy). As each nation pursues its self-interest, the pay-off pattern of the Prisoner's Dilemma leads both nations to choose the *juste retour* strategy.

Table 7.10 Work allocation

		Nation 2	
		Efficient allocation	*Juste retour*
Nation 1	*Efficient allocation*	10,10	7,12
	Juste retour	12,7	8,8

The arrangements for work sharing and government decision-making lead to departures from the ideal model of collaboration resulting in cost penalties and delays. On development work, the costs of collaboration are sometimes approximated by the square root rule: collaborative development costs can be estimated by the square root of the number of nations involved in the project (Sandler and Hartley 1995: 236). For example, with four nations, collaborative development actually costs twice as much as an equivalent national programme. On production work, the official UK view is that collaboration results in 'little savings' and there are indications that the unit production costs of a collaborative programme might be higher than a national equivalent: a view which suggests substantial inefficiencies (for example, up to a 10 per cent cost penalty: HCP 247, 1991). There is also a general belief that collaborative development programmes take longer to develop and deliver to the Armed Forces, with delays being approximated by the cube root of the number of partner nations involved. Some estimates suggest collaborative development might take an extra two years or over 50 per cent longer than a national project; but generally such claims are not supported by statistical tests (HCP 436, 1995; Hartley and Martin 1993).

The four-nation Eurofighter 2000 project illustrates the problems of collaborative programmes (see Table 7.9). Between 1988 when it started and 1995, the costs to the UK of the EF2000 development programme had risen by about 23 per cent (£662 million, 1993–94 prices) and the project was at least three years late (HCP 724, 1995). These cost increases and delays reflected the rigid work-sharing requirements and the political and financial uncertainties surrounding the programme, rather than any major technical difficulties (HCP, 724, 1995). The rigid work-sharing arrangements specified by the partner nations in the main development contracts '. . . and the requirement to provide a balanced spread of technology between the participating nations, have often resulted in industry placing work with specially-formed consortia with complex managerial and working structures and variable levels of technical expertise rather than on grounds of value for money'

(HCP 724, 1995: 25). In each of these specially-created consortia there are complex industrial interfaces to manage which place a premium on industry to establish suitable systems to coordinate the work of each company located in different nations. The Flight Control System (FCS) for the EF2000 is a classic example of all the worst features of collaborative work sharing and a major source of programme delays. One parliamentary view is that the industrial arrangements for the FCS had all the characteristics of an 'accident waiting to happen. Even though British companies, ... had demonstrated their competence to carry out the work, other companies became involved who were either not up to the job or whose involvement made arrangements unduly cumbersome' (HCP 222, 1994: xiv). GEC-Marconi has estimated that a solo bid for the work would have been a third cheaper than the consortium bid.

The EF2000 project has also been subject to considerable political and financial uncertainties. For example, these uncertainties delayed for more than one year the formal agreement by the partner nations on the 1992 re-orientation of the programme, with Germany being a major source of the uncertainty and delay. Further uncertainty arose in the mid-1990s as the partner nations reviewed their future budgetary positions, their likely orders and work-sharing requirements prior to a contractual commitment to production.

There are at least two lessons from the EF2000 programme. First, care is needed in identifying the criteria to be used in evaluating collaborative programmes. Perfect problem-free projects do not exist. Most hi-tech defence projects, whether they be national or collaborative, are characterised by problems reflecting 'poor' procurement management and ambitious technical requirements leading to cost overruns, delays and sometimes cancellation. Interestingly, though, whilst EF2000 is a third generation collaboration (after Jaguar and Tornado), it is characterised by the traditional problems of work sharing and government decision-making. Of course, it might be claimed that these problems and inefficiencies would be even greater without the benefits of previous collaborative experience.

Second, there remain considerable opportunities for improving the efficiency of collaborative programmes. Efficiency could be improved by applying the following three policy guidelines:

Rule 1 Allocate work on the basis of each nation's comparative advantage using competition to determine work shares.

Rule 2 Select a single prime contractor for the programme and ensure that the prime contractor is subject to contractual incentives placing it at risk (via competitively-determined fixed price or target price incentive contracts).

Rule 3 The principle of compensation. Adequate arrangements are needed to compensate the losers from policies designed to improve efficiency in collaborative programmes. Compensation need not be organised within the programme but could involve offsets on other defence projects or more general regional aid and manpower policies (for example, training and mobility).

6. The Costs of Change

Extending the Single European Market to defence procurement and proposals to improve the efficiency of collaborative projects are not costless. Some firms, industries and regions will lose from changes which open up national defence markets to competition and these changes will be additional to those already resulting from disarmament following the end of the Cold War. Market liberalisation is likely to favour large defence companies able to undertake the development of major projects and able to exploit economies of scale and scope as well as being able to survive in competitive markets. Vulnerable sectors include defence firms which have not been exposed to competition; firms in developing defence industries; and smaller companies, although some of these might survive through specialisation in niche markets.

Defence firms will respond to these market changes through reductions in capital and labour inputs, through seeking new military, civil and export markets, through national and international mergers and alliances and some firms will exit the market. The direct conversion of defence plants to civil production appears an attractive option (for example, tanks to tractors), but one which in practice is difficult and costly. New civil markets have to be identified; there are costs involved in retraining managers and the workforce and in re-equipping the plant; and there are the transaction costs of entering new civil markets. Furthermore, changing the firm's culture from one of dependency to enterprise takes time and involves further costs; and, after bearing all these costs of conversion and entry, questions arise as to whether the new civil markets are expected to be profitable (Hartley 1996; Sandler and Hartley 1995).

7. Conclusion

Disarmament and rising equipment costs will force EU states to re-appraise their traditional procurement policies. Proposals for extending the Single Market to defence procurement appear attractive and offer substantial savings in the long run. However, efforts to introduce competition into previously protected markets will encounter problems of creating a 'level playing field' since national procurement agencies can always justify any preferences for national suppliers on the grounds of military requirements. Moreover, if competition is restricted to EU firms, there are problems of monopoly, cartels and collusive tendering, especially for hi-tech equipment (for example, aerospace). In these circumstances, to maintain competition, it will be necessary to open up the EU defence market to firms from the rest of the world, with implications for the future of the European defence industrial base. Alternatively, major EU defence producer groups will lobby their governments to create 'Fortress Europe' to protect the European DIB, resulting in all the worst features of protectionism: managed or no competition, subsidies and inefficiencies.

Notes

1 This chapter is the result of research funded by the ESRC as part of its Single Market Programme (Grant no. L113251028).

8

EUROPEAN UNION REGULATIONS AND CORPORATE GOVERNANCE

Alistair Alcock

1. Introduction

The Anglo-Saxon system of corporate governance for large quoted companies is under a sustained attack, both populist and academic.[1] There are two basic criticisms made:

1 Public company directors are a self-perpetuating oligarchy, in practice answerable to no-one; and
2 They are socially and economically too powerful to be left to 'maximise profits' for their shareholders.

In respect of the first criticism, it was in 1932 that Berle and Means highlighted, in *The Modern Corporation and Private Property*,[2] the Anglo-Saxon phenomenon of public companies owned by dispersed passive shareholders leaving self-perpetuating directors controlling the business and answerable to no-one.[3] In the same year, Coase first delivered a lecture on the importance of 'the institutional structure of production' and the use of the firm to avoid market 'transaction costs'.[4]

From these two sources others, like Jensen and Meckling, have developed the argument that the separation of corporate ownership and control leads to conflicts of interest between the directors and shareholders which, even if they can be limited, involve 'agency costs'.[5] As Coase pointed out in his 1991 Nobel Lecture, 'if we move from a regime of zero transaction costs to one of positive transaction costs, what becomes immediately clear is the crucial importance of the legal system in this new world'.[6]

In dealing with this criticism, it must be admitted that the UK legal framework for corporate governance is weak. Even with concentration in the hands of institutions, shareholders' votes in a general meeting are not an effective method of control.[7] Individual shareholder actions through the courts, meanwhile, offer no threat while companies' articles grant all management power to the directors, who owe very limited duties of competence and are procedurally protected by the rule in *Foss v Harbottle*.[8]

Yet there seem to be few abuses by directors of major UK public companies, except perhaps for their own remuneration. That Robert Maxwells are not two a penny is due to one reason: publicity. Directors of major UK public companies live in a goldfish bowl of published information.[9] The Cadbury Committee has been unfairly maligned for sticking to its narrow brief of examining the financial aspects of corporate governance,[10] since the publication of clear and accurate financial information is central to the control of professional managers of quoted companies. Greater publicity may yet re-establish some control over directors' remuneration.[11]

It is on the second criticism that I wish to concentrate. Berle and Means actually thought that the separation of ownership and control of large corporations would lead to 'a purely neutral technocracy balancing a variety of claims by various groups in the community and assigning to each a portion of the income stream on the basis of public policy rather than private cupidity'.[12] With minor exceptions this has generally not happened in the UK, but should it?

2. Social Responsibility

Critics of large corporations reject the classical economists' view that corporate behaviour is no more than a reflection of the popular will, expressed not through the ballot box, but via individual purchase decisions. The imperfections of oligopolistic markets and information dissemination, the 'want-creation' of advertising, the discretion of 'delegated decisions' on technology, organisation of the work force, plant location, and executive prerogatives – all these allow large corporations discretionary decisions and thus power.

The critics reject both the public concession and private contract theories of the company as bases for justifying or opposing state intervention into corporate affairs respectively. They maintain that even if the system of corporate enterprises 'owned' by shareholders were the most efficient for the creation of wealth, the only justification for those shareholders' rights would be their consequences for the public good. To the extent that companies affect other interests – like those of employees, local communities and consumers – the state thus can and does interfere. However, the mechanism for such interference in the UK is to impose external limits on the freedom of companies through the civil and criminal law, but only to impose on company directors the duty of trying to maximise profits within that law.

The critics believe that the duty on directors and the internal structures of major companies should be altered to take account of these other interests beyond the point necessary to comply with external legal limits or to create favourable relations with these other interests in order to maximise profits. They believe in 'profit-sacrificing social responsibility', the 'stakeholder' theory of corporate governance. Directors should not be seeking to maximise profits for shareholders alone, but be considering the interests of other 'stakeholders' in the company, creditors, employees, the local community, the environment at large. To this end many look to Europe.

3. Europe

The European Commission's Paper, *Employee Participation and Company Structure in the European Community*, justifies employee participation as:

> the democratic imperative that those who will be substantially affected by decisions made by social and political institutions must be involved in the making of those decisions. In particular, employees are increasingly seen to have interests in the functioning of enterprises which can be as substantial as those of shareholders, and sometimes more so...[13]

This philosophy underpinned the initial draft of the 5th Directive on Company Law that attempted to impose a German codetermination and two-tier board structure on all major European public companies. The concept involved a supervisory board up to half of whose members were to be elected by European employees, although the majority of members were to remain elected by shareholders (or the state). The supervisory board's functions were to employ the management, control conflicts of interest with them, check their key decisions and supervise their overall performance.

Under intense pressure from, *inter alia*, the Conservative Government in the UK, the proposals were watered down so that the option was given to individual governments to accept or reject codetermination and two-tier boards for their companies. With the stuffing knocked out of it, progress on the 5th Directive ground to a halt. However, a change of government in the United Kingdom might resurrect the directive. Certainly some close to Tony Blair, like Will Hutton, favour the German model of corporate governance. If the 5th Directive was introduced, a future Labour government could, in theory, elect to impose the German model upon the United Kingdom under its terms.

Some critics of the UK system have, in any case, found the German experience of codetermination disappointing, in that worker representation on the supervisory boards of public companies does not seem to have affected the decisions of those boards to any significant extent.[14] Parkinson, for one, flirts with the idea of developing worker cooperatives, although he admits that there is little chance of major European public companies converting to this form of ownership in the near future. There is such a movement encouraged by tax breaks in the US.

However, there are some powerful arguments against the whole stakeholder view of corporate governance and the associated, but not necessarily consistent belief in employee participation.

4. Economic Developments

My first criticism of the critics is that large public companies no longer resemble the picture painted by the critics of all powerful colossus bestriding the world. They have probably never had so little room for manoeuvre. Global competition has broken down domestic oligopolies. Take, for example, the European car market. In the 1960s and early 1970s, most major countries' car markets were dominated by one or two local manufacturers, the UK with British Leyland, France with Renault and Citroën, Germany with Volkswagen and Mercedes, Italy with Fiat. All that is changing and, in the UK, has already changed beyond recognition. No manufacturer has more than about 20 per cent of the UK market.

At the same time, Coase's examination of why companies exist, and what benefits the firm brings by comparison with market transactions, has been applied by businesses in examining what activities do not need to be conducted by the firm and can in fact be contracted out (that is to say, returned to the market).

Far from major industrial companies controlling more and more of the developed world's work force, the work force of these companies is shrinking rapidly. I see no reason why the work force employed in industry in Europe and the United States should not shrink well below 10 per cent early in the next century. Look at what has happened to the percentage of the work force employed on the land in the last 50 years, and there is certainly no shortage of food now being produced in the United States or Europe. Why are these changes happening?

It is not just a matter of GATT treaties and world markets opening up. It is also a function of the growing sophistication of capital markets and technology, particularly information technology. The changes are not confined to traditional manufacturing industry. Take the airlines. No longer are the major players safe. Panam is no more and the fastest-growing airline in the United States recently has been South West, which did not exist a few years ago. Why? Because some managers realised that a modern airline is not about owning routes (which are being opened up) or even aircraft (they can be leased). It is about ticketing, marketing and the provision of a lean, efficient service. What has happened to the airlines is even beginning to happen to the heart of the process, the information technology industry itself.[15]

Amidst this whirlwind of change, not even a 'Fortress Europe' policy is going to allow large UK public companies much room for manoeuvre, since the challenges come just as much from new businesses within Europe as from major established competitors without. Nevertheless, even if I have greater faith in the market's ability (at least over time) to correct its own failings and a more limited faith in the state's ability to do so than the critics, I do accept their basic belief that the state has a residual right to intervene in the exercise of private power, whether in contracting in the marketplace or through institutional structures like public companies. But do the critics' proposals assist in controlling corporate power?

5. Governance Chaos

My second criticism of the critics is that their main proposal for taming corporate power by increasing the influence of employees might only produce bad governance for public companies. To explain this, I need to go back to the question, why has the market itself not developed worker-controlled firms?

Hansmann has pointed out in his article 'Ownership of the Firm'[16] that, although pure worker-controlled firms are rare, they do exist in America in certain service industries (like taxicabs and rubbish collection) and control by senior employees exists around the world in service professions (such as law, accounting, investment banking, stockbroking and management consulting) through the form of partnerships. Indeed, many of these partnerships extend the other attribute of 'ownership', the distribution of surpluses, across the firm through firm wide bonus schemes.[17]

Hansmann notes that all these organisations have at least two out of three attributes, namely: (1) a low requirement for risk capital; (2) a homogeneity of jobs and skills among the owners; and (3) an easily measurable productivity for each owner. He comments that 'it is, in fact, extremely difficult to find successful examples of worker-owned firms in which there is substantial hierarchy or division of labor among the worker-owners'.[18]

Ironically, the tendency of public companies and public sector bodies to contract out any support services they require opens up wider opportunities for this sort of worker involvement in the competing small service organisations thereby created. It does not, of course, tackle the position of the streamlined public companies (and, indeed, public sector organisations).

The problem for complex organisations is that there is no homogeneous employee interest. Management decisions on reducing capital employed in one area by slimming or closing down operations and raising it in other areas with new investment is inherently likely to set one group of employees against another. Furthermore, no organisation can have its strategic decisions held hostage by internal sectional interest groups.[19] Whatever the European Commission believes, democracy is not necessarily an answer to all problems.

The German example is difficult to interpret. To what extent has co-determination been a cause or an effect of social solidarity to reestablish their economy after the Second World War? It certainly seems that it has had little noticeable effect on management decisions in public companies (for example, the employees' representatives seem to have been 'captured' by management[20]).

One effect may have been to discourage privately owned and controlled German companies from 'going public' (and thus be fully subject to co-determination) in the first place. Ironically, it is these privately owned, tightly controlled companies that have been the foundation of the great German economic success story, rather than the co-determinist public ones.

Another effect may have been to discourage overseas diversification, at least until recently. However, if co-determination was introduced into the largest UK public companies now, this might increase the pressure to invest overseas, since, in the largest manufacturing companies at least, the majority of employees are probably outside the UK. I presume, of course, that whatever the 5th Directive may require, the critics do not intend to discriminate against non-European employees.

It must also be noted that the German and Japanese models have been supported and to some extent disciplined by a highly protected and cartelised banking system, which in both countries is breaking down under competitive pressures. The open UK economy could not possibly hope to create such a system now.

Returning, however, to the apparent 'management capture' of the minority employee representatives on German supervisory boards – this is not entirely surprising. Those representatives become part of a structure, the very *raison d'être* of which is not to allow conflicting interests to be balanced (what might be termed the 'John Major school of management') but to make strategic decisions despite the conflicts (the 'Thatcher' school). The prospect of companies being led by boards where a form of governance is adopted so that such interests battle it out in the board room is likely, in Hansmann's view, to be a recipe for disaster.

Hansmann's point that homogeneity of interest across owners lessens decision costs, and that this may be one reason as to why the vast majority of firms are owned by shareholders rather than workers, has received indirect support recently from Drucker in his book *Post Capitalist Society*.[21] Drucker describes the modern world as a 'Society of Organisations':

> Organisations are special-purpose institutions. They are effective because they concentrate on *one* task. If you go to the American Lung Association and say: 'Ninety per cent of all adult Americans ... suffer from ingrown toenails; we need your expertise in research, health education, and prevention to stamp out this dreadful scourge,' you'd get the answer: 'We are interested only in what lies

> between the hips and the shoulders'... Only a clear, focused and common mission can hold the organization together and enable it to produce results.[22]

The public quoted company is the quintessential late-20th century organisation. Just as President Clinton has pinned up a notice in the Oval Office to remind him that 'It's the Economy' that matters, the legal system and the structures of corporate governance need to remind directors (albeit gently) that 'It's the Bottom Line' – that is, shareholders' interest – that counts. This brings me to my third criticism of the critics.

6. Social Irresponsibility

Ironically, to allow directors to take into consideration the competing interests of all the stakeholders, the law would have to give directors of public companies a wider discretion than they have at present (even in Germany). How would it be used? To the extent that directors already divert resources to social projects in the UK, the answer would appear to be – rather randomly. Some studies suggest that the prime consideration is the pet interest of the chairman (or perhaps his spouse). Even if it became a recognised duty of the board and more organised, American critics of the social responsibility movement like Levitt have pointed out:

> What we have, then, is the frightening spectacle of a powerful economic functional group (for example, management) whose future and perception are shaped in a tight materialistic context of money and things but which imposes its narrow ideas about a broad spectrum of unrelated non-economic subjects on the mass of man and society...[23]
>
> (Levitt 1970)

If you doubt this, consider the baleful influence of business' involvement in education in this country.

It is to counteract this tendency that the critics of UK corporate governance seek to strengthen the influence of employees, even to the extent of worker-controlled firms. However, in the current economic climate, giving employees of large public companies partial or total control over those companies could just strengthen management's social irresponsibility.

Supporters of worker-controlled firms accept that one of the abiding arguments against such firms is that, if they require any substantial degree of capital and it is supplied by the workers, those workers are hopelessly tied, economically speaking, to the fortunes of the firm. They, unlike arms-length investors, cannot diversify their risk by taking on a portfolio of jobs with different employers. Parkinson, for one, proposes separating the two key elements of 'ownership', residual control and residual earnings.

Parkinson, I believe, consistently underrates the necessity for, and vulnerability of, risk capital. The American economy was nearly brought to its knees in the late 1980s by a fatal combination of substituting debt for equity (through take-overs financed by junk bonds) and governmental profligacy forcing up interest rates and dampening down economic demand. The costs of corporate failure were borne, not just by the new junk bondholders, but by existing longstanding bondholders who found the contractual protections contained in the original terms of their bonds did not prevent the erosion of the equity base of the companies in which they were invested (that is to say capital maintenance provisions were easily circumvented).[24]

Investment theorists, like Modigliani and Miller,[25] argue that the debt-equity ratios of companies do not matter since they are merely allocating the risks/returns of the underlying projects of the company. However, such arguments have to assume that corporate distress, let alone bankruptcy, is costless. It is not. Although those costs do not affect the fixed assets of a company that can merely be redeployed, they do affect the human capital. In particular, management, from its own self-interest and from emotional ties to the firm and its employees, is likely to be bankruptcy-risk averse. The management of a highly geared company is likely to reject high risk projects, and if most companies in an economy lack risk capital, the whole economy could become risk averse, unless supported by a cartelised and protected banking system as in Germany and until the recent meltdown, Japan.

Modigliani and Miller would presumably take the view that this is illogical because the project risks have not changed, however the potential returns are allocated between investors, and therefore any equity cushion needed could be obtained by adjusting the terms of the debt instruments issued. However, as I have already pointed out, the protection of debt instruments depends upon pre-arranged contractual terms which are no substitute for the flexibility of equity's open-ended commitment in return for voting protection (even if that protection is mainly a defensive one of depriving others of the ultimate right of control).

Attacking voting protection for risk capital in the present economic climate runs particular dangers. Drucker highlights the threat to social cohesion presented by recent economic developments. He sees the rise of what he terms the 'knowledge worker', the worker with the skills particularly required to exploit the new productive technologies, as not tied to particular fixed assets, but free to sell his skills at a very high price in a global marketplace. Others are relegated to being 'service workers', at least in the United States, but in Europe they may just become permanently unemployed. It is critical, in his view, that the productivity of those service workers improves if post-capitalist society is not to fall apart.

In the meantime, as large public companies contract-out non-core activities, these knowledge workers are likely to become key players in the productivity gains to be made by the streamlined public companies. Changes in corporate governance which might reinforce their economic power in such organisations could lead to an unholy alliance of interests between the management and their knowledge workers. The area that the present corporate governance structure has most difficulty controlling is management remuneration. This problem is already extending to the control of the remuneration of other key employees in the financial services industry. It must be remembered that the diversion of returns from the equity holders is nowadays a reduction of the returns to the pension funds (that is to say, the deferred remuneration) of the bulk of other employees, for example, the service workers.[26]

Indeed, proponents of worker-controlled firms believe all employees are, in some sense, exploited contracting parties. But in Europe, employees, at least of large well-financed companies, have become one of the most privileged contracting groups in society. Nevertheless, as contracting out continues, most service workers are going to find themselves working for small organisations that have to negotiate ordinary trade creditor type contracts with these major public companies. This will only serve to highlight how heterogeneous employees' interests are. What special stakeholders' rights have the employees within the organisation, as against outsiders, to justify strengthening their position?

Employees are, after all, only a 'private' group liable to act self-interestedly, and their representatives would be no more accountable to society as a whole than are managers owing responsibilities exclusively to shareholders. The critics' belief that employees are more likely to be interested in the economic well-being of the local community and the local physical environment is just not borne out by experience. Which local community? A BMW workers' representative may have very different views from a Rover's representative. Also it is Brazilians who wish to cut down the rain forest to advance their economic well-being; it is Arthur Scargill who wants power stations to continue to pollute the atmosphere by burning coal.

This is not to say that employee participation will not grow, even in major public companies. Hierarchical command structures are already being replaced by flatter, participative management arrangements. Formal representation on works committees or public company boards is irrelevant to this process, which requires much more flexible two-way communication. I can see that formal worker representative arrangements might feel circumvented and threatened by these new developments and resist such changes. It would be ironic if the Anglo-Saxon governance model, condemned for so long as old-fashioned and out-of-date, in the end proves more adaptable than more academically respectable and apparently 'socially responsible' systems.

7. Conclusion

Arguments for social responsibility and the representation of all 'stakeholders' in an enterprise sound attractive, but at their heart lies a terrible dilemma that even the critics cannot escape. To allow directors to take into consideration all stakeholders' interests, the scope of directorial discretion (and therefore the range of justifications directors can offer for any particular course of action) has to be widened. To counteract this increase in directors' power, structural checks and balances need to be incorporated; but the only stakeholders whom it is easy to incorporate are employees. State appointees do not have a happy track record, and others, like suppliers and customers, can hardly be incorporated for fear of creating multiple restrictive practices.

With public companies contracting out all but key activities, however, what special rights do their remaining employees have over other contracting (and non-contracting) interests? They are merely a heterogeneous private interest group, sufficient of whom may form an alliance with the directors against any other interests, so that the directors' increased power may be exploited to the eventual cost of all concerned when the day of market retribution comes – as come it will – in an open global economy.

Notes

1 Hutton (1995); Parkinson (1993).
2 Berle and Means (1937).
3 That this structure of ownership is largely confined to the Anglo-Saxon world is discussed by E. Wymeersch (1993).
4 R.H. Coase (1991).
5 M.C. Jensen and M. Meckling (1976), where agency costs are described as comprising three elements: 'The *principal* can limit divergences from his interest by establishing appropriate incentives for the agent and by incurring monitoring costs designed to limit aberrant activities of the agent. In addition in some situations it will pay the *agent* to expend resources (bonding costs) to guarantee that he will not take certain actions which would harm the principal ... in addition there will be some divergence between the agent's decisions and those decisions which would maximize the welfare of the principal ... we refer to this latter cost as the "residual loss".'
6 O.E. Williamson and S.G. Winter (eds) (1993).
7 Parkinson assumes, as do other commentators, that institutions managing pension fund portfolios actually have the power to decide how the shares they hold shall vote. Traditionally, management contracts with pension fund trustees specifically prevent the manager from voting to avoid all the complications of declaring shareholdings under Companies Act 1985, Part VI, particularly following the introduction of 'concert party' rules, now Companies Act 1985, ss 204 to 206.
8 (1843) 2 Hare 461, as elaborated upon in *Edwards v Halliwell* (1950) 2 All ER 1064, 1066, severely restricts the right of any shareholder to start an action against directors or others for harm that they have done to the company (and thus, indirectly, the shareholder).
9 This includes not just the report and accounts and share and other disclosures required by Companies Act 1985, Parts VI, VII and X, but all the additional information required by The Stock Exchange's Listing Rules (aka the 'Yellow Book') and the Take-over Code.
10 *Report of the Committee on the Financial Aspects of Corporate Governance* (London: Gee, 1992) (aka the 'Cadbury Report').

11 The Greenbury Committee set up by the CBI, has recommended full disclosure of remuneration packages as has become the norm in the United States, although the method of calculating accruing pension benefits remains a controversial issue.
12 A.A. Berle and G.C. Means (1967).
13 Commission of the European Communities (1975).
14 E. Batstone and P.L. Davies (eds) (1976).
15 The fates of IBM and Apple.
16 H. Hansmann (1988).
17 This was the arrangement in the London stockbroking firm for which I worked until 'Big Bang' and the changes in ownership and working practices introduced to the stock market in 1986.
18 Hansmann (1988: 296).
19 Classic examples being consultants in NHS hospitals and prison officers in HM prisons.
20 Batstone and Davies (eds) (1976).
21 P.F. Drucker (1993).
22 Drucker (1993: 53).
23 T. Levitt (1970).
24 I do accept the arguments that the gearing created by buy-outs can, and in many cases did, increase economic efficiency, see O.E. Williamson (1988), but, as with many market movements, it developed a life of its own, outstripping its own basic economic rationale.
25 F. Modigliani and M.H. Miller (1958).
26 Pension funds and insurance companies hold about half of all UK listed shares and account for about one third of the UK personal sector's net wealth, *CSO Social Trends 25: 1995 Edition*. Generally the trustees and managers of pension funds owe a fiduciary duty to their members to maximise the return to the fund, subject to not accepting an undue level of risk, *Cowan v Scargill* (1985) Ch 270. Parkinson's proposals amount to a direct or indirect relaxation of that fiduciary duty that might not seem such an attractive proposition after the Maxwell affair.

9

SUPPLIER RELATIONS IN THE MULTINATIONAL AUTOMOTIVE INDUSTRY

Mari Sako, Richard Lamming and Susan R. Helper

This chapter reports on extensive field research conducted in the worldwide automobile industry, on the subject of developing close relationships between vehicle manufacturers and their component suppliers. A postal survey was conducted in Europe, Japan and the US in 1993 and 1994, receiving detailed responses from over 1400 suppliers.[1] Using a simple definition for supply partnerships, the chapter concludes that suppliers in some regions are observing improved collaborative attitudes on the part of their customers but that the expected benefits from such strategies have yet to be realised. Some reasons are suggested for this. The chapter focuses especially on the UK industry, in comparison with other regions.

This is a turbulent time for the UK automotive industry. Traditionally, vehicle manufacturers have relied on the pressure of head-to-head competition to obtain low prices from their suppliers. Over a very long period, this has created a norm of 'arm's-length' relationships between customer and supplier, which typically degenerated into adversarial mistrust of each other. More recently, however, it appears that European vehicle manufacturers have been asking their suppliers to work in close collaboration in order to speed up the rate of improving their performance to meet global competition (Lamming 1993).

Despite performance advantages of partnerships in supply which have been demonstrated in other parts of the world,[2] mutual suspicion is said to be hindering their formation in the UK automotive industry. A recent report (SMMT and DTI 1994) on relationships between vehicle manufacturers and their components suppliers in the UK, concluded that the national industry was plagued by poor communications, a general lack of trust between individuals and between companies, and a resultant loss of opportunity for generating mutual benefits through collaboration – so called supply partnerships. Components suppliers, it was observed, clearly did not believe that their customers took sufficient care in managing their supply chain relationships, while the responses of the vehicle manufacturers showed clearly that there was a preoccupation with optimising individual supply base structures, without consideration for the general development of the industry. It concluded: 'suppliers are still wary of their customers' rhetoric, while the vehicle manufacturers speak privately and publicly of dissatisfaction with their component suppliers' performance'. These conclusions had to be viewed in the European context – some would argue that it makes no sense to speak of a national industry. The prosperity and development of companies operating in the UK is, however, of great importance to the nation and thus research revealing a significant problem in this industry must be taken seriously.[3]

Suppliers might be reluctant to commit to investment with a long payback period if they believe that the customer's commitment would last only until the next round of rationalising its supplier base. Suppliers may also suspect that vehicle manufacturers are asking them to share sensitive information, including cost breakdowns, for the sole purpose of cutting prices. When mistrust is entrenched, a shift from adversarial to more cooperative relations is evidently not easy (Briggs 1995).

How much has really changed in the nature of supplier relations in the UK automotive industry? How do the trends in the UK compare with those in the rest of Europe, Japan and the US? What types of relationship are likely to lead to good performance by *both* suppliers and customers? Do suppliers in close partnerships with vehicle manufacturers perform better in all respects than those without such relationships? What is the effect on suppliers of trading with Japanese vehicle manufacturers in the UK?

1. Partnership in Supplier Relations: A Definition

Traditional studies of purchasing have emphasised the distinction between 'make' and 'buy'. However, in order to analyse different options within the buy alternative, another framework is necessary. Research papers and theories on this are plentiful and can be traced to well known works such as Coase (1937), Williamson (1975) and more recently, Landeros and Monczka (1989), Ring and Van de Ven (1992), Macbeth (1994), Macbeth and Ferguson (1994), Ellram and Krause (1994) and Dale and Burns (1995). Attempts have frequently been made to define partnership, and also to refute definitions (Cousins 1994). Partnership in supply has been described as a step on the way to a further development and as a doubtful 'fad' (Kearney 1994). Other terms have been developed such as 'voice' in contrast to 'exit' (Hirschman 1970) and obligational contracting relations in contrast to arm's-length contracting relations (Sako 1992).

Here, we employ a contrast between the extremes of 'partnership' and 'arm's-length relationship' ('partnership' and 'non-partnership'). Expressed simply, in a partnership, customer and supplier commit to continuous improvement and shared benefits, by exchanging relevant information openly and by resolving problems by working together rather than by finding a new trading partner (SMMT 1994).

In principle, a partnership should be more efficient, since a rich flow of information between the parties makes possible effective use of techniques such as value analysis and value engineering. This should result in decreasing costs, as the benefits of learning are shared and improved confidence leads to higher levels of investment. Better development solutions are also likely to be found through involving suppliers at an early stage in new projects (Lamming 1993; Clark 1989).

However, a customer company which wants to establish a partnership with its suppliers must make a commitment to them. The level of this commitment is reflected in the supplier's degree of certainty that the customer will continue to buy its products for some length of time. This assurance can be provided by any mechanism that makes it harder for the customer to switch to alternative suppliers, most typically by retaining suppliers' trust (Sako 1992). Commitment is necessary both to obtain suggestions for improvement (which may be based on proprietary information) and to make investments that respond to these suggestions.

The debate in the literature and the observation of implementation projects in practice indicate that partnership in supply is a complex concept. To measure development of partnerships over time in research, it is necessary to provide a pragmatic, working definition. For the purposes of this survey, it was specified that a partnership in supply exists when:

- the supplier provides the customer with details of its manufacturing (and other) process steps;
- the supplier believes that there is a high probability that it will continue to provide products to the customer for more than three years;
- if another supplier offers a lower price for a product, the supplier expects the customer to help it to make necessary process improvements to match the competitor's expertise, rather than automatically re-source the business, or engage in arbitrary bargaining.

This framework is used in this chapter to investigate the trends in adopting these partnerships and the types of relationship that are associated with good supply performance. We focus on similarities and differences in supplier relations and performance in the four regions, namely the UK, the rest of Europe, Japan and the US. Responses are classified according to their location, not by the nationality of ownership. However, in order to gauge the impact of Japanese transplants in the UK, those suppliers which answered the survey with respect to a Japanese customer are shown as a subcategory of the UK sample (labelled Jap/UK) in some of the figures.

2. Survey Methodology

In order to address the questions posed above, international postal surveys of first-tier[4] component suppliers were conducted in 1993 and 1994.[5] The respondents were asked about their situation now (at the time of the survey) and four years ago (around 1989/1990). The surveys yielded an unusually comprehensive database with a total of 1409 responses. In the US, 675 responses were received from independent US-owned firms, Japanese transplants and vertically integrated divisions of US vehicle manufacturers, representing a response rate of 55 per cent. In Japan, 472 responses were received from independent Japanese-owned firms, vertically-integrated divisions of Japanese vehicle manufacturers and a few foreign-owned companies, representing a response rate of 30 per cent. In Europe, 262 completed questionnaires were received – a response rate of 16 per cent. The 116 UK-based responses (constituting a UK response rate of 25 per cent) are shown separately in this chapter for the purpose of comparison with the rest of Europe, the US and Japan.

In spring 1993, the North American survey was mailed to every automotive supplier and vehicle manufacturer component division named in the *Elm Guide to Automotive Sourcing*.[6] This guide lists the major first-tier suppliers (both domestic and foreign-owned) to manufacturers of cars and light trucks in the US and Canada.

The target respondent was the divisional director of marketing at independent firms, and the divisional business manager or director of strategic planning at vehicle manufacturer components divisions. These individuals were selected on the grounds that they would have the broadest knowledge about both customer relationships and about their firms' products and processes. The respondents had a wealth of experience: they averaged more than 18 years in the auto industry and more than 11 years with their company.

In Japan, the survey (in Japanese) was sent out in July 1993 to all members of the Japan Auto Parts Industries Association (JAPIA), all automotive suppliers named in *Nihon no Jidosha Buhin Kogyo 1992/1993* (Japanese Automotive Parts Industry) (published by Auto Trade Journal Co. Inc. and JAPIA, Tokyo, 1992), and vehicle manufacturers' component divisions. This publication lists all the first-tier suppliers (both domestic and foreign-owned) to the 11 assemblers of cars and trucks in Japan. In order to maintain consistency with the US sample, respondents were asked not to respond with respect to heavy trucks and buses.

The target respondent in Japan was the director of sales and marketing at independent firms. For member companies of JAPIA, the survey was sent to the main contacts named by JAPIA, many of whom were either chief executives or marketing directors. JAMA (Japan Auto Manufacturers Association) took responsibility for identifying the respondents for vehicle manufacturer components divisions. The Japanese respondents were generally well experienced; they had worked on average 22 years at their company.

In spring 1994, the European survey was sent out to around 1600 major automotive suppliers located in western Europe. This sample was compiled from several sources including trade associations and the major vehicle manufacturers in Europe. The target respondent was the director of sales and marketing at each firm. These individuals were selected on the grounds that they would have the broadest knowledge about both customer relationships and about their firms' products and processes. The respondents had a wealth of experience: they averaged 16 years in the automotive industry and eight years with their company.

Because many companies supply their customers with several different types of product, and their relationships with their customers differ by product, respondents in Europe, North America and Japan were asked to answer the survey for their *most important or significant* customer regarding one product which was typical of their company's output. Many of the questions asked respondents to compare their current situation (at the time of the survey) with that four years ago.

The responses were far above the norm for business surveys. The response rates were 55 per cent in North America, 30 per cent in Japan (45 per cent among JAPIA members) and 16 per cent in Europe (25 per cent among UK-based suppliers), after taking into account those firms which were unreachable (mail sent to them was returned undelivered), and those which were not eligible to answer the survey (they were not first-tier automotive suppliers, or they specialised in supplying for heavy trucks and buses). In Europe, 44 per cent of responses were from UK-based suppliers, 24 per cent from Germany, 9 per cent from France and 10 per cent from Italy.

3. Limited Convergence in Supplier Relations Practices

Suppliers sharing process information

In order to discover how widely the practice of partnership sourcing has spread from the suppliers' viewpoint, we examined the extent of change in each of the three dimensions given above.

Figure 9.1 shows that in the last four years, an increasing proportion of suppliers in the UK have come to provide their customers with a detailed breakdown of the steps they use in their production process. If used properly, this information should help vehicle manufacturers ensure that their component designs are compatible with suppliers' processes, thus improving productivity and quality. The proportion of UK suppliers providing their

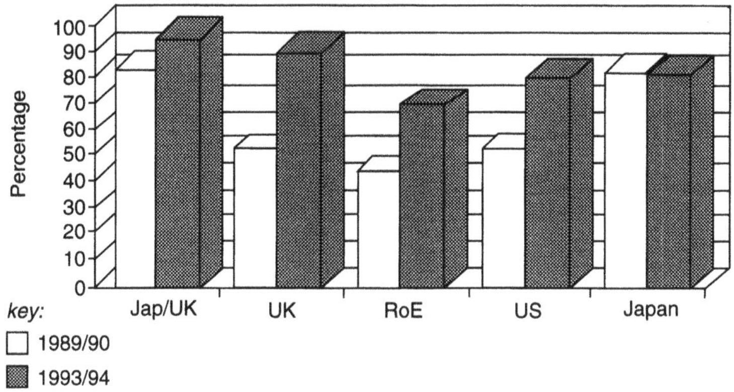

Figure 9.1 Percentage of suppliers providing customers with detailed breakdown of process steps

customers with such information has nearly doubled, from an average of 51 per cent in 1990 to 90 per cent in 1994, a much faster increase than that in the rest of Europe (from 42 to 68 per cent). Among the UK suppliers, all except one of those that supply the Japanese customers were providing such information by 1994. The practice of information disclosure has also spread in the US, from an average of 50 per cent in 1989 to 80 per cent in 1993. In Japan the level was already high, at around 80 per cent but has not increased since 1989.

Customer commitment

A measure of the customer's approach to partnership relationships is provided by the length of contracts given to suppliers. Some progress appears to have been made in terms of this form of customer commitment. In the UK, average contract lengths have increased from one year in 1990 to three years in 1994. Similarly in the US, median contract lengths have increased from one year in 1989 to one and a half years in 1993. (However, the increase in the average conceals a sharp decrease in contract lengths reported by suppliers to one particular vehicle manufacturer in the US.)

In Japan, two-thirds of the supply described by the respondents in both 1989 and 1993 was covered by the practice of having no product-specific contracts. Where they do exist, the implicit contracts in Japan tend to be longer than a basic contract which is renewed annually. It is not sufficient, therefore, to use contract lengths alone as a true reflection of differences in customer commitment in Europe, the US and Japan.

An alternative measure of customer commitment is the duration over which the supplier believes there is a high probability that it will continue supplying to the same customer. As shown in Figure 9.2, the median level

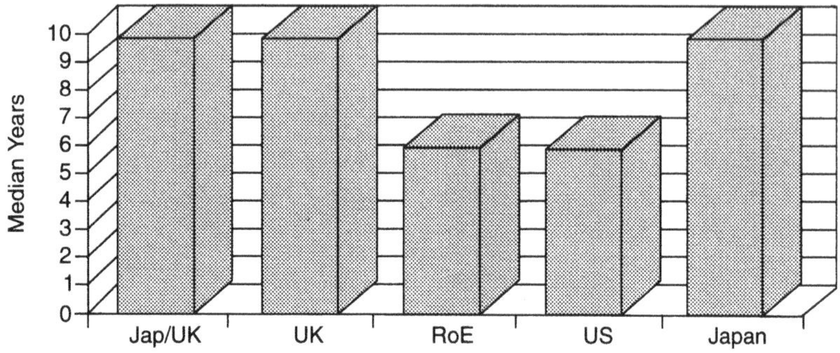

Figure 9.2 Gap in perceived customer commitment 1993/4

of commitment was ten years for the UK and Japan, six years in the US and seven years in the rest of Europe. The length of commitment by Japanese customers in the UK, as perceived by UK suppliers, was also ten years on average.

Solving problems with customers

The third indicator of partnership is an orientation towards joint problem solving. Suppliers were asked how the customer would react if a competitor offered a lower price for a product of equal quality. An increasing proportion of UK suppliers (from an average of 39 per cent in 1990 to 80 per cent in 1994) said their customers would help them to match a competitor's effort (see Figure 9.3). The expectation of such a partnership-style reaction was particularly high (65 per cent in 1990 rising to 86 per cent in 1994) among those UK suppliers supplying the Japanese car manufacturers in the UK.

Figure 9.3 Europe and the US move towards partnership

In the US and the rest of Europe, the move towards partnership according to this measure was not as dramatic, from an average of 34 per cent in 1989 to 53 per cent in 1993 in the US, and from 33 per cent in 1990 to 53 per cent in 1994 in the rest of Europe.

The European and the US move towards a partnership-type reaction is in contrast to a slight shift away from partnership in Japan. Japanese suppliers which expected their customers to offer help, declined from 45 to 40 per cent, while those which expected them to switch to the competitor 'as soon as is technically feasible' or 'at the end of the current model' *rose* from 40 to 49 per cent between 1989 and 1993. By contrast in the UK, those who expected their customers to switch to the competitor 'as soon as is technically feasible' or 'at the end of the current contract' fell from 40 to 37 per cent between 1990 and 1994. Moreover, in the UK, only 16 per cent in 1994, as compared to 30 per cent in 1990, expected their customers to switch to the competitor as soon as it was technically feasible (see Figure 9.4). Thus UK suppliers appeared least likely to experience customer behaviour which is detrimental to building partnerships in this situation, when compared to suppliers in the rest of Europe, Japan and the US.

To summarise, an increasing proportion of suppliers in the UK, the rest of Europe and the US have provided their customers with a detailed breakdown of process steps, so that the gap between the US and Europe on the one hand and Japan on the other in this respect has been more or less eliminated. At the same time, customer commitment, measured by suppliers' future projections, is higher in Japan and in the UK than in the US or the rest of Europe. With respect to the orientation towards joint problem-solving, suppliers' expectations of partnership-style response have increased in the UK, the US and Europe but declined slightly in Japan.

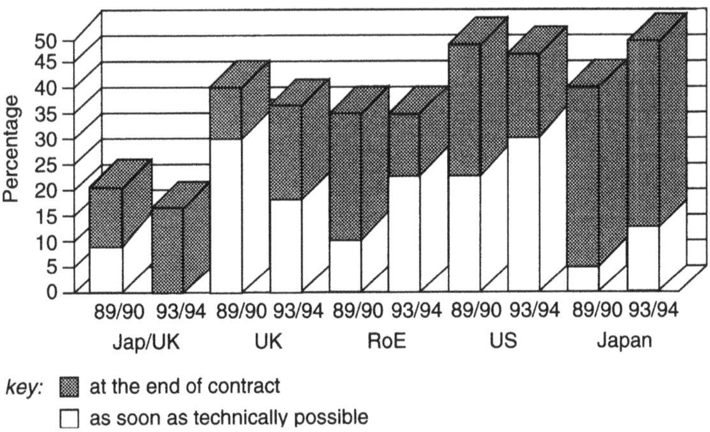

Figure 9.4 Japan moves towards non-partnership

Suppliers trading with Japanese car manufacturers in the UK – constituting 19 per cent of the UK sample – are clearly in the lead in establishing partnerships along all the three dimensions. Thus, there has been a limited, yet noticeable, convergence in the nature of supplier-customer links in all the regions.

4. Supply Partnerships and Automotive Industry Performance

What difference does partnership make to performance? The survey enables the examination of four indicators of performance:

- in overall supply performance, as indicated by success in winning 'supplier awards' (for example, for total quality, etc.);
- in production and logistics, as measured by reductions in production and delivery batch sizes;
- in financial performance, as measured by control of costs and profit margins;
- in technology management, as measured by suppliers' involvement in new product development.

Overall supply performance: Winning customer's awards for excellence

There may be several reasons for customers to give awards to their suppliers, but the rate at which certain types of suppliers win such accolades may be taken as a measure of overall supply performance.

US firms with partnership relationships do better than those without: they receive 28 per cent more awards for excellent performance from the vehicle manufacturers and their market-share growth for the product line as a whole is 1.5 percentage points greater.

Japanese firms with such relationships also perform much better than those without. A supplier with a partnership relationship receives on average 18 per cent more awards from the vehicle manufacturers. No market-share growth advantage was evident for partnership suppliers in Japan.

UK suppliers who have embraced partnership also did slightly better, receiving 14 per cent more awards from the vehicle manufacturers than their non-partnership competitors. However, the performance advantage of partnership suppliers over non-partnership suppliers is not so marked as in the US or Japan, nor was there an advantage in market share growth for partnership suppliers in the UK and the rest of Europe. In the rest of Europe, also, partnership suppliers did not receive significantly more awards than non-partnership suppliers.

Performance in production and logistics: Moving towards true just-in-time operation

If they are to improve logistics performance for the supplier, partnerships should help to narrow the gap between just-in-time (JIT) delivery and JIT production. To assess this, the survey measured the gap between production batch size and delivery batch size, as an indication of an approach to achieving true JIT. Responses indicate that US partnership suppliers are 10 per cent more likely than non-partnership suppliers to adopt JIT delivery without a cost increase, while Japanese partnership suppliers are 50 per cent more likely to benefit in this way. In Europe and the UK, these benefits do not seem to be so clearly in evidence.

In Europe, excluding the UK, median batch sizes for both production and delivery have become smaller between 1990 and 1994. By 1994, partnership suppliers were both delivering and producing in smaller batches than non-partnership suppliers (see Figure 9.5). During the period 1990–1994, the

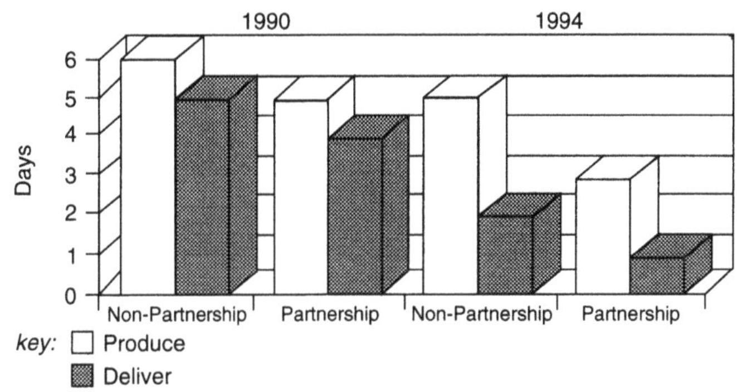

Figure 9.5 Median number of days batch lasts customer in Europe

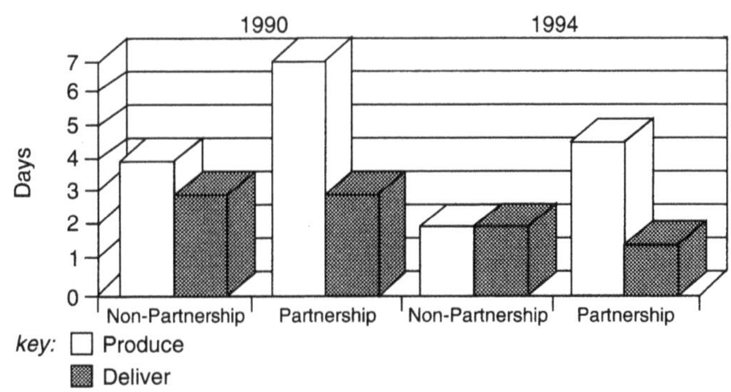

Figure 9.6 Median number of days batch lasts customer in the UK

partnership firms have made investments that have allowed them to reduce production batch sizes from five to three days. Improvements were also made in delivery batch sizes which declined from four to one day for partnership suppliers.

In the UK, the most impressive improvement by partnership suppliers has been in the reduction of production batch sizes, from an average of seven days in 1990 to four and a half days in 1994. However, in the UK, non-partnership suppliers have even smaller production batch sizes – reduced from four to two days. Moreover, by 1994, there are no clear advantages of being in partnerships as far as average production and delivery performance are concerned – non-partnership suppliers appear to have equalised production and delivery batches at two days – arguably achieving JIT operation – whereas there is a gap of three days between median production and delivery batches for partnership suppliers (see Figure 9.6).

In the US, in 1993, over half of US suppliers were delivering in batches smaller than those in which they produced, indicating that they were stockpiling inventory. The median difference between production and delivery batch sizes has shrunk for all firms since 1989 but the median batch sizes for both production and delivery are now significantly smaller for firms which have partnership relationships. Four years ago, the median production batch size was the same for both non-partnership and partnership firms – lasting the customer ten days. Since then, however, the American partnership firms have made investments that have allowed them to reduce production batch sizes to five days. In contrast, non-partnership firms have only reduced their production batch sizes to seven days. Delivery performance for partnership suppliers is also superior: they deliver every two days, while non-partnership firms deliver every three days.

In Japan, there has apparently been no significant improvement in the average production and delivery batch sizes since 1989. Without comparable survey observations before 1989, we must refer to other studies which show that production and delivery batches were reduced a great deal in Japan in the 1970s and early 1980s (Lieberman 1994). What the 1993 survey does show, however, is that partnership suppliers perform better than non-partnership suppliers in developing JIT operation. In 1989, the median batch size for delivery was the same for partnership and non-partnership suppliers. Since then, only the partnership suppliers have achieved a reduction in delivery batches. Moreover, median production batches have been significantly smaller for partnership suppliers since 1989. In 1993, partnership suppliers produced in batches that would last the customer 12 hours, and delivered every five hours.

Overall, despite dramatic improvements in the last four years in Europe, European suppliers on average produce in batches which are seven times as large, and deliver in batches four times as large, as in Japan (if one day is converted to 16 hours, with two shifts per day). Again, UK suppliers to Japanese car manufacturers in the UK appear to be in the lead, having achieved smaller

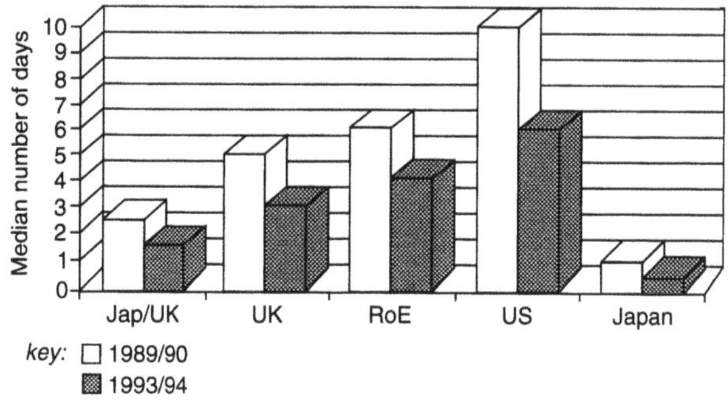

Figure 9.7 Production batch sizes remain largest in US

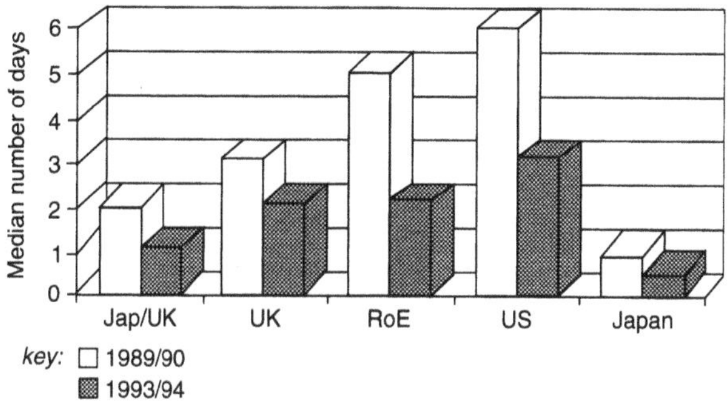

Figure 9.8 Delivery batch sizes remain smallest in Japan

production and delivery batch sizes than the UK averages in 1990 and 1994 (see Figures 9.7 and 9.8). American suppliers, on average, produce in batches which are four times as large as Japanese suppliers, while Japanese suppliers deliver six times more frequently than US suppliers. As in the US and Europe, however, around half of the Japanese suppliers were delivering in batches smaller than those in which they produced, indicating that they were stockpiling inventory.

The continuing gap between production and delivery batch size explains why over half of all suppliers in the US, nearly half (46 per cent) in Europe, and just over a third of all suppliers in Japan agree with the statement: 'JIT only transfers inventory responsibility from customers to suppliers'. In both the US and Japan, the statement was less likely to be endorsed by suppliers with partnerships (one-third in the US and 30 per cent in Japan).

Costs and margins

Figures 9.9 and 9.10 show one area in which partnership-type relations have had differential effects in different regions, namely costs and profits. The

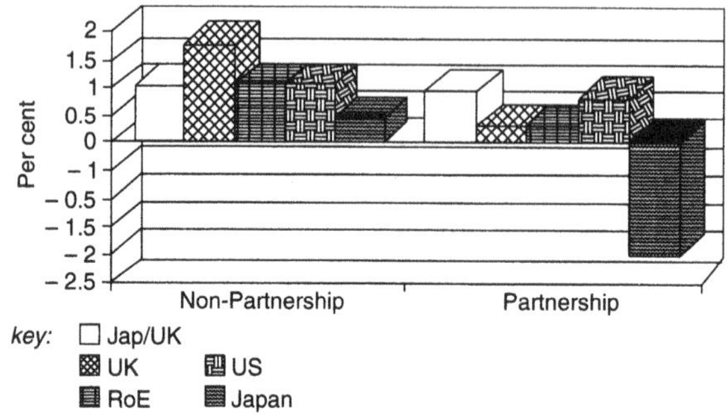

Figure 9.9 Average annual cost change (1988/90–1992/3)

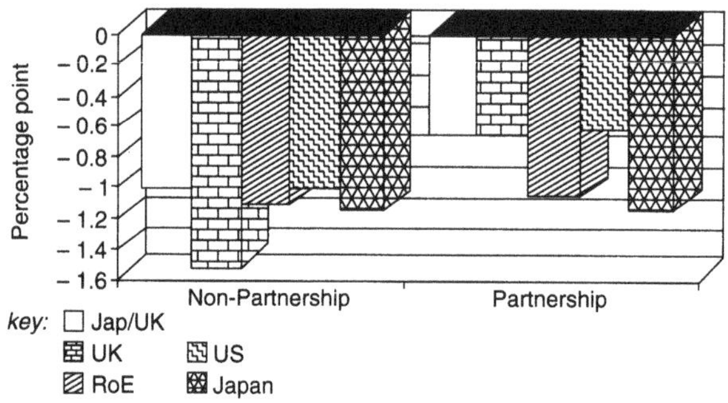

Figure 9.10 Average annual margin change (1988/9–1992/3)

only suppliers which have achieved a significant degree of cost reduction during the period 1988/9—1992/3 were those in Japan that have partnership relations.

Despite the promise of 'continuous improvement', little has occurred in the way of cost reduction by suppliers. In the UK, average supplier costs actually rose almost 2 per cent per annum for non-partnership suppliers, over the period 1989–1993. Partnership suppliers, however, were able to contain cost increases better, experiencing an increase of just less than 1/2 per cent per year. UK-based partnership suppliers felt that their profit margins were squeezed less (by half a percentage point) than suppliers without partnerships (by 1.5 percentage points).[7]

The picture is different in Japan, where partnership suppliers felt just as squeezed on their profit margin as non-partnership suppliers. Customers in Japan apparently demand that the benefit of suppliers' cost reduction is passed on to the customer over the medium term. In Japan, average supplier costs declined at 0.2 per cent per year in nominal terms between 1988 and 1992, but 0.7 per cent in 1991/2. Supplier margins also fell, at one percentage point per year between 1988 and 1992. In contrast to US firms, Japanese partnership suppliers did outperform non-partnership suppliers in cost reduction by 1.5 per cent per annum, but they were not significantly better at defending their profit margins. In Japan, suppliers are reducing their costs, but since prices are falling even faster, supplier margins are squeezed.

In the US, average supplier costs actually rose almost 2 per cent per year in nominal terms between 1988 and 1992, although costs did fall slightly between 1991 and 1992 (see Figure 9.8). Supplier margins fell almost one percentage point per year between 1988 and 1992, and at an even faster rate between 1991 and 1992. In Europe (outside the UK) also, average supplier costs actually rose 1 per cent per year in nominal terms between 1989 and 1993, while supplier margins fell one percentage point per year between 1989 and 1993, and at an even faster rate between 1992 and 1993. Partnership suppliers did not have any greater success at cost reduction than non-partnership suppliers, and were not significantly more able to defend their margins. It appears that suppliers' price reductions may be due to reduced margins rather than reduced costs.

Developing new products

Another area in which partnership-style relationships have had a mixed performance is the product development process. There is a general trend towards joint development and, over time, more suppliers appear to be developing their products in consultation with the customer. For example in the UK, 52 per cent of suppliers developed their products jointly with their customers for the previous model, while as many as 87 per cent of suppliers did so for the current model. Similarly, the proportion of suppliers engaged in joint product development with customers increased from 58 to 84 per cent in the rest of Europe, from 51 to 67 per cent in the US and from 59 to 63 per cent in Japan. In all regions, partnership suppliers are more likely to engage in joint development with their customer than non-partnership suppliers. For instance, in the UK, 92 per cent of partnership suppliers, as compared to 79 per cent of non-partnership suppliers, developed their products jointly with the customer for the current model.

There is, however, an increasing number of suppliers which design proprietary parts with no customer involvement. They tend *not* to be partnership suppliers, but they possess the technological capability which customers find valuable. For instance, 14 per cent of non-partnership suppliers in Japan, as compared to only 10 per cent of partnership suppliers, said they took entire responsibility in designing their product. By far the most dramatic difference was seen among non-UK European suppliers: 36 per cent of non-partnership suppliers, as compared to 16 per cent of partnership suppliers, designed their products with no customer involvement (see Figure 9.11). They have a greater European market share for their specific products

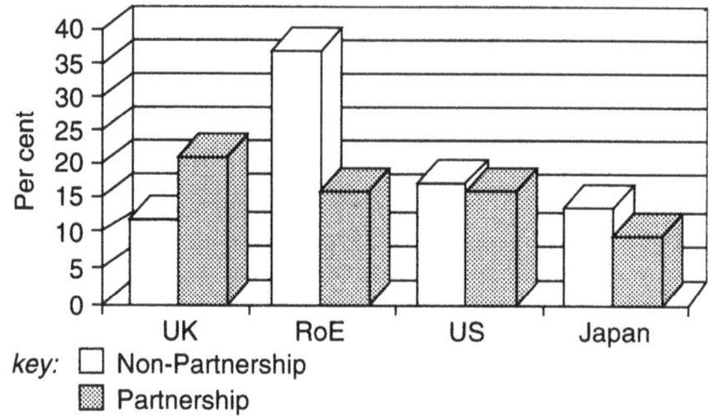

Figure 9.11 New product development process: per cent of suppliers with sole responsibility for design

than other suppliers, and they have experienced a faster growth in business with their automotive customers in the last four years.

The UK appears to be exceptional: suppliers with sole responsibility for design are *more* likely to be partnership suppliers. This is not inconsistent with the above results, however: UK partnership suppliers are being asked to develop some products jointly with customers and, at the same time, to take on full responsibility for others. This may be an encouraging reflection of confidence in the UK firms, as customers relinquish control of technologies.

5. Conclusions

The UK industry shows some interesting signs of development towards partnership relationships, as defined for the purposes of this research. The international survey results used in this chapter show that such supply arrangements can provide significant business benefits to companies practising them. However, the widespread commitment to partnerships does not seem to be resulting in practical benefits in the UK, where non-partnership suppliers appear to be doing just as well as partnership suppliers, particularly in some aspects of JIT operation.

It is interesting, for instance that 64 per cent of suppliers responding in the UK were developing supply partnerships with the vehicle manufacturers – a higher rate than all other parts of the world. It is also remarkable that the proportion of UK-based suppliers providing process information to their customers – 91 per cent – is higher than that for their American and European counterparts, and even for those in Japan. It is especially interesting to see that nearly all the UK firms which supply the Japanese vehicle assemblers are providing such information.

The increase in the proportion of UK suppliers that feel that customers would help them to improve their performance in the face of new competition is also remarkable, especially so for suppliers to UK-based Japanese plants. Once again, the UK compares well with Japan in this respect and in the low number of UK suppliers which expect their customer to re-source 'as soon as is technically feasible' in such situations.

UK suppliers with partnership relations were able to contain cost increases and to defend a squeeze on profit margins better than non-partnership suppliers but not as well as partnership suppliers in other parts of the world. In particular, it has often been pointed out that partnership cannot be a cosy arrangement and perhaps there is a false sense of security within UK partnership suppliers who do not feel as squeezed as their non-partnership competitors: in Japan, all suppliers recognise the need to face a major squeeze. The results on margins make worrying reading: it does appear that suppliers' price reductions may be due to reduced margins rather than reduced costs.

The conclusions on product design are also interesting: the increase in the number of suppliers designing new products in conjunction with the vehicle manufacturers, and the growth in proprietary suppliers who are recognised as the best people to develop technologies, both show a move towards making better use of the technical expertise that is spread throughout the industry.

On balance, the evidence shows that a fully developed partnership model of supplier relations is not yet firmly in place in the UK automotive industry. It is clear that not all suppliers are convinced of the efficacy of partnership-style supplier relations although there is some improvement in perceptions of trust between them and their customers.

Given that Europe-based vehicle manufacturers share much of the same supplier base, it may be damaging to the industry as a whole for some of them to use partnerships in an attempt to promote investment, while other customers are reducing supplier margins in a short-term effort to cut their own costs. The partnership strategy, which must be attributed at least in part to the advent of Japanese firms in Europe, has led to a significant improvement in some aspects of supplier performance and promises much more. Another strategy, used by vehicle manufacturers *in extremis* has been to exhibit very adversarial attitudes, eschewing partnerships and placing the automotive market pressures firmly on the shoulders of suppliers. Both strategies are internally consistent and it remains to be seen whether they are compatible with each other. In particular, there are different implications for customer's risk between the two: forming partnerships requires much greater commitment from the customer and can only be countenanced in the light of greater expected long-term benefits.

Another possible reason why partnership suppliers in the UK are not performing much better than non-partnership suppliers is that it takes time to develop such relationships, and four years is simply not long enough to realise the benefits. If so, the UK suppliers may be expected to develop much further.

Finally, the survey shows that the partnership suppliers in the UK have a greater number of customers on average than non-partnership suppliers for any given product, and expect to have an even greater number in four years' time (a difference not as marked elsewhere in Europe). This evidence may indicate a lack of understanding or an unwillingness to recognise the need for suppliers themselves to make a long-term commitment with each of their customers. UK-based suppliers may be required to make some significant readjustment in business strategies to benefit from partnerships in the future.

Notes

1 The surveys were funded by the International Motor Vehicle Programme, based at the Massachusetts Institute of Technology, and by the UK Department of Trade and Industry, Vehicles Division. Parts of this chapter were issued as a report by the DTI in April 1995.

2 There is empirical evidence to show that close relationships between customers and suppliers can have beneficial effects on performance in several areas. For example, Clark (1989) found that early supplier involvement in product design was a key part of Japanese car manufacturers' edge in introducing new models both faster and with fewer total labour hours than their US and European counterparts. Heide and John (1988) found that customers and suppliers who were mutually dependent invested more in specific assets. See also Partnership Sourcing Ltd (1991–1994)

3 See SMMT & DTI (1994:6). Note that this report was based on a survey and a series of workshops with both first-tier and second-tier suppliers, as well as vehicle manufacturers.

4 For a discussion on the definition of 'first tier' see Lamming (1993) chapter 7.

5 Susan Helper conducted a survey in the US in 1993, while Mari Sako conducted similar surveys in Japan in 1993 and in Europe in 1994. All of the three regional surveys were sponsored by the International Motor Vehicle Program (IMVP) at MIT. The European and UK survey was also sponsored by the DTI Vehicles, Metals and Minerals Division. Funding was also provided by the Sloan Foundation and the Ameritech Foundation. The North American survey received support from the Center for Regional Economic Issues at Case Western Reserve University. The Japanese survey received support from the Japan Auto Parts Industries Association (JAPIA) and the Economic Research Institute of the Japan Society for the Promotion of Machine Industry (Helper, 1991, 1995).

6 *Elm International Inc., East Lansing, Michigan.*

7 A percentage point change measures the difference between one rate and another rate. For example, the change between a 6 per cent margin and a 4 per cent margin is two percentage points. Also, note that the rate of inflation during the period covered by the survey was 6.7 per cent in the UK, 4.4 per cent in the USA and 2.6 per cent in Japan.

REFERENCES

ACDA (1995) *World Military Expenditures and Arms Transfers 1993–94*, Washington DC: US Arms Control and Disarmament Agency.

Akerlof, G.A. (1970) 'The Market for "Lemons": Qualitative Uncertainty and the Market Mechanism', *Quarterly Journal of Economics*, **84**(3): 488–500.

Alchian, A. and Demsetz, H. (1972) 'Production, Information Costs and Economic Organization', *American Economic Review*, **62**(5): 777–95.

Axelrod, R. (1984) *The Evolution of Cooperation*, New York: Basic Books.

Badarocco, J.L. (1991) *The Knowledge Link: How Firms Compete Through Strategic Alliances*, Boston, Mass.: Harvard Business School Press.

Bakos, J. and Brynjolfsson, E. (1993) 'From vendors to partners: Information Technology and Incomplete Contracts in Buyer–Supplier Partnerships', *Journal of Organizational Computing*, **3**(3): 301–28.

Ballew, P.D. and Schnorbus, R.H. (1994) 'Realignment in the Auto Supplier Industry: The Rippling Effects of Big Three Restructuring', *Federal Reserve Bank of Chicago Economic Perspectives*, Jan.–Feb.: 2–9.

Barclift, J.A. (1991) 'Strategic partnership: Competitive Advantage or Risky Business?', *NAPM Insights*, January: 7.

Barnevik, P. (1994) *Global Strategies: Insights from the World's Leading Thinkers*, Boston: Harvard Business School Press.

Bartlett, C. A. and Ghoshal, S. (1989) *Managing Across Borders: The Transnational Solution*, Boston: Harvard Business School Press.

Batstone, E. and Davies, P. L. (eds) (1976) *Industrial Democracy: The European Experience*, London: HMSO.

Baumol, W.J. (1982) 'Contestable Markets: An Uprising in the Theory of Industrial Structure', *American Economic Review*, **72**, March: 1–15.

Baumol, W.J., Panzar, J.C. and Willig, R.D. (1982) *Contestable Markets and the Theory of Industrial Structure*, New York: Harcourt Brace Jovanovich.

Beaudreau, B.C. (1986) *Managers, Learning and the Multinational Firm: Theory and Evidence*, PhD Dissertation, University of Western Ontario (unpublished).

Berger, H., Noorderhaven, N.G. and Nooteboom, B. (1993) 'Determinants of Supplier Dependence: An Empirical Study' Proceedings of the EAEPE Conference, October.

Bergman, S. (1991) 'Reverse Marketing in 1991', *NAPM Insights*, July: 26–7.

Berle, A. A. and Means, G. C. (1932) *The Modern Corporation and Private Property*, New York: Macmillan (revised edn, 1967)

Bertin, G.V. and Wyatt, S. (1988) *Multinationals and Industrial Property: The Control of the World's Technology*, Hemel Hempstead: Harvester Wheatsheaf.

Bleeke, J., and Ernst, D. (1993) 'The Way to Win in Cross-Border Alliances', in J. Blecke and D. Ernst (eds) *Collaborating to Compete*, New York: Free Press: 17–34.

Blomstrom, M. and Lipsey R. (1991) 'Firm Size and Foreign Operations of Multinationals', *The Scandinavian Journal of Economics*, **93** (1): 101–7.

Blomstrom, M. Lipsey, R. and Kulchycky K. (1988) 'U.S. and Swedish Direct Investment and Exports', in R.E. Baldwin (ed.) *Trade Policy Issues and Empirical Analysis*, Chicago: University of Chicago Press: 259–97.

Blomstrom, M. and Zejan, M. (1991) 'Why Do Multinational Firms Seek Out Joint Ventures?', *Journal of International Development*, **3** (1): 53–63.

Bolton, P. and Dewatripont, M. (1994) 'The Firm as a Communication Network', *Quarterly Journal of Economics*, **109**: 819–39.

Brainard, S.Lael (1993a) 'A Simple Theory of Multinational Corporations and Trade with a Trade-off between Proximity and Concentration', NBER Working Paper No. 4269, February.

Brainard, S. Lael (1993b) 'An Empirical Assessment of the Factor Proportions Explanation of Multinationals Sales', NBER Working Paper No. 4580, December.

Brainard, S. Lael (1993c) 'An Empirical Assessment of the Proximity–Concentration Tradeoff between Multinational Sales and Trade', NBER Working Paper No. 4583, December.

Briggs, P. (1995) 'Eliminating Mistrust and Maintaining Competitive Advantage Without the use of Competitive Tendering', *Proceedings of the 4th International IPSERA Conference*, University of Birmingham: CPRU.

Brzoska, M. (1996) 'Dilemma and Practices of Defense Industry Restructuring in West European countries', *Conference on Politics and Economics of Defense Industries in a Changing World*, Tel Aviv, Israel: Bar Ilan University: January.

Buckley, P.J. and Carter, M.J. (1996) 'The Economics of Business Process Design: Motivation, Information and Coordination Within the Firm', *International Journal of the Economics of Business*, **3**: 5–25.

Buckley, P.J. and Casson, M. (1976) *The Future of Multinational Enterprise*, London: Macmillan.

Buckley, P.J., Mirza, H. and Sparkes, J.R. (1987) 'Direct Foreign Investment in Japan as a Means of Market Entry,' *Journal of Marketing Management*, **2**(3): 241–58.

Buckley P.J. and Casson M. (1985) *The Economic Theory of Multinational Enterprise*, London: Macmillan.

Buckley, P.J. and Casson, M. (1988) 'A Theory of Cooperation in International Business', in F.J. Contractor and P. Lorange (eds) *Cooperative Strategies in International Business*, Lexington: Lexington Books.

Buckley, P.J. and Casson M. (1989) (2nd edn) *The Future of Multinational Enterprise*, London: Macmillan.

Buckley, P.J. and Casson, M. (1992) 'Organising for Innovation: The Multinational Enterprise in the Twenty-first Century', Chap. 12 of P.J. Buckley and M. Casson (eds) *Multinational Enterprise in the World Economy: Essays in Honour of John Dunning*, Aldershot: Edward Elgar.

Buckley, P.J. and Casson, M. (1996) 'An Economic Model of International Joint Venture Strategy', *Journal of International Business Studies*, **27**(5), 849–76.

Buckley, P.J. and Ghauri, P. (1991) *The Internationalisation of the Firm*, Oxford: Oxford University Press.

Buckley, P.J. and Glaister, K. (1994) 'UK International Joint Ventures: An Analysis of Patterns of Activity and Distribution', *British Journal of Management*, **5**: 33–41.

Buckley, P.J., Pass, C.L. and Prescott, K. (1992) *Servicing International Markets: Competitive Strategies of Firms*, Oxford: Blackwell.

Burgers, W.P., Hill, C.W. and Kim, W.C. (1993) 'A Theory of Global Strategic Alliances: The Case of the Global Auto Industry', *Strategic Management Journal*, **14**: 419–32.

Burton, J. (1994) 'Competition over Competition Analysis: A Guide to Some Contemporary Economics Disputes', in J. Lonbay (ed.) *Frontiers of Competition Law*, Chichester, UK: Chancery Law Publishing: 1–23.

Burton, J. (1995a) 'Composite Strategy: The Combination of Collaboration and Competition', *Journal of General Management*, **21**(1): Autumn: 1–23.

Burton, J. (1995b) 'Partnering with the Japanese: Threat or Opportunity for European Businesses?', *European Management Journal*, **13**(3): 304–15.

Burton, J., and Hanlon, P. (1994) 'Airline Alliances: Cooperating to Compete?', *Journal of Air Transport Management*, **1**(4): 209–27.

Business Week (1994) 'Can Nike do it?' April (18): 86–90.

Carlos, A. (1994) 'Bonding and the Agency Problem: Evidence from the Royal African Company 1672–1691', *Explorations in Economic History*, July **31** (3): 313–35.

Carlos, A. and Nicholas S. (1990) 'Agency Problems in Early Chartered Companies: The Case of the Hudson's Bay Company', *Journal of Economic History*, December, **50** (4): 853–75.

Carter, M.J. (1995) 'Information and the Division of Labour: Implications for the Firm's Choice of Organisation', *Economic Journal*, **105**: 385–97.

Carter, M.J. (1996) 'Is the Customer Always Right: Information, Quality and Organisational Architecture', *University of Bradford Working Paper Series*, No. 9603.

Casson, M.C. (1979) *Alternatives to the Multinational Enterprise*, London: Macmillan.

Casson, M. (1982) *The Entrepreneur: An Economic Theory*, Oxford: Martin Robertson.

Casson, M. (1985a) 'Transaction Costs and the Theory of Multinational Enterprise', Chap. 2 of P.J. Buckley and M. Casson (eds) *The Economic Theory of the Multinational Enterprise*, London: Macmillan.

Casson, M. (1985b) 'Entrepreneurship and the Dynamics of Foreign Direct Investment', Chap. 8 of P.J. Buckley and M. Casson (eds) *The Economic Theory of the Multinational Enterprise*, London: Macmillan.

Casson, M. (1987) *The Firm and the Market: Studies on Multinational Enterprise and the Scope of the Firm*, Oxford: Blackwell, Cambridge, Mass.: MIT Press.

Casson, M.C. (1991) *The Economics of Business Culture: Game Theory, Transaction Costs and Economic Performance*, Oxford: Clarendon Press.

Casson, M.C. (1994) 'Why are Firms Hierarchical?', *International Journal of the Economics of Business*, **1**(1): 47–76.

Casson, M.C. (1995a) 'Information Costs and the Organisational Structure of the Multinational Enterprise', *The Organisation of International Business*, Aldershot: Edward Elgar: Chapter 4.

Casson, M.C. (1995b) 'Cultural Factors in Bargaining: How Leaders can Persuade People to Signal Truthfully', *University of Reading Discussion Papers in Economics*, No. 306.

Casson, M.C. (1996a) 'The Nature of the Firm: Information Synthesis and Entrepreneurial Organisation', *Management International Review*, **36** (1): 55–94.

Casson, M.C. (1996b) 'A Reappraisal of the Theory of the Firm', Department of Economics, University of Reading, *mimeo*.

Caves, R.E. (1996) *Multinational Enterprise and Economic Analysis – Cambridge Surveys of Economic Literature*, 2nd edn Cambridge: Cambridge University Press.

Caves, R.E. and Murphy II W.F. (1976) 'Franchising: Firms, Markets, and Intangible Assets', *Southern Economic Journal*, April: 572–86.

Chakravarty, B.S. and Perlmutter, H.V. (1985) 'Strategic Planning for a Global Business', *Columbia Journal of World Business*, Summer: 3–10.

Chalmers, M. and Greene, O. (1995) *Taking Stock: The UN Register After Two Years*, Bradford: Westview Press.

Champy, J. (1995) *Reengineering Management: The Mandate for New Leadership*, London: Harper Collins.

Chandler, A.D. (1992) 'Organizational Capabilities and the Economic History of the Industrial Enterprise', *Journal of Economic Perspectives*, **6**(3): 79–100.

Clark, K. (1989) 'Project Scope and Project Performance: The Effect of Parts Strategy and Supplier Involvement on Product Development' *Management Science* **35**: 1237–63.

Cmnd 9430-Z (1985) *Statement on the Defence Estimates 1985*, London: HMSO.

Cmnd 1022-Z (1990) *Statement on the Defence Estimates 1990*, London: HMSO.

Cmnd 2800-Z (1995) *Statement on the Defence Estimates 1995*, London: HMSO.

Coase, R. H. (1937) 'The Nature of the Firm', *Economica* (New series), **4**: 386–405.

Coase, R. H. (1993) 'Nobel Lecture: The Institutional Structure of Production', in O.E. Williamson and S.G. Winter (eds) *The Nature of the Firm: Origins, Evolution and Development*, New York: Oxford University Press.

Cousins, P. D. (1994) 'Partnership Sourcing: A Misused Concept', in Lamming, R. C. and Cox, A. W. (eds) *Strategic Procurement in the 1990s: Concepts and Cases*, Earlsgate: UK.

Cranshaw, M., Davies, E. and Kay, J. (1994) 'On Being Stuck in the Middle or Good Food Costs Less at Sainsbury', *British Journal of Management*, **5**: 19–32.

Cusumano, M.A. and Takeishi, A. (1991) 'Supplier Relations and Management: A Survey of Japanese, Japanese-transplant, and U.S. auto plants', *Strategic Management Journal*, **12**: 563–88.

Czinkota, M.R., Ronkainen, I.A. and Moffett, M.H. (1996) *International Business*, 4th edn., New York: Dryden Press (Harcourt Brace).

Dale, B. G. and Burns, B. (eds) (1995) *Developing Partnerships*, McGraw Hill: London.

Davenport, T.H. (1993) *Process Innovation: Reengineering Work Through Information Technology*, Boston, Mass.: Harvard Business School Press.

Davenport, T.H. and Short, J.E. (1990) 'The New Industrial Engineering: Information Technology and Business Process Redesign', *Sloan Management Review*, **31**(4) Summer: 11–27.

Davidson W.H. and McFetridge D. G. (1984) 'International Technology Transactions and the Theory of the Firm', *Journal of Industrial Economics*, **32**: 253–64.

De Vestel, P. (1995) *Defence Markets and Industries in Europe: Time for Political Decisions?*, Chaillot Papers 21, Paris: Institute for Security Studies.

Deming, W.E. (1988) *Out of Crisis*, Cambridge MA: MIT Center for Advanced Engineering Study.

Demsetz, H. (1995) 'The Firm of Theory: Its Definition and Existence', *The Economics of the Business Firm: Seven Critical Commentaries*, Cambridge: Cambridge University Press, 1–14.

Denekamp, J. and Ferrantino M.J. (1992) 'Substitution and Complementarity of U.S. Exports and Foreign Based Affiliate Sales in a Demand Based Gravity System', Working paper.

Dick, A.R. (1993) 'Strategic Trade Policy and Welfare: The Empirical Consequences of Cross-Ownership', *Journal of International Economics*, **35**: 227–49.

Dicken, P. (1992) *Global Shift: The Internationalization of Economic Activity*, London: Paul Chapman.

Dnes, A.W. (1992) '"Unfair" Contractual Practices and Hostages in Franchise Contracts', *Journal of Institutional and Theoretical Economics*, **148**(3): 484–504.

Doz, Y., Prahalad, C.K. and Hamel, G. (1990) 'Control, Change and Flexibility: The Dilemma of Transnational Collaboration', in A. Bartlett, Y. Doz and G. Hedland (eds) *Managing the Global Firm*, London: Routledge: 117–43.

Drucker, P.F. (1988) 'The Coming of the New Organisation', *Harvard Business Review*, January–February: 45–53.

Drucker, P. F. (1993) *Post Capitalist Society*, New York: Harper Collins.

Dunning, J.H. (1977) 'Trade, Location of Economic Activity and MNE: A Search for an Eclectic Approach', in B. Ohlin, P.O. Hesselborn, and P.M. Wijkman (eds) *The International Allocation of Economic Activity* London: Macmillan.

Dunning, J.H. (1981) *International Production and the Multinational Enterprise*, London: Allen and Unwin.

Dunning, J.M. (1993) *Multinational Enterprises and the Global Economy*, Reading, Mass.: Addison Wesley.

EC (1995) Memorandum of Evidence by DGXV, in HCP 333, *Aspects of Defence Procurement and Industrial Policy*, House of Commons Paper 333, London: HMSO: London: 99–100 (this contains the key points from the summary of the unpublished report by Hartley and Cox 1992).

Economist (1993) 'The Global Firm: R.I.P.', 6 February: 85.

Ekholm, K. (1995) 'Multinational Production and Trade In Technological Knowledge', *Lund Economic Studies*, no. 58.

Ellram, L.M. (1990) 'The Supplier Selection Decision in Strategic Partnerships, *Journal of Purchasing and Materials Management*, **26** (Fall): 8–14.

Ellram, L. M. and Krause, D. R. (1994) 'Supplier Partnerships in Manufacturing Versus Non-manufacturing Firms', *International Journal of Purchasing and Logistics Management* **5** (1).

Ethier, W.J. (1986) 'The Multinational Firm', *Quarterly Journal of Economics*, **101**: 805–33.

Ethier, W.J. (1994) 'Multinational Firms in the Theory of International Trade', in E. Bacha, (ed.) *Development, Trade and the Environment*, London: Macmillan.

Ethier, W.J. and Markusen J.R. (1996) 'Multinational Firms, Technology Diffusion and Trade', *Journal of International Economics*, **41** (1–2): 1–28.

Faulkner, D. (1995) *Strategic Alliances: Co-operating to Compete*, Maidenhead, Berks: McGraw-Hill.

Feldstein, M., Hines, J.R., Jr. and Glenn Hubbard, R. (eds) (1995) *The Effects of Taxation on Multinational Corporations*, Chicago: University of Chicago Press.

Ford, D. (1980) 'The Development of Buyer-Seller Relationships in Industrial Markets', *European Journal of Marketing*, **14** (5/6): 339–53.

Freidheim, C. (1993) 'The Global Corporatian – Obsolete so soon?', *World Economic Forum*, Dovos: Switzerland (*mimeo*).

Froot, K.A. (1993) *Foreign Direct Investment*, Chicago: University of Chicago Press.

Galt, J.D.A. and Dale, B.G. (1991) 'Supplier Development: A British Case Study', *International Journal of Purchasing and Materials Management*, **27** (Winter): 16–22.

Gialloreto, L. (1988) *Strategic Airline Management: The Global War Begins*, London: Pitman.

Graham, E.M. and Krugman P.R. (1993) 'The Surge in Foreign Direct Investment in the 1980s', in Kenneth A. Froot (ed.) *Foreign Direct Investment*, Chicago: University of Chicago Press: 13–36.

Grant, R.M. (1995) *Contemporary Strategy Analysis: Concepts, Techniques, Applications*, 2nd edn, Oxford: Blackwell.

Gross, T., Turner, E. and Cederholm, L. (1987) 'Building Teams for Global Operations', *Management Review*, June: 32–6.

Grossman, S. and Hart, O.D. (1986) 'The Costs and Benefits of Ownership: A Theory of Vertical and Lateral Integration', *Journal of Political Economy*, **94**(4): 691–719.

Grubaugh, S. (1987) 'Determinants of Direct Foreign Investment', *Review of Economics and Statistics*, February **69**: 149–51.

Grubert, H. and Mutti, J. (1991) 'Taxes, Tariffs, and Transfer Pricing in Multinational Corporate Decision Making', *Review of Economics and Statistics*, **73** (2): 285–93.

Hackett, S.C. and Srinivasan, K. (1997) 'Do Supplier Switching Costs Differ Across Japanese and US Firms?', *Japan and the World Economy*, forthcoming.

Haddad, M. and Harrison A. (1993) 'Are There Positive Spillovers from Direct Foreign Investment?', *Journal of Development Economics*, **42**: 51–74.

Hammer, M. (1990) 'Reengineering Work: Don't Automate, Obliterate', *Harvard Business Review*, July–August: 104–12.

Hammer, M., and Champy, J. (1993) *Reengineering the Corporation: A Manifesto for Business Revolution*, London: Nicholas Brealey.

Hansmann, H. (1988) 'Ownership of the Firm', *Journal of Law, Economics and Organization*, **4**: 267–403.

Hartley, K. (1995) *The Economic Case for Subsidising the Aerospace Industry*, Research Monograph 6, University of York, York: Centre for Defence Economics.

Hartley, K. (1996) 'Defence Industries Adjusting to Change', *Defence and Peace Economics*, **7** (2): 169–84.

Hartley, K. and Cox, A. (1992) *The Cost of Non-European Defence Procurement*, EC DGIII, Brussels (14 volumes plus Executive Summary, unpublished: see EC 1995).

Hartley, K. and Martin, S. (1993) 'Evaluating collaborative programmes', *Defence Economics*, **4** (2): 195–211.

Harvard Business School (1985a) 'Nike', Case 9–385–328.

Harvard Business School (1985b) 'Nike', Case 9–386–037.

Hayek, F.A. von (1937) 'Economics and Knowledge', *Economica* (New Series), **4**: 33–54.

HCP 247 (1991) *Ministry of Defence: Collaborative Projects*, National Audit Office, London: HMSO.

HCP 222 (1994) *Progress on the Eurofighter 2000 Programme*, Defence Committee, House of Commons, London: HMSO.

HCP 436, (1995) *Ministry of Defence: Major Projects Report 1994*, National Audit Office, London: HMSO.

HCP 724 (1995) *Ministry of Defence: Eurofighter 2000*, National Audit Office, London: HMSO.

HCP 209, 210 (1996) *Government's Reply to the First Reports from the Defence and Trade and Industry Committees Session 1995–96 on Aspects of Defence Procurement and Industrial Policy*, London: HMSO.

Head, K., Ries, J. and Swenson, D. (1995) 'Agglomeration Benefits and Location Choice: Evidence from Japanese Manufacturing Investments in the United States', *Journal of International Economics*, **38**: 223–47.

Hedlund, G. and Nonaka, I. (1993) 'Models of Knowledge Management in the West and Japan', Chap. 5 of P. Lorange, B. Chakravarthy, J. Roos and A. Van de Ven (eds) *Implementing Strategic Processes: Change, Learning and Co-operation*, Oxford: Basil Blackwell.

Hegert, M. and Morris, D. (1988) 'Trends in International Collaborative Arrangements', in F.J. Contractor and P. Lorange (eds) *Cooperative Strategies in International Business*, Lexington, Mass: Lexington Books: 99–110.

Heide, J. and John, G. (1988) 'The Role of Dependence Balancing in Safeguarding Transaction-specific Assets in Conventional Channels', *Journal of Marketing* **54**: 20–35.

Heide, J. and John, G. (1992) 'Do Norms Matter in Marketing Relationships?', *Journal of Marketing*, **56** (April): 32–44.

Helper, S. (1991) 'How Much has Really Changed Between U.S. Automakers and Their Suppliers?', *Sloan Management Review*, **15** (Summer): 15–28.

Helper, S. and Mudambi, R. (1994) 'When do Customers Switch Suppliers? Some Empirical Evidence from the U.S. Auto Industry', paper presented at the 20th Annual EEA Conference, Boston, MA: March.

Helper, S. and Mudambi, R. (1995) 'When do Customers Switch Suppliers?', paper presented at the 11th Annual IMP Conference, Manchester, England: September.

Helper, S. and Sako, M. (1995) 'Supplier Relations in Japan and the United States: Are They Converging?', *Sloan Management Review*, (Spring): 77–84.

Helpman, E. (1984) 'A Simple Theory of Trade with Multinational Corporations', *Journal of Political Economy*, **92**: 451–71.

Helpman, E. (1985) 'Multinational Corporations and Trade Structure', *Review of Economic Studies*, **52**: 443–58.

Helpman, E. and Krugman, P.R. (1985) *Market Structure and Foreign Trade*, Cambridge: MIT Press.

Hennart, J-F. (1986) 'What is Internalisation?', *Weltwirtschaftliches Archiv*, **122**: 791–804.

Henzler, H.A. (1992) 'The New Era of Eurocapitalism', *Harvard Business Review*, July/August: 57–69.

Henzler, H. and Rall, W. (1986) 'Facing Up to the Globalization Challenge', *McKinsey Quarterly* (Winter): 52–68.

Hirschman, A.O. (1970) *Exit, Voice, and Loyalty: Responses to Decline in Firms, Organisations and States*, Harvard University Press: Cambridge MA.

Hladik, K.J. (1988) 'R&D and International Joint Ventures', in F.J. Contractor and P. Lorange (eds) *Cooperative Strategies in International Business*, Lexington, Mass.: Lexington Books: 187–204.

Holmstrom, B. (1979) 'Moral Hazard and Observability', *Bell Journal of Economics* **10**(1): 74–91.

Hood, N. and Young, S. (1979) *The Economics of Multinational Enterprise*, London: Longman.

Horstmann, I.J. and Markusen J.R. (1987a) 'Strategic Investments and the Development of Multinationals', *International Economic Review*, **28**: 109–21.

Horstmann, I.J. and Markusen, J.R. (1987b) 'Licensing Versus Direct Investment: A Model of Internalization by the Multinational Enterprise', *Canadian Journal of Economics*, **20**: 464–81.

Horstmann, I.J. and Markusen, J.R. (1992) 'Endogenous Market Structures in International Trade,' *Journal of International Economics*, **32**: 109–29.

Horstmann, I.J. and Markusen, J.R. (1996) 'Exploring New Markets: Direct Investment, Contractual Relations, and the Multinational Enterprise', *International Economic Review*, **37**: 1–19.

Hout, T., Porter, M.E. and Rudden, E. (1982) 'How Global Companies Win Out', *Harvard Business Review*, Sept.–Oct.: 98–108.

Hu, Y.-S. (1992) 'Global or Stateless Corporations are National Firms with International Operations', *California Management Review*, **34**(2): Winter: 107–26.

Hummels, D.L. and Stern, R.M. (1994) 'Evolving Patterns of North American Merchandise Trade and Foreign Direct Investment, 1960–1990', *The World Economy*, January 17 (1): 5–29.

Hutton, W. (1995) *The State We're In*, London: Jonathan Cape.

Hymer, S.H. (1960) *The International Operations of National Firms: A Study in Foreign Direct Investment*, PhD dissertation, MIT. Cambridge, MA: MIT Press, 1976.

Jensen, M.C. and Meckling, M. (1976) 'The Theory of the Firm: Managerial Behaviour, Agency Costs and Ownership Structure', *Journal of Financial Economics*, **3**: 305–60.

Julius, A. De (1990) *Global Companies and Public Policy*, London: Royal Institute of International Affairs.

Kanter, R.M. (1989) *When Giants Learn to Dance*, London: Simon and Schuster.

Kanter, R.M. (1996) *World Class: Thriving Locally in a Global Economy*, London: Simon and Schuster.

Kay, J.A. (1992) 'Innovations in Corporate Strategy', in Bowen, A. and Ricketts, M. (eds) *Stimulating Innovation in Industry*, London: Kogan Page: 117–31.

Kay, J.A. (1993) *Foundations of Corporate Success*, London: Oxford University Press.

Kearney, A.T. (1994) *Partnership or Powerplay: What is the Reality of Forming Closer Relationships with Suppliers and Customers along the Supply Chain?*, a report on the findings of a joint research programme into supply chain integration in the UK: London/UMIST: Manchester.

Keller, M. (1993) *Collision: GM, Toyota, Volkswagen and the Race to Own the 21st Century*, New York: Doubleday.

Kindleberger, C.P. (1969) *American Business Abroad*, New Haven: Yale University Press.

Kindleberger, C.P. (1978) *Multinational Excursions*, Cambridge: MIT Press.

Kirkpatrick, D.L. (1995) 'The Rising Unit Cost of Defence Equipment – the Reasons and Results', *Defence and Peace Economics*, **6** (4): 263–88.

Kirzner, I.M. (1979) *Perception, Opportunity and Profit*, Chicago: University of Chicago Press.

Klein, B., Crawford, R.G. and Alchian, A.A. (1978) 'Vertical Integration, Appropriable Rents and the Competitive Contracting Process', *Journal of Law and Economics*, **21**: 297–326.

Kogut, B. and Zander, U. (1993) 'Knowledge of the Firm and the Evolutionary Theory of the Multinational Corporation', *Journal of International Business Studies*, **24**: 625–45.

Krubashik, E., and Lautenschlagger, F. (1993) 'Forming Successful Strategic Alliances', in J. Bleeke and D. Ernst (eds) *Collaborating to Compete*, New York: Free Press: 55–65.

Lamming, R.C. (1993) *Beyond Partnership: Strategies for Innovation and Lean Supply* Hemel Hempstead, UK: Prentice Hall.

Landeros, R. and Monczka, R.M. (1989) 'Cooperative Buyer–Seller Relationships and a Firm's Competitive Posture', *Journal of Purchasing and Materials Management*, **25** (Fall): 9–18.

Larkin, J. (1995) 'The "GM Potential" Supplier Conference', *Automotive Sourcing*, 2(3): 162–75.

Levinsohn, J.A. (1989) 'Strategic Trade Policy when Firms can Invest Abroad: When are Tariffs and Quotas Equivalent?', *Journal of International Economics*, August **27** (1–2): 129–46.

Levitt, T. (1970) 'The Dangers of Social Responsibity', in H.D. Marshall (ed.) *Business and Government: The Problem of Power*, Lexington: D.C. Heath.

Lieberman, M. (1994) The Diffusion of 'Lean Manufacturing' in the Japanese and US Automotive Industry (Working Paper): Anderson Graduate School of Management, UCLA.

Lipsey, R.E. (1993) 'Foreign Direct Investment in the United States: Changes over Three Decades', in K.A. Froot (ed.) *Foreign Direct Investment*, Chicago: University of Chicago Press: 113–72.

Lipsey, R.E. (1994) 'Outward Direct Investment and the U.S. Economy', NBER Working Paper No. 4691, March.

Lohtia, R., Brooks, C.M. and Krapfel, R.E. (1994) 'What Constitutes a Transaction-Specific Asset? An Examination of the Dimensions and Types', *Journal of Business Research*, **30**: 261–70.

Lorange, P. (1993) *Strategic Planning and Control: Issues in the Strategy Process*, Oxford: Basil Blackwell.

Lynch, R.P. (1993) *Business Alliances Guide: The Hidden Competitive Weapon*, New York: Wiley and Sons.

Macbeth, D.K. (1994) 'The Role of Purchasing in a Partnering Relationship', *European Journal of Purchasing and Supply Management* 1 (1): 19–25.
Macbeth, D.K. and Ferguson, N. (1994) *Partnership Sourcing* London: Pitman.
Malmgren, H.B. (1961) 'Information, Expectations and the Theory of the Firm', *Quarterly Journal of Economics*, **75**: 399–421.
Mansfield, E. and Romeo, A. (1980) 'Technology Transfer to Overseas Subsidiaries by U.S. Firms', *Quarterly Journal of Economics*, **94**: 737–50.
Markusen, J.R. (1984) 'Multinationals, Multi-Plant Economics, and the Gains from Trade', *Journal of International Economics* **16**: 205–26.
Markusen, J.R. (1995) 'The Boundaries of Multinational Firms, and the Theory of International Trade', *Journal of Economic Perspectives* **9**: 169–89.
Markusen, J.R. (1997) 'Incorporating the Multinational Enterprise into the Theory of International Trade', this volume.
Markusen, J.R., Rutherford, T.F. and Hunter L. (1995) 'Trade Liberalization in a Multinational-Dominated Industry', *Journal of International Economics*, **38**: (1–2): 95–117.
Markusen, J.R. and Venables, A.J. (1995) 'The Increased Importance of Multinationals in North American Economic Relationships: A Convergence Hypothesis', in M. W. Canzoneri, Wilfred J. Ethier, and Vitoria Grilli (eds) *The New Transatlantic Economy*, London: Cambridge University Press.
Markusen, J.R. and Venables A.J. (1996) 'Multinational Firms and the New Trade Theory', NBER and University of Colorado Working Paper.
Martin, R. (1988) 'Franchising and Risk Management', *American Economic Review*, **78**(5): 954–68.
Martin, S. (ed.) (1996) *The Economics of Offsets*, Reading: Harwood.
Marschak, J. and Radner, R. (1972) *The Economic Theory of Teams*, New Haven, Conn.: Yale University Press.
Mathewson, G.F. and Winter, R.A. (1985) 'The Economics of Franchise Contracts', *Journal of Law and Economics*, **28**: 503–26.
Metcalf, L.E., Frear, C.R., and Krishnan, R. (1992) 'Buyer–Seller Relationships: An Application of the IMP Interaction Model', *European Journal of Marketing*, **26**(2): 27–46.
Miller, M.S. (1987) 'How to Analyze Supplier Price Proposals', *Purchasing World*, **31** (May): 55–7.
Modigliani, M. and Miller, M.H. (1958) 'The Cost of Capital, Corporate Finance and the Theory of Investment', *American Economic Review*, **48**(3): 261–97.
Morck, R. and Yeung, B. (1991) 'Why Investors Value Multinationality', *Journal of Business*, **64** (2): 165–87.
Morck, R. and Yeung, B. (1992) 'Internalization: An Event Study Test', *Journal of International Economics*, August **33** (1–2): 41–56.
Morgan, J. and Dowst, S. (1988) 'It Takes More Than a Low Bid to be World Class', 10, November: 50–62.
Morgan, R.M. and Hunt, S.D. (1994) 'The Commitment–Trust Theory of Relationship Marketing', *Journal of Marketing*, **58** (July): 20–38.
Motta, M. (1992) 'Multinational Firms and the Tariff-Jumping Argument', *European Economic Review*, **36**: 1557–71.
Mudambi, R. (1990) 'Entry Deterrence: The Case of a Buyer with Market Power', *Review of Industrial Organization*, **5**(1): 111–38.

Mudambi, R. (1995) 'The MNE Investment Location Decision: Some Empirical Evidence', *Managerial and Decision Economics*, **16**(3): 249–57.
Mudambi, R. and Dobson, P. (1993) 'Contract Renewal and the Value of Incumbency in Supplier Bidding Competition', *School of Management & Finance Discussion Paper* 10/93, October: University of Nottingham.
Mudambi, R. and Ricketts, M.J. (1997) 'Economic Organisation and the Multinational Firm', this volume.
Mudambi, R. and Schründer, C.P. (1995) 'Progress Towards buyer–supplier partnerships: Evidence from Small and Medium Sized Manufacturing Firms', *European Journal of Purchasing and Supply Management*, **2** (2/3): 119–27.
Nelson, R.R. and Winter, S.C. (1982) An Evolutionary Theory of Economic Change, Cambridge, MA: Harvard University Press.
Newman, R.G. (1989) 'Single Sourcing: Short-term Savings Versus Long-term Problems', *Journal of Purchasing and Materials Management*, **25** (Summer): 20–5
Newman, R.G. (1992) *Supplier price analysis*, New York: Quorum Books.
Newman, R.G. and Rhee, K.A. (1990) 'A Case Study of NUMMI and its Suppliers', *Journal of Purchasing and Materials Management*, **26** (Fall): 15–20.
Nicholas, S. (1982) 'British Multinational Investment Before 1939', *Journal of European Economic History*, **11**: 605–30.
Nicholas, S. (1983) 'Agency Contracts, Institutional Modes, and the Transition to Foreign Direct Investment by British Manufacturing Multinationals Before 1939', *Journal of Economic History*, **43**: 675–86.
Noordewier, T.G., John, G. and Nevin, J.R. (1990) 'Performance Outcomes of Purchasing Arrangements in Industrial Buyer–Vendor Relationships', *Journal of Marketing* **54** (October): 80–93.
Nooteboom, B. (1993) 'Networks and Transactions: Do they Connect?', in J. Groenewegen (ed.) *Dynamics of the Firm*, Aldershot: Edward Elgar: 9–26.
Nooteboom, B. (1994a) 'Cost, Quality and Learning Based Governance of Transactions: Western, Japanese and a Third Way', paper presented at the EMOT workshop, Como: October.
Nooteboom, B. (1994b) 'Governance of Transactions: A Strategic Process Model', paper presented at the EAEPE Conference, Copenhagen. October.
North, D.C. (1990) *Institutions, Institutional Change and Economic Performance*, Cambridge: Cambridge University Press.
Ohmae, K. (1985) *Triad Power: The Coming Shape of Global Competition*, New York: The Free Press.
Ohmae, K. (1987) 'The Triad World View', *Journal of Business Strategy*, **7**, (Spring): 8–19.
Ohmae, K. (1990) *The Borderless World*, New York: The Free Press.
Ohmae, K. (1993) 'The Global Logic of Strategic Alliances', in J. Bleeke and D. Ernst (eds) *Collaborating to Compete*, New York: The Free Press: 35–54.
Ohmae, K. (1995) *The End of the Nation State: The Rise of Regional Economies*, New York: The Free Press.
Parkinson, C. (1993) *Corporate Power and Responsibility*, Oxford: Clarendon Press.
Partnership Sourcing Ltd. (1991) *Partnership Sourcing* London, UK: CBI.
Partnership Sourcing Ltd. (1992) *Making Partnership Sourcing Happen* London, UK: CBI.

Partnership Sourcing Ltd. (1993) *Partnership Sourcing: Creating Service Partnerships* London, UK: CBI.

Partnership Sourcing Ltd. (1994) *Partnership Sourcing: A Practical Guide for Self Assessment* London, UK: CBI.

Pascale, R.T. and Athos, A.G. (1981) *The Art of Japanese Management*, London: Allen Lane.

Perks, H. (1993) 'Inter-Firm Collaboration in Western Europe – Some Preliminary Findings', University of Salford: North West Centre for European Marketing, Working Paper 9515.

Peters, T.J. and Waterman, R.H. (1982) *In Search of Excellence: Lessons from America's Best Run Companies*, New York: Harper and Row.

Pilling, B.K., Crosby, L.A. and Jackson, D.W. Jr (1994) 'Relational Bonds in Industrial Exchange: An Experimental Test of the Transaction Cost Economic Framework', *Journal of Business Research*, 30(3): 237–52.

Pitelis, C.N. and Sugden, R. (eds) (1991) *The Nature of the Transnational Firm*, London: Routledge.

Porter, M.E. (1980) *Competitive Strategy: Techniques for Analysing Industries and Competitors*, New York: The Free Press.

Porter, M.E. (1985) *Competitive Advantage: Creating and Sustaining Superior Performance*, New York: The Free Press.

Porter, M.E. (1986) 'Competition in Global Industries: A Conceptual Framework', in M.E. Porter (ed.) *Competition in Global Industries*, Boston: Harvard Business School Press: 15–60.

Porter, M.E. (1990) *The Competitive Advantage of Nations*, New York: The Free Press.

Pratt, J.W. and Zeckhauser, R.J. (eds) (1985) *Principals and Agents: The Structure of Business*, Boston: Harvard Business School Press.

Pugh, P. (1993) 'The Procurement Nexus', *Defence Economics*, 4 (2) 179–94.

Radner, R. (1992) Hierarchy: 'The Economics of Managing', *Journal of Economic Literature*, 30: 1382–415.

Ramasesh, R.V., Ord, J.K., Hayya, J.C. and Pan, A. (1991) 'Sole Versus Dual Sourcing in Stochastic Lead-time (s,Q) Inventory Models', *Management Science* 37(4): 428–43.

Rich, N. (1995) 'The Use of Quality Function Deployment for Relationship Assessment: Adversary, Associate or Partner?' *Proceedings of the 4th IPSERA Conference: Manufacturing and Production Procurement*, Contracts and Procurement Unit, University of Birmingham.

Richardson, G.B. (1960) *Information and Investment*, Oxford: Oxford University Press.

Richardson, J. (1993) 'Parallel Sourcing and Supplier Performance in the Japanese Automobile Industry', *Strategic Management Journal* 14: 339–50.

Ricketts, M. (1994) *The Economics of Business Enterprise*, 2nd edn. Hemel Hempstead: Harvester Wheatsheaf.

Ricks, D.A. (1993) *Blunders in International Business*, Oxford: Blackwell.

Ring, P.S. and Van de Ven A.H. (1992) 'Structuring co-operative relationships between organizations', *Strategic Management Journal*, 13: 483–498.

Rubin, P.H. (1978) 'The Theory of the Firm and the Structure of the Franchise Contract', *Journal of Law and Economics*, 21(1): 223–33.

Rugman, A.M. (1981) *Inside the Multinationals: The Economics of Internal Markets*, London: Croom Helm and New York; Columbia University Press.

Rugman, A.M. (1985) 'Internalization is Still a General Theory of Foreign Direct Investment', *Weltwirtschaftliches Archiv*, **121** (3): 570–87.

Rugman, A.M. (1986) 'New Theories of the Multinational Enterprise: An Assessment of Internalization Theory', *Bulletin of Economic Research*, **38** (2): 101–18.

Rugman, A.M. and Hodgetts, R.M. (1995) *International Business: A Strategic Management Approach*, New York: McGraw-Hill.

Sah R.K. and Stiglitz, J.E. (1986) 'The Architecture of Economic Systems: Hierarchies and Polyarchies', *American Economic Review*, **76**: 716–27.

Sako M. (1992) *Prices, Quality and Trust: Inter-firm Relations in Britain and Japan* Cambridge, UK: Cambridge University Press.

Sandler, T. and Hartley, K. (1995) *The Economics of Defense*, Cambridge: Cambridge University Press.

Schneider, F. and Frey, B.S. (1985) 'Economic and Political Determinants of Foreign Direct Investment', *World Development*, 1985, **13**: 161–75.

Segal, M.N. (1989) 'Implications of Single vs Multiple Buying Sources', *Industrial Marketing Management*, **18**: 163–78.

Sheridan, J.H. (1990) 'Suppliers: Partners in Prosperity', *Industry Week*, March 19: 12–19.

Simonian, H. (1996) 'The House That Jack Built', *Financial Times*, 5 March: 15.

SIPRI (1995) *Yearbook: Armaments, Disarmament and National Security*, SIPRI, Oxford: Oxford University Press.

Smith, A. (1987) 'Strategic Investment, Multinational Corporations and Trade Policy', *European Economic Review*, **31**: 89–96.

SMMT Industry Forum (1994) *Guidelines on Customer/Supplier Partnerships in the UK Automotive Industry*, February.

SMMT and DTI (1994) *A Review of the Relationships between Vehicle Manufacturers and Suppliers*, February, Department of Trade and Industry, Vehicles Division, London.

Sriram, V. and Mummalaneni, V. (1991) 'Determinants of Source Loyalty in Buyer–Supplier Relationships', *Journal of Purchasing and Materials Management*, **26** (Fall): 21–6.

Stigler, G.J. (1968) 'A Theory of Oligopoly' in *The Organization of Industry*, Homewood, Ill: R. D. Irwin: 39–63.

Taylor, W. (1991) 'The Logic of Global Business', *Harvard Business Review*, March/April: 90–105.

Teece, D. (1977) 'Technology Transfer By Multinational Firms: The Resource Cost of Transferring Technological Know-How', *Economic Journal*, **87**: 242–61.

Teece, D. (1986) *The Multinational Corporation and the Resource Cost of International Technology Transfer*, Cambridge: Ballinger.

Thompson, A.G. (1994) 'Relational Problems in Australian Business Ventures in Southeast Asia', *mimeo*: University of Melbourne.

Turnbull, P., Oliver, N. and Wilkinson, B. (1992) 'Buyer–Supplier Relations in the UK Automotive Industry: Strategic Implications of the Japanese Manufacturing Model', *Strategic Management Journal*, **13**: 159–68.

United Nations, (1994) *World Investment Report 1994*, New York: United Nations.

UNCTAD (1993) *World Investment Report 1993: Transnational Corporations and Integrated International Production*, New York: United Nations.

Urban, S. and Vendemini, S. (1992) *European Strategic Alliances: Co-operative Corporate Strategies in the New Europe*, Oxford: Blackwell.

Waterson, M. (1982) 'Vertical Integration, Variable Proportions and Oligopoly', *Economic Journal*, **92**: 129–44.

Wheeler, D. and Mody, A. (1992) 'International Investment Locations: The Case of US Firms,' *Journal of International Economics*, **33**: 57–76.

Wheeler, D. and Mody, A. (1992) 'International Investment Location Decisions', *Journal of International Economics*, **33** : 57–76.

Williamson, O.E. (1975) *Markets and Hierarchies: Analysis and Antitrust Implications: A Study in the Economics of Internal Organization*, New York: The Free Press.

Williamson, O.E. (1981) 'The Modern Corporation: Origins, Evolution, Attributes', *Journal of Economic Literature*, **19** (4): 1537–68.

Williamson, O.E. (1985) *The Economic Institutions of Capitalism: Firms, Markets and Relational Contracting*, New York: Collier Macmillan.

Williamson, O.E. (1988) 'Mergers, Acquisitions and Leveraged Buyouts: An Efficiency Assessment', in G.D. Libecap (ed.) *Corporate Reorganization through Mergers, Acquisitions and Leveraged Buyouts*, Greenwich: JAI Press.

Williamson, O.E. and Winter, S.G. (eds) (1993) *The Nature of the Firm: Origins, Evolution and Development*, New York: Oxford University Press.

Wilson, R.W., (1977) 'The Effect of Technological Environment and Product Rivalry on R&D Effort and Licensing of Inventions', *Review of Economics and Statistics*, **59**: 171–78.

Winter, S.G. (1988) 'On Coase, Competence and the Corporation', *Journal of Law, Economics and Organisation*, **4**: 163–80.

Wolf, H. (ed.) (1993) *Arms Industry Limited*, Oxford: Oxford University Press.

Womack, J.R., Jones, D.T. and Roos, D. (1990) *The Machine That Changed the World*, New York: Rawson Associates.

Wymeersch, E. (1993) 'The Corporate Governance Discussion in Some European States', in D.D. Prentice and P.R.J. Holland (eds) *Contemporary Issues in Corporate Governance*, Oxford: Clarendon Press.

Zeile, W.J. (1993) 'Merchandise Trade of U.S. Affiliates of Foreign Companies', *Survey of Current Business*, October 52–65.

AUTHOR INDEX

SUBJECT INDEX

For Product Safety Concerns and Information please contact our EU representative GPSR@taylorandfrancis.com
Taylor & Francis Verlag GmbH, Kaufingerstraße 24, 80331 München, Germany

www.ingramcontent.com/pod-product-compliance
Ingram Content Group UK Ltd.
Pitfield, Milton Keynes, MK11 3LW, UK
UKHW011006180926
475701UK00004B/587

* 9 7 8 1 1 3 8 8 8 0 9 1 7 *